Strategic Monoliths

Pearson Addison-Wesley
Signature Series

  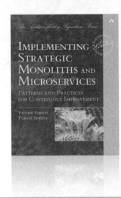 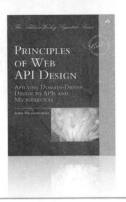

Visit informit.com/awss/vernon **for a complete list of available publications.**

The **Pearson Addison-Wesley Signature Series** provides readers with practical and authoritative information on the latest trends in modern technology for computer professionals. The series is based on one simple premise: great books come from great authors.

Vaughn Vernon is a champion of simplifying software architecture and development, with an emphasis on reactive methods. He has a unique ability to teach and lead with Domain-Driven Design using lightweight tools to unveil unimagined value. He helps organizations achieve competitive advantages using enduring tools such as architectures, patterns, and approaches, and through partnerships between business stakeholders and software developers.

Vaughn's Signature Series guides readers toward advances in software development maturity and greater success with business-centric practices. The series emphasizes organic refinement with a variety of approaches—reactive, object, and functional architecture and programming; domain modeling; right-sized services; patterns; and APIs—and covers best uses of the associated underlying technologies.

Make sure to connect with us!
informit.com/socialconnect

the trusted technology learning source

Praise for Strategic Monoliths and Microservices

"Most books address either the business of software or the technical details of building software. *Strategic Monoliths and Microservices* provides a comprehensive approach to blending the needs of business and technology in an approachable way. It also dispels many of today's myths while offering practical guidance that any team or organization can apply immediately and with confidence."

—*James Higginbotham, Executive API Consultant, Founder of LaunchAny, and author of* Principles of Web API Design

"Digital Transformation cannot succeed as a 'grass roots' effort. Vaughn and Tomasz offer C-level execs a roadmap to software excellence that includes establishing the culture necessary to foster and sustain software innovation. Written with real-world understanding, Vaughn and Tomasz help the reader to appreciate that moving software development from a cost center to a profit center involves tradeoffs that need not sacrifice innovation. A must-read for decision makers."

—*Tom Stockton, Principal Architect, MAXIMUS*

"In this book, Vaughn Vernon and Tomasz Jaskuła use their extensive experience with DDD to present a comprehensive guide to using the many different aspects of DDD for modern systems development and modernization. It will be a valuable guide for many technical leaders who need to understand how to use DDD to its full potential."

—*Eoin Woods, software architect and author*

"There are common misconceptions and roots of failure around software engineering. One notable example is neglecting the rugged trek towards digital transformation. Such an endeavor comprises breakthrough innovations, failure culture, emphasis on the role of software architecture, as well as on the importance of efficient and effective inter-human communication. Fortunately, the authors offer the necessary help for mastering all hurdles and challenges. What I like most about this book is the holistic view it provides to all stakeholders involved in digital transformation and innovation. Vaughn Vernon and Tomasz Jaskuła introduce a clear path to successful innovation projects. They provide insights, tools, proven best practices, and architecture styles both from the business and engineering viewpoint. Their book sheds light on the implications of digital transformation and how to deal with them successfully. This book deserves to become a must-read for practicing software engineers, executives, as well as senior managers. It will always serve me as a precious source of guidance and as a navigator whenever I am entering unchartered territories."

—*Michael Stal, Certified Senior Software Architect, Siemens Technology*

Strategic Monoliths and Microservices

Driving Innovation Using Purposeful Architecture

Vaughn Vernon
Tomasz Jaskuła

◆▼ Addison-Wesley

Boston • Columbus • New York • San Francisco • Amsterdam • Cape Town
Dubai • London • Madrid • Milan • Munich • Paris • Montreal • Toronto • Delhi • Mexico City
São Paulo • Sydney • Hong Kong • Seoul • Singapore • Taipei • Tokyo

For information about buying this title in bulk quantities, or for special sales opportunities (which may include electronic versions; custom cover designs; and content particular to your business, training goals, marketing focus, or branding interests), please contact our corporate sales department at corpsales@pearsoned.com or (800) 382-3419.

For government sales inquiries, please contact governmentsales@pearsoned.com.

For questions about sales outside the U.S., please contact intlcs@pearson.com.

Visit us on the Web: informit.com/aw

Library of Congress Control Number: 2021943427

Copyright © 2022 Pearson Education, Inc.

Cover image: John I Catlett/Shutterstock

Figures 1.5, 1.6, 1.7: illustration by grop/Shutterstock

Pages 109 and 152: Dictionary definitions from Merriam-Webster. Used with Permission.

ISBN-13: 978-0-13-735546-4
ISBN-10: 0-13-735546-7

2 2021

Contents

Foreword

We met the founders of Iterate in April 2007. Three of them had attended our first workshop in Oslo and invited us out to dinner. There, we learned they had just quit their jobs at a consulting firm and founded their own, so they could work in a place they loved using techniques they believed in. I thought to myself, "Good luck with that." After all, they were just a few years out of college and had no experience running a business. But I kept my skepticism to myself as we talked about how to find good customers and negotiate agile contracts.

We visited Iterate many times over the next decade and watched it grow into a successful consulting firm that was routinely listed as one of Norway's best places to work. They had a few dozen consultants and evolved from writing software to coaching companies in Test-Driven Development to helping companies innovate with design sprints. So I should have seen it coming, but when they decided to transform the company in 2016, I was surprised.

We decided to change course, they told us. We want to be a great place to work, where people can reach their full potential, but our best people are limited as consultants. They are always pursuing someone else's dream. We want to create a company where people can follow their own passion and create new companies. We want to nurture startups and fund this with our consulting revenue.

Once again I thought to myself, "Good luck with that." This time I did not keep my skepticism to myself. We talked about the base failure rate of new ventures and the mantra from my 3M days: "Try lots of stuff and keep what works." That's a great motto if you have a lot of time and money, but they had neither. One of the founders was not comfortable with the new approach and left the company. The others did what they had always done—move forward step-by-step and iterate toward their goal.

It was not easy and there were no models to follow. Wary of outside funding, they decided to merge the diametrically opposed business models of consulting and venture funding by limiting to 3% the amount of profit they could make from consulting, pouring the rest back into funding ventures. They had to make sure that consultants did not feel like second-class citizens and those working on new ventures were committed to the success of the consulting business. And they had to learn how to successfully start up new businesses when all they'd ever started was a consulting business.

It's been five years. Every year we visited to brainstorm ideas as the company struggled to make their unique approach work. When the pandemic hit, not only did their consulting business grind to a halt, but the farm-to-restaurant business they had nurtured for three years had no restaurants left to buy local farm goods. But think about it: Iterate had top talent with nothing to do and a venture that was poised to collect and deliver perishable goods. It took two weeks to pivot—they offered the food to consumers for curbside pickup—and the venture took off. While most Oslo consulting firms suffered in 2020, Iterate saw one venture (last-mile delivery) exit through a successful acquisition and three others spin off as separate entities, including a ship-locating system and a three-sided platform for knitters, yarn suppliers, and consumers. As a bonus, Iterate was number 50 on *Fast Company*'s 2020 list of Best Workplaces for Innovators, ahead of Slack and Square and Shopify.

So how did Iterate succeed against all odds? They started by realizing that a consulting approach to software development did not give them the freedom to take a lead role. With software becoming a strategic innovation lever, they felt it was time to claim a seat at the decision-making table. This was scary, because it involved taking responsibility for results—something consultants generally avoid. But they were confident that their experimental approach to solving challenging problems would work for business problems as well as technical problems, so they forged ahead.

You might wonder what Iterate's transformation has to do with the enterprise transformations that are the subject of this book. There is nothing in Iterate's story about Monoliths or Microservices or agile practices—but these are not the essence of a transformation. As this book points out, a transformation begins with the articulation of a new and innovative business strategy, one that provides real, differentiated value to a market. The pursuit of that strategy will be a long and challenging journey, requiring excellent people, deep thinking, and plenty of learning along the way. For those who are starting out on such a transformation, this book provides a lot of thinking tools for your journey.

For example, as you head in a new direction, you probably do not want to blow up the structures that brought your current success, however outmoded they might be. You need that old Big Ball of Mud Monolith (or consulting services) to fund your transition.

Another example: The first thing you want to consider is the right architecture for your new business model, and it probably won't be the same as the old one. Just as Iterate moved from having a pool of consultants to having clearly distinct venture teams, you will probably want to structure your new architecture to fit the domain it operates in. This usually means clarifying the business capabilities that fit the new strategy and structuring complete teams around these capabilities. So instead of having a layered architecture, you are likely to want one based on the natural components and subcomponents of your product (also known as *Bounded Contexts*).

Think of SpaceX: The architecture of a launch vehicle is determined by its components—first stage (which contains nine Merlin engines, a long fuselage, and some landing legs), interstage, second stage, and payload. Teams are not formed around engineering disciplines (e.g., materials engineering, structural engineering, software engineering), but rather around components and subcomponents. This gives each team a clear responsibility and set of constraints: Teams are expected to understand and accomplish the job their component must do to ensure the next launch is successful.

As you clarify the product architecture in your new strategy, you will probably want to create an organization that matches this architecture because, as the authors point out, you can't violate Conway's Law any more than you can violate the law of gravity. The heart of this book is a large set of thinking tools that will help you design a new architecture (quite possibly a modular Monolith to begin with) and the organization needed to support that architecture. The book then offers ways to gradually move from your existing architecture toward the new one, as well as presents ideas about when and how you might want to spin off appropriate services.

Over time, Iterate learned that successful ventures have three things in common:

- Good market timing

- Team cohesion

- Technical excellence

Market timing requires patience; organizations that think transformations are about new processes or data structures tend to be impatient and generally get this wrong. Transformations are about creating an environment in which innovation can flourish to create new, differentiated offerings and bring them to market at the right time.

The second element of success, team cohesion, comes from allowing the capabilities being developed (the Bounded Contexts) and the relevant team members to evolve over time, until the right combination of people and offering emerges.

The third element, technical excellence, is rooted in a deep respect for the technical complexity of software. This book will help you appreciate the complexity of your existing system and future versions of that system, as well as the challenge of evolving from one to the other.

The Iterate story contains a final caution: Your transition will not be easy. Iterate had to figure out how to meld a consulting pool with venture teams in such a way that everyone felt valuable and was committed to the organization's overall success. This is something that every organization will struggle with as it goes through a transition. There is no formula for success other than the one offered in this book: highly skilled people, deep thinking, and constant experimentation.

There is no silver bullet.

—*Mary Poppendieck, co-author of* Lean Software Development

Preface

Chances are good that your organization doesn't make money by selling software in the "traditional sense," and perhaps it never will. That doesn't mean that software can't play a significant role in making money for your organization. Software is at the heart of the wealthiest companies.

Take, for example, the companies represented by the acronym FAANG: Facebook, Apple, Amazon, Netflix, and Google (now held by Alphabet). Few of those companies sell any software at all, or at least they do not count on software sales to generate the greater part of their revenues.

Approximately 98% of Facebook's money is made by selling ads to companies that want access to the members of its social networking site. The ad space has such high value because Facebook's platform provides for enormous engagement between members. Certain members care about what is happening with other members and overall trends, and that keeps them engaged with people, situations, and the social platform. Capturing the attention of Facebook members is worth a lot of money to advertisers.

Apple is for the most part a hardware company, selling smartphones, tablets, wearables, and computers. Software brings out the value of said smartphones and other devices.

Amazon uses a multipronged approach to revenue generation, selling goods as an online retailer; selling subscriptions to unlimited e-books, audio, music, and other services; and selling cloud computing infrastructure as a service.

Netflix earns its revenues by selling multilevel subscriptions to movie and other video streaming services. The company still earns money through DVD subscriptions, but this part of the business has—as expected—fallen off sharply with the rising popularity of on-demand streaming. The video streaming is enhanced for, and controlled by, the experience with user-facing software that runs on TVs and mobile devices. Yet, the real heavy lifting is done by the cloud-based system that serves the videos from Amazon's AWS. These services provide video encoding in more than 50 different formats, serving up content through content delivery networks (CDN) and dealing with chaotic failures in the face of cloud and network outages.

Google also makes its money through ad sales; these ads are served along with query results from its search engine software. In 2020, Google earned approximately $4 billion from direct software usage, such as via Google Workspace. But the Google Workspace software does not have to be installed on user computers, because it is provided in the cloud using the Software as a Service (SaaS) model. According to recent reports, Google owns nearly 60% of the online office suite market, surpassing even the share claimed by Microsoft.

As you can see from these industry leaders' experiences, your organization doesn't need to sell software to earn market-leading revenues. It will, however, need to use software to excel in business both now and over the years to follow.

What is more, to innovate using software, an organization must recognize that a contingent of software architects and engineers—the best—matter. They matter so much that the demand for the best makes them ridiculously difficult to hire. Think of the significance of landing any one of the top 20 picks in the WNBA or NFL draft. Of course, this description does not apply to every software developer. Many or even most are content to "punch a clock," pay their mortgage, and watch as much of the WNBA and NFL on TV as they possibly can. If those are the prospects you want to recruit, we strongly suggest that you stop reading this book right now. Conversely, if that's where you've been but now you want to make a meaningful change, read on.

For those organizations seeking to excel and accelerate their pace of innovation, it's important to realize that software development achievers are more than just "valuable." If a business is to innovate by means of software to the extent of ruling its industry, it must recognize that software architects and engineers of that ilk are "The New Kingmakers," a term coined by Stephen O'Grady in his 2013 book *The New Kingmakers: How Developers Conquered the World* [New-Kingmakers]. To truly succeed with software, all businesses with audacious goals must understand what drives this ilk of developer to transcend common software creation. The kinds of software that they yearn to create are in no way ordinary or obvious. The most valuable software developers want to make the kind of software that determines the future of the industry, and that's the recruiting message your organization must sound to attract (1) the best and (2) those who care enough to become the best.

This book is meant for C-level and other business executives, as well as every role and level involved in leading software development roles. Everyone responsible for delivering software that either directly results in strategic differentiation, or supports it, must understand how to drive innovation with software.

The authors have found that today's C-level and other executives are a different breed than their predecessors from decades past. Many are tech savvy and might even be considered experts in their business domain. They have a vision for making things better in a specific place, and they attract other executives and deeply technical professionals who grok what the founder or founders are driving to accomplish:

- CEOs who are close to the technology vision, such as startup CEOs, and those who want to be informed about the role of software in their future

- CIOs who are responsible for facilitating and enabling software development as a differentiator

- CTOs who are leading software vision through innovation

- Senior vice presidents, vice presidents, directors, project managers, and others who are charged with carrying the vision to realization

- Chief architects, who will find this book inspiring and a forceful guide to motivate teams of software architects and senior developers to drive change with a business mindset and purposeful architecture

- Software architects and developers of all levels, who are trying to firmly fix a business mentality in themselves—that is, a recognition that software development is not merely a means to a good paycheck, but to prospering beyond the ordinary and obvious through software innovation

This is a vital message that all software professionals must learn from by consuming, ruminating on, and practicing the expert techniques explored in this book.

Strategic Monoliths and Microservices: Driving Innovation Using Purposeful Architecture is not a book on implementation details. We'll provide that kind of information in our next book, *Implementing Strategic Monoliths and Microservices* (Vernon & Jaskuła, Addison-Wesley, forthcoming). This volume is very much a book on software as part of business strategy.

This book is definitely of interest to leaders who lack deep knowledge or experience in the software industry. It informs by showing how every software initiative must discover big ideas, architect with purpose, design strategically, and implement to defeat complexity. At the same time, we vigorously warn readers to resist dragging accidental or intentional complexity into the software. The point of driving change is to deliver software that works even better than users/customers expect. Thus, this book is meant to shake up the thinking of those stuck in a rut of the status quo, defending their jobs rather than pushing forward relentlessly as champions of the next generation of ideas, methods, and devices—and perhaps becoming the creators of the future of industry as a result.

The authors of this book have worked with many different clients and have seen firsthand the negative side of software development, where holding on to job security and defending turf is the aim rather than making the business thrive by driving prosperity. Many of the wealthiest companies are so large, and are engaged in so many initiatives under many layers of management and reporting structure, that their vision-to-implementation-to-acceptance pathway is far from a demonstration of continuity. With that in mind, we're attempting to wake the masses up to the fact that the adage "software is eating the world" is true. Our lessons are served up with a dollop of realism, demonstrating that innovation can be achieved by means of progressive practical steps rather than requiring instantaneous gigantic leaps.

There is always risk in attempting innovation. That said, not taking any risk at all will likely be even more risky and damaging in the long run. The following simple graph makes this point very clear.

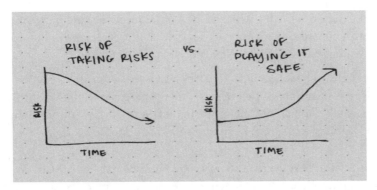

Figure P.1 *There is a risk in taking a risk, but likely even a greater risk in playing it safe.*

As Natalie Fratto [Natalie-Fratto-Risk] suggests, it is generally the case that the risk of taking risks diminishes over time, but the risk of playing it safe increases over time. The venture investor side of Natalie can be seen in her TED Talk [Natalie-Fratto-TED], which explains the kinds of founders in whose businesses she invests. As she explains, many investors seek business founders with a high intelligence quotient (IQ), whereas others look for entrepreneurs with a high emotional quotient (EQ). She looks primarily for those with a high adaptability quotient (AQ). In fact, innovation calls for a great amount of adaptability. You'll find that message repeated in this book in several forms. Everything from experimentation to discovery to architecture, design, and implementation requires adaptability. Risk takers are unlikely to succeed unless they are very adaptable.

As we discuss our primary topic of innovation with software, it's impossible to entirely avoid the highly controversial topic of iterative and incremental development. Indeed, some form of the "A-word"—yes, agile/Agile—cannot be sidestepped. This book stays far away from promoting a specific and ceremonial way to use Agile or to be a lean business. Sadly, the authors have found that most companies and teams creating software claim to *use* Agile, yet don't understand how to *be* agile. *The desire is to emphasize the latter rather than reinforce the former.* The original message of agile is quite simple: It's focused on collaborative delivery. If kept simple, this approach can be highly useful. That said, this is nowhere near our primary message. We attempt only to draw attention to where "un-simple" use causes damage and how *being agile* helps. For our brief discussion on how we think *being agile* can help, see the section "Don't Blame Agile," in Chapter 1, "Business Goals and Digital Transformation."

Given our background, it might surprise some readers to learn that we do not view *Strategic Monoliths and Microservices* as a Domain-Driven Design (DDD) book. To be sure, we introduce and explain the domain-driven approach and why and how it is helpful—but we haven't limited our range. We also offer ideas above and beyond DDD. This is a "software is eating the world, so be smart and get on board, innovate, and make smart architectural decisions based on real purpose, before you are left behind" book. We are addressing the real needs of the kinds of companies with which we have been engaged for decades, and especially based on our observations over the past five to ten years.

We have been slightly concerned that our drumbeat might sound too loud. Still, when considering the other drums beating all around technology-driven industries, we think a different kind of drumming is in order. When many others are on high mountains, constantly beating the "next over-hyped products as silver bullets" drum, there must be at least an equalizing attempt at promoting our brains as the best tooling. Our goal is to show that thinking and rethinking is the way to innovate, and that generic product acquisition and throwing more technology at hard problems is not a strategic plan. So, think of us as the people on an adjacent mountain beating the other drum to "be scientists and engineers" by advancing beyond the ordinary and obvious, by being innovative and just plain different. And, yes, we definitely broke a sweat doing that. If our intense drumbeat leaves readers with a lasting impression that our drums made that specific brain-stimulating rhythm, then we think we've achieved our goal. That's especially so if the stimulation leads to greater success for our readers.

Legend/Key for Diagrams

Figure P.2 (on page xxii) shows the modeling elements used in most of the architecture diagrams in this book. The elements used range from large- to small-scale, and those in between, depending on the topic of the diagram. Some are taken from EventStorming described on page 87.

In Figure P.2, the top half, from the upper left, are strategic and architectural elements: Business/Bounded Context is a software subsystem and model boundary of a business capability and a sphere of knowledge; Big Ball of Mud is the "unarchitecture" in which most enterprises languish; Ports and Adapters Architecture is both a foundational and versatile style; and Modules are named packages that contain software components.

Figure P.2 *Modeling elements used in architecture diagrams throughout this book.*

The bottom half of Figure P.2 depicts eight tactical component types, occurring within a subsystem and that sometimes flow to other subsystems: Commands cause state transitions; Events capture and carry record of state transitions across subsystem boundaries; Policy describes business rules; Aggregate/Entity holds state and offers software behavior; User Role interacts with the system and often represents a persona; View/Query collects and retrieves data that can be rendered on user interfaces; Process manages a multi-step operation through to an eventual completion; and Domain Service provides cross-cutting software behavior.

Refer to Figure P.2 for the legend/key of element types, especially when reading the black-and-white print book, which uses patterns in lieu of colors.

References

[Natalie-Fratto-Risk] https://twitter.com/NatalieFratto/status/1413123064896921602

[Natalie-Fratto-TED] https://www.ted.com/talks/natalie_fratto_3_ways_to_measure_your_adaptability_and_how_to_improve_it

[New-Kingmakers] https://www.amazon.com/New-Kingmakers-Developers-Conquered-World-ebook/dp/B0097E4MEU

Acknowledgments

Writing a book is hard work. Readers might think that the more books written, the better the process is for the author. Multi-book authors would probably agree that the writing flows better as experience grows. Yet, most multi-book authors probably aim higher each time than they knew how to do previously. Knowing what lies ahead before the writing begins can be unnerving. The experienced author knows that each book has a life of its own and requires more mental energy and writing precision than even their own expectations could predict.

It happens every time, at least to one author involved in this effort. In the case of this book, one author knows what to fear and still did it anyway. The second author had translated a book from English to French, but his willingness to sign up for pure writing was based on the experienced author telling him not to worry.

That might be what a shark cage guide says just before the steel around the rank amateur plunges them into the breathtakingly cold waters off of Cape Town, South Africa. Truth is, the spectators who gaze upon great whites in action are fairly safe, at least by statistical accounts, because no one has ever died from that extreme viewing melee. Still, it's a good thing that sharks aren't as attracted to yellow and even brown in water as they are to blood. (We'll leave the close-call research to you.) So, trying to write a book probably won't kill you. Even so, have you ever wondered about the ratio between the people who have said they are going to write a book, but don't, and those who actually do write a book? It's probably similar to those who say they will one day dive with great white sharks and those who actually do.

It might take one, two, or a few people to author a book. But it takes an army to review, edit, edit, edit—add more edits—produce, and publish that book. The first draft manuscript of this book was considered "very clean," but there were still hundreds of additions, deletions, and general corrections made in every single chapter. And don't bring up the illustrations. Please. Even the very best of writers—which these authors would never claim to be—are subject to a daunting battery of "live rounds" before their book is ready for the public. Actually, we'll clarify that. That's the case if you are an author under the prestigious Addison-Wesley brand. (We won't go into the number of obvious errors you can find in the first few pages of books produced by other tech publishers.) The analogy of "live rounds" seems appropriate, because Pearson supports a small army of the best editors with the best aim that can be hired.

We are grateful to Pearson Addison-Wesley for giving us the opportunity to publish under their highly respected label. They have guided us through the process of writing this book until the publication was in sight. Special thanks go to our executive editor, Haze Humbert, for driving the process of acquisition, review, development, and full editorial production so smoothly, and coddling the process when an overly optimistic author didn't deliver all chapters as early as he anticipated. Haze's assistant editor, Menka Mehta, kept correspondence and calendars in sync and flowing. Our development editors Sheri Replin and Chris Cleveland offered high-level edits and prepared our chapters for page layout. Thanks to Rachel Paul for keeping the publication process clipping along. Thanks also to Jill Hobbs for being so kind as she made our "very clean" manuscript read superbly; it's amazing what a fine copy editor can do for a book, and especially a book written by tech authors. When you see things happening steadily but don't know how, it's probably due to a very competent director of product management, and in our case that is Julie Phifer.

In case it is not abundantly clear, the vast majority of editorial professionals with whom we work are women, and we think it is fair to include this team as "women in tech." If you are a woman in tech and want to be a book author, you can't hope for a better team to work with. These authors are not only proud to collaborate with this team, but highly honored that they have trusted us enough to be their extended members. So, future women authors, or future multi-book women authors, please allow me to introduce Haze Humbert, as your gateway to the best experience that book authoring can offer.

This book would not have been the same without the valuable feedback from our reviewers. In particular, we would like to thank Mary Poppendieck, who provided an extensive review of our book and offered rich feedback, and wrote a great foreword. Mary gave us her in-depth perspective on the difference between a software developer and a software engineer. Of course, any company can hire for the position of software engineer, but Mary describes a role that goes far beyond a title. Readers will find many of her viewpoints highlighted by sidebars and boxes, but her gifts to our project are in no way "side anything"—her input is nothing less than pure gold. Pay attention to what she has to say.

Other reviewers who offered particularly valuable reviews have served in such roles as CTO, chief architect, principal architect, and similar, and in a range of companies from very large to nimble startups. They are listed here in order by given (first) name: Benjamin Nitu, Eoin Woods, Frank Grimm, Olaf Zimmermann, Tom Stockton, and Vladik Khononov. There were several others who offered helpful feedback, including C-level executives, vice presidents, and other executives, who shall remain unnamed. We are honored to have gathered a group of highly experienced tech executives who were early readers, and we are thrilled that they were very impressed with our book. We would be remiss if we did not mention the many people who offered to read and review our manuscript early on. We would have taken pleasure in that, but for various reasons it was not possible to include them. For every bit of help you provided and the confidence that you showed in us, thank you one and all.

Vaughn Vernon

This book would truly not have been possible without Haze Humbert. When Haze took over from my previous executive editor at Addison-Wesley, she actively suggested and discussed ideas for future books that I might write. Haze was very patient with me. After having three books published in roughly five years, I didn't look forward to authoring another one anytime soon. I wasn't burned out, just keenly aware of the commitment necessary to bring a new book to the world. And I was enjoying designing and creating software more than writing books. Being a creative person, during my discussions with Haze I pitched a number of ideas about which she could have laughed out loud. Yet, her kind demeanor and patience covered my audacious and/or ludicrous project pitches.

In early 2020, Haze offered an opportunity that was much more realistic, but completely unexpected and quite difficult to believe and digest, and whose acceptance seemed daunting. Her offer was to become the editor of my own Vaughn Vernon Signature Series. Knowing that my previous books had been successful—even best sellers—and appreciating that I could possibly achieve that feat again with another book, was far less earthshaking than fathoming the inception and delivery of a signature series. It was mind-blowing stuff. After a few weeks and several discussions with my trusted advisor, Nicole, the idea sank in. One thought that solidified the possibility of succeeding was this: If Pearson Addison-Wesley, with its unmatched experience as an elite publisher, thought enough of my work to make that offer, it meant that the company was confident that I would succeed. There's no way that such a publisher would pitch, invest in, and back this effort if it thought anything otherwise.

Based on that alone, not on my own abilities, I accepted. So here I am today, deeply thankful to Haze and the others with whom she works and represents. Thank you all so much.

I am grateful to Tomasz Jaskuła for accepting my offer to co-author this book with me. I hope the sharks didn't get too close for comfort. Tomasz is smart and tenacious, and has also been a worthy business partner in our training and consulting efforts. He's also done nearly all of the heavy lifting for the .NET implementation of our open source reactive platform, VLINGO XOOM.

Both of my parents have been a stabilizing force for me, and have taught me and supported my efforts for as long as I can remember. When I wrote my first published book, *Implementing Domain-Driven Design,* my parents were still full of life and mobile. More than eight years since, and after many months of lockdown have accumulated due to the pandemic, they now face additional challenges. It's a relief that in-person visits with them are once again permitted, and our time together is so enjoyable. Mom still has her witty sense of humor, and her stamina has not entirely abandoned her. I am happy that Dad still yearns for handheld computers, books, and other tools that enable him to remain in touch with engineering. I look forward to seeing his eyes light up when I drop by with a new gadget or book. Mom and Dad, I can't thank you enough.

I can't say enough about the ongoing support from my wife and our son. As crazy as the past 18 months or so have been, we've managed to grow together under continually changing circumstances. Nicole has been incredibly resilient through what seemed like unavoidable damage to our businesses. Despite the challenges, she has led us to new highs in the growth of both our training and consulting company, Kalele, and our software product startup VLINGO. VLINGO XOOM, our open source reactive platform and our initial product, is healthy and its adoption is growing. VLINGO is also building two new SaaS products. Not only have our teams been effective, but Nicole's business savvy has only expanded under greater challenges. It is inconceivable that I could have succeeded with anything at all, let alone a signature series and new book authoring, without her.

Tomasz Jaskuła

Back in 2013, Vaughn Vernon authored an outstanding book, *Implementing Domain-Driven Design.* He followed that with a world tour of workshops under the same name. His was the first book in which Domain-Driven Design was described from a practical point of view, shedding light on many theoretical concepts that were previously misunderstood or unclear for years in the Domain-Driven Design community. When I first learned about Vaughn's IDDD Workshop, I didn't hesitate to attend as soon as possible. It was a time when I was applying Domain-Driven Design on different projects, and I couldn't miss the opportunity to meet one of the most prominent members of the community. So, in 2013 I met Vaughn in Leuven, Belgium, where one of the workshops took place. This was also where I met most of the Domain-Driven Design community influencers, who were there to learn from Vaughn! A few years later, I'm proud to have coauthored this book with Vaughn, who has become a friend. He has been supportive of me through the years and I'm really grateful for the confidence he has in me. Writing this book was a great learning experience. Thank you, Vaughn, for all your help, your confidence in me, and your support.

I would also like to thank Nicole Andrade, who, with all the kindness in the world, has supported us through the effort of writing this book. She has played an important role in strengthening the friendship between Vaughn and me through the years, and I know she will continue to do so for years to come.

Writing the book without the support from my friend and business partner François Morin of our company, Luteceo, would have been much more difficult. His encouragement of my writing, and his willingness to take care of running the company while I was not available, gave me the space I needed to take on this project.

I would like to thank my parents Barbara and Stefan, who have always believed in me and supported me through my personal challenges. They taught me early the importance of being curious and learning continuously, which is one of the greatest pieces of advice I could have ever received.

Finally, I would not have been able to write this book without the unconditional support and love from my wife Teresa and my lovely daughters Lola and Mila. Their encouragement and support were essential for me to complete this book. Thank you so much.

About the Authors

Vaughn Vernon is an entrepreneur, software developer, and architect with more than 35 years of experience in a broad range of business domains. Vaughn is a leading expert in Domain-Driven Design and reactive architecture and programming, and champions simplicity. Students of his workshops are consistently bowled over by the breadth and depth of what he teaches and his unique approaches, and as a result have become ongoing students attending his other well-known workshops. He consults and trains around Domain-Driven Design, reactive software development, as well as EventStorming and Event-Driven Architecture, helping teams and organizations realize the potential of business-driven and reactive systems as they transform their businesses from technology-driven legacy web implementation approaches. Vaughn is the author of four books, including the one you are now reading. His books and his Vaughn Vernon Signature Series are all published by Addison-Wesley.

Kalele: https://kalele.io

VLINGO: https://vlingo.io

Twitter: @VaughnVernon

LinkedIn: https://linkedin.com/in/vaughnvernon/

Tomasz Jaskuła is CTO and co-founder of Luteceo, a software consulting company in Paris. Tomasz has more than 20 years of professional experience as a developer and software architect, and worked for many companies in the e-commerce, industry, insurance, and financial fields. He has mainly focused on creating software that delivers true business value, aligns with strategic business initiatives, and provides solutions with clearly identifiable competitive advantages. Tomasz is also a main contributor to the OSS project XOOM for the .NET platform. In his free time, Tomasz perfects his guitar playing and spends time with his family.

Twitter: @tjaskula

LinkedIn: https://linkedin.com/in/tomasz-jaskula-16b2823/

Transformational Strategic Learning through Experimentation

Executive Summary

Part I of the book introduces the goals of this book by establishing digital transformation as a revenue-generating business strategy. Every nontrivial business must take seriously the vital need to focus on software building as the only way to survive the next few decades of interindustry competition. Yet, survival all too often results from delivering from a position of weakness and fear, or simply lack of innovative thinking.

To lead with boldness, courage, and confidence requires delivering business-driven differentiating software that transcends the obvious and ordinary benefits that the survivors manage to shove in front of users. The clear winners turn up the dial on innovation. This kind of success can be fostered by improving what a given industry has already achieved, and by realizing the improvements as software products. Some winners will, as inventors, entirely change the way an industry works. Even so, invention is not necessary to be a winning innovator.

Accomplishing innovation as an industry leader happens deliberately. The greatest innovations have come from relentless experimentation coupled with continuous improvement. The mindset and tools that support this kind of drive are taught in the first three chapters.

Chapter 1: Business Goals and Digital Transformation

SpaceX didn't invent the rocket or space travel and exploration. Instead, SpaceX innovated to the extreme in a preexisting but relatively closed industry.

- Understand that the real goal is business-driven breakthroughs rather than a steady stream of shiny new technical products to excite the geeks. Unless the shiny things have a clear and justifiable purpose, they will likely serve only to sidetrack real business-centric innovations. The focus should be on innovation with software products.

- Recognize that innovation in general consists of realizing breakthrough improvements on what exists. There is a strong possibility that the potential for uniquely innovative products that can capture new markets has been staring everyone in the face. What exists can be the catalyst for innovation that delivers even greater value than was available yesterday, given new delivery mechanisms and revenue models.

- Perceive where software efforts go wrong. Doing so can be a great way to recognize when the same problems start to happen in a local system project, or already have occurred. Such problems usually begin with a lack of effective collaborative communication, or when communication occurs but without recognizing when topics shift from one area of expertise to another. Both situations lead to large, mud-like software that just won't die.

- Communication is about knowledge, and knowledge sharing is the only way to go beyond the obvious and ordinary. Continuously challenging assumptions that are based on ordinary thinking—what is obvious—is the first step toward experimentation that leads to discovery.

- Thinking like a product company is not wrong for any business. Many businesses sell nontechnology products. When businesses invest in software as products, that adds a new dimension in quality and elicits motivations to improve through clear customer-based revenue goals rather than the internal desire for endless pet features. If a business is not there yet, it's time to get unstuck.

Chapter 2: Essential Strategic Learning Tools

SpaceX would not have been successful as quickly as it was, or possibly not ever, unless team members allowed themselves to crash rockets in an effort to learn quickly. Crashing rockets is a lot more expensive than rapidly failing software experiments. The SpaceX outcome led to market domination.

- Put business initiatives before software architecture and technical platforms. Tell potential customers that the software they should use sports a Microservices architecture or runs in the cloud, and that message will likely be received with blank stares. Users don't care about Microservices or the cloud; they care about outcomes.

- The quickest way to deliver the best outcomes for users is by driving in the straightest possible lines of incremental improvement. Select from the best service-level architecture and deployment options based on full knowledge of need and purpose.

- Experiments fail, and failure is not a bad thing. Every fast failure results in rapid learning. Employ an engineering model that depends on an experimentation mindset, not a contractor model that freezes in the face of the unknown.

- Embrace failure culture, but understand that failure culture is not blame culture. Innovation is difficult enough without troubling the vulnerable scientific minds with threats of reprisals for tiptoeing on the razor's edge. When controlled failures lead to success, those failures look like the red carpet leading to a pot of gold.

- Recognizing the business capabilities of the business enterprise is a sound way to see where investing in strategic software initiatives matters most. Don't build what you can buy or download for free, because these solutions are generic and non-differentiating, and often complex to implement. Your business is defined by its core capabilities and will deliver value if given proper focus and investment.

Chapter 3: Events-First Experimentation and Discovery

How can the broad range of personality types overcome communication challenges to achieve deep dives into collaborative communication, learning, experimentation- and discovery-based innovation, and improved software construction?

- Don't segregate the extroverts and the introverts. Pushing business and technical minds in separate directions will lead to software that reflects that intentional segregation. It won't be fulfilling—more so the polar opposite. Find ways to bring the two mindsets together with an unending drive toward discovery-based innovation. The "ways" are introduced in Chapter 3 and further explored in Part 2.

- "Events-first" might sound foreign or even intimidating. It need not be. Considering that nearly everything (and possibly everything) in everyday life is done due to events that stimulate our reactions. In software, events are records of things that have happened and that cause additional things to happen in response. Focusing on events as a learning and discovery tool is first-rate experience in experimentation.

- Experimentation is effective when your organization is iterating quickly by means of rapid learning tools. Rapid learning requires collaborative communication between business and technical experts. These fundamental skills are enhanced with lightweight modeling tools that are as expensive as paper and pens, or the use of free online collaboration tools.

- Whether in-person or remote, or a hybrid experimentation session of mixed in-person and remote participants, inexpensive and free tools are available to support a lightweight, exploratory activity, known as EventStorming. The important detail is to make sure that the session includes both business and technical experts who can answer the obvious questions and are willing to challenge the ordinary.

Prepare for a potentially new way of thinking. Computing and software are no longer ways to avoid repetitive, manual, paper-based tasks. That thinking is at least 30 years behind the curve. Don't treat software as a cost center. Today's thinking seeks to deliver software that changes everything, as a new era of business emerges in every industry. Promote software to a profit center, and demand strategic innovation as the only acceptable results.

Chapter 1

Business Goals and Digital Transformation

The most outstanding business achievement is to create a product that is needed by a great number of consumers, is completely unique, and is optimally priced. Historically, and in a general sense, the realization of such an accomplishment has depended on the ability to identify what is essential or highly desirable for a key market demographic. This is reflected in a maxim captured by the writings of Plato: "Our need will be the real creator." Today, this statement is better known as "Necessity is the mother of invention."

Yet, the most profound innovators are those who invent an ingenious product even before consumers realize it is needed. Such achievements have occurred serendipitously, but have also been born from those daring enough to ask, "Why not?"[1] Perhaps mathematician and philosopher Alfred North Whitehead struck on this notion when he argued that "the basis of invention is science, and science is almost wholly the outgrowth of pleasurable intellectual curiosity" [ANW].

Of course, the vast majority of businesses face a stark reality: Breakthroughs in product development that lead to far-reaching market impact aren't an everyday happening. Inventing entirely unique products that capture whole markets might seem as likely as aiming at nothing and hitting the center of a pot of gold.

As a result, the predominant business plan is to create competition. The uniqueness is seen in pricing the replica rather than in creating the original. Hitting such a large target is entirely ordinary and lacking in imagination and is not even a sure means of success. If creating (more) competition seems to be the best play, consider Steve Jobs's advice: "You can't look at the competition and say you're going to do it better. You have to look at the competition and say you're going to do it differently."

---

1. (George) Bernard Shaw: "Some men see things as they are and ask why. Others dream things that never were and ask why not."

SpaceX Innovation

Between the years 1970 and 2000, the cost to launch a kilogram to space averaged $18,500 US per kilogram. For a SpaceX Falcon 9, the cost is just $2,720 per kilogram. That's a factor of 7:1 improvement, and so it's no secret why SpaceX has almost all of the space launch business these days. How did they do it? What they did not do was work under contract to the government—that is, the only funding mechanism up until then. Their goal was to dramatically reduce the cost to launch stuff into space. Their main sub-goal under that was to recover and reuse booster rockets. There's a wonderful YouTube video of all the boosters they crashed in order to achieve their goal. The strategy of integrating events (in this case, test booster launches) is how multiple engineering teams rapidly try out their latest version with all the other teams. Government contracts would never have tolerated the crashes that SpaceX suffered. Yet, the crashes speeded up the development of a reliable, cheap booster rocket by perhaps a factor of 5, simply by trying things out to discover the unknown unknowns, instead of trying to think everything through in excruciating detail. That is a pretty classic engineering approach, but would never be allowed in a contracting model. The SpaceX team said it was far cheaper to have crashes and find the problems than to try to wait forever until there was no risk. [Mary Poppendieck]

Imitation is not a strategy. Differentiation is.

Differentiation is the strategic business goal that must be constantly sought after. If pure invention seems nearly impossible, continuous and tenacious improvement toward innovation should not. In this book, we have undertaken the task of helping readers achieve strategic business differentiation through relentless improvement in digital transformation.

Digital Transformation: What Is the Goal?

Understanding that the making of the unordinary is a major feat should not dissuade anyone from taking small, scientific steps with ongoing determination toward actual innovation. No matter the complexity in reaching Z, performing the science of experimentation to arrive at B when starting from A is a realistic expectation. After that, reaching C is doable, which then leads to D. It's a matter of keeping our lab coat and pocket protector on, and acknowledging that unique products that can capture new markets have likely been staring us in the face all along.

Whether Microsoft Office was considered a worker-productivity innovation from the outset, it certainly has been the most successful suite in that market. With Office 365, Microsoft didn't have to reinvent the word processor and the spreadsheet to innovate. It did, however, add a new delivery mechanism and capabilities to enable full teams to collaborate, among other features. Did Microsoft win yet again by innovating through digital transformation?

Digital transformation is left to the eye of the business innovator, but commonly businesses lose sight of the innovation part of transformation. Transformative innovation requires that the business understands the difference between changing infrastructural platforms and building new product value. For example, although taking business digital assets from the on-premises datacenter to the cloud might be an important IT initiative, it is not in itself a business initiative in innovation.

Does migrating your software to the cloud qualify as a digital transformation? Possibly, but more so if the move supports future differentiation. It best qualifies if the cloud delivers new opportunities to innovate or at least to unburden the extremely high cost of digital asset operations and channel those funds to new products. Think of the cloud as creating opportunities by freeing you from most traditional datacenter responsibilities. It won't be transformative, however, if the shift to the cloud amounts to trading one set of costs for a different set of costs. Amazon offering its already successful computing infrastructure to the outside world was a digital transformation for the company that resulted in cloud innovation. Paying a subscription to Amazon to use its cloud is not a transformative innovation to the subscriber. The lesson is clear: Innovate or be innovated on.

Just as migrating to the cloud is not an innovation, neither is creating a new distributed computing architecture. Users don't care about distributed computing, Microservices, or Monoliths, or even features. Users care about outcomes. Improved user outcomes are needed rapidly and without negatively impacting their workflows. For software to stand a chance at meaningful transformation, its architecture and design must support the delivery of better user outcomes as rapidly as possible.

When using the cloud, an improved architecture and design approach (and any additional well-tuned steps that lead to productivity gains) make reaching innovative transformational goals possible. Using infrastructure as a service frees the business to work on innovative business software rather than churning on trying to innovate on its infrastructure. Not only are infrastructure innovations time-consuming and costly, but they might not benefit the business's bottom line, and developing infrastructure in-house might never address infrastructure and operational needs as well as AWS, Google Cloud Platform, and Azure. Yet, this is not always the case. For some businesses, it would be much more cost-effective to bring operations in-house or keep them there [a16z-CloudCostParadox].

Remember, it's A to B, B to C, C to D. . . . Be willing to iterate on any of these steps so that you can learn enough to take the next one. Understanding that going back from J to G before reaching K is expected, and that Z need not ever happen, is liberating. Teams can innovate, but none of these transformational steps can tolerate lengthy cycles. Chapter 2, "Essential Strategic Learning Tools," shows how experimentation is the friend of innovation and the enemy of indecision.

Software Architecture Quick Glance

This section introduces the term *software architecture*—a term that is referred to often herein. It's a rather broad topic that is covered in more detail throughout this book.

For now, think of software architecture as similar to building architecture. A building has structure, and it reflects the results of communication that has taken place between the architect and the owner regarding the design features, by providing the features as specified. A building forms a whole system of various subsystems, each of which has its own specific purpose and role. These subsystems are all loosely or more tightly connected with other parts of the building, working separately or in conjunction with others to make the building serve its purpose. For example, a building's air conditioning requires electrical power, duct work, a thermostat, insulation, and even a closed area of the building to cool, if that subsystem is to be effective.

Likewise, a software architecture provides structural design—that is, the formulation of many structures, not one. The structural design organizes the system components, affording them the means to communicate as they work together. The structure also serves to segregate clusters of components so they can function independently. The structures must, therefore, help achieve quality attributes rather than functional ones, while the components within implement the functionality specified by teams of system builders.

Figure 1.1 illustrates two subsystems (showing only a fragment of a whole system), each having components that work together internally but in isolation from the other subsystem. The two subsystems exchange information through a communication channel, with the box in between representing the information that is exchanged. Assume that these two subsystems are physically separated into two deployment units, and communicate via a network. This forms a portion of a distributed system.

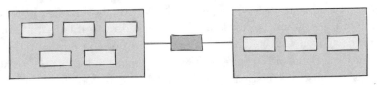

Figure 1.1 *A software architecture provides structure within subsystems and supports communication between them.*

Another important aspect of both building and software architecture is that they must support inevitable change. If existing components fail to meet new demands in either architecture, they must be replaceable without extreme cost or effort. The architecture must also be able to accommodate possible needed expansion, again without major impact to the overall architecture.

Why Software Goes Wrong

We don't want to overstate the seriousness of the poor state of enterprise software development, and we don't think it can be overstated.

When discussing enterprise software system conditions with *Fortune* and Global companies, we quickly learn about their major pain points. These are always related to aged software that has undergone decades of maintenance, long after innovation took place. Most discussions identify that software development is considered a cost center to the business, which makes it that much more difficult to invest in improvements. Today, however, software should be a profit center. Unfortunately, the collective corporate mindset is stuck 30-plus years back when software was meant to make some operations work faster than manual labor.

A specific application (or subsystem) starts with a core business reason to be built. Over time, its core purpose will be enhanced or even altered considerably. Continuous additions of features can become so extensive that the application's original purpose is lost and it likely means different things to different business functions, with the full diversity of those understandings not readily known. This often leads to many hands stirring the pot. Eventually the urgent development transitions from strategic to keeping the software running by fixing urgent bugs and patching data directly in the database in an effort to compensate for failures. New features are generally added slowly and gingerly in an attempt to avoid producing even more bugs. Even so, injecting new bugs is inevitable: With the ever-increasing level of system disorder and lost historical perspective, it's impossible to determine the full impact a single given change will have on the greater body of software.

Teams admit that there is no clear and intentional expression of software architecture, either in individual applications (subsystems) or even overall in any large system. Where some sense of architecture exists, it is generally brittle and obsolete given advances in hardware design and operational environments such as the cloud. Software design is also unintentional, and thus appears to be nonexistent. In consequence, most ideas behind an implementation are implicit, committed to the memories of a few people who worked on it. Both architecture and design are by and large ad hoc and just plain weird. These unrecognized failures make for some really sloppy results due to slipshod work.

Just as dangerous as producing no well-defined architecture at all is introducing architecture for merely technical reasons. A fascination often exists among software architects and developers with regard to a novel development style relative to what they previously employed, or even a newly named software tool that is the subject of a lot of hype and industry buzz. This generally introduces accidental complexity[2] because the IT professionals don't fully understand what impacts their ill-advised decisions will have on the overall system, including its execution environment and operations. Yes, Microservices architecture and tools such as Kubernetes, although duly applicable in the proper context, drive a lot of unqualified adoption. Unfortunately, such adoption is rarely driven by insights into business needs.

The prolonged buildup of software model inaccuracies within the system from failure to perform urgent changes is described as the *debt metaphor*. In contrast, the accumulation from accepting uncontrolled changes to a system is known as *software entropy*. Both are worth a closer look.

Debt Metaphor

Decades ago, a very smart software developer, Ward Cunningham, who was at the time working on financial software, needed to explain to his boss why the current efforts directed toward software change were necessary [Cunningham]. The changes being made were not in any way ad hoc; in fact, they were quite the opposite. The kinds of changes being made would make it look as if the software developers had known all along what they were doing, and serve to make it look like it was easy to do. The specific technique they used is now known as *software refactoring*. In this case, the refactoring was done in the way it was meant to be implemented—that is, to reflect the acquisition of new business knowledge into the software model.

To justify this work, Cunningham needed to explain that if the team didn't make adjustments to the software to match their increased learning about the problem domain, they would continue to stumble over the disagreement between the software that existed and their current, refined understanding. In turn, the continued stumbling would slow down the team's progress on continued development, which is *like paying interest on a loan*. Thus, the *debt metaphor* was born.

Anyone can borrow money to enable them to do things sooner than if they hadn't obtained the money. Of course, as long as the loan exists, the borrower will be

---

2. Accidental complexity is caused by developers trying to solve problems, and can be fixed. There is also essential complexity inherent in some software, which is caused by the problems being solved. Although essential complexity cannot be avoided, it can often be isolated in subsystems and components specifically designed to tackle them.

paying interest. The primary idea in taking on debt in the software is to be able to release sooner, but with the idea that you must pay the debt sooner rather than later. The debt is paid by refactoring the software to reflect the team's newly acquired knowledge of the business needs. In the industry at that time, just as it is today, software was rushed out to users knowing that debt existed, but too often teams had the idea that you never have to pay off the debt.

Of course, we all know what happens next. If debt continues to stack up and the person borrows more and more, all the borrower's money goes to paying interest and they reach a point where they have zero buying power. Matters work the same way with software debt, because eventually developers deep in debt will be severely compromised. Adding new features will take longer and longer, to the point where the team will make almost no progress.

One of the major problems with the contemporary understanding of the debt metaphor is that many developers think this metaphor supports deliberately delivering poorly designed and implemented software so as to deliver sooner. Yet, the metaphor doesn't support that practice. Attempting that feat is more like borrowing on subprime loans[3] with upward adjustable interest rates, which often results in the borrower becoming financially overextended to the point of defaulting. Debt is useful only as long as it is controlled; otherwise, it creates instability within the entire system.

Software Entropy

Software entropy[4] is a different metaphor but closely related to the debt metaphor in terms of the software system conditions it describes. The word *entropy* is used in statistical mechanics in the field of thermodynamics to measure a system's disorder. Without attempting to go too deep into this topic: "The second law of thermodynamics states that *the entropy of an isolated system never decreases over time.* Isolated systems spontaneously evolve towards thermodynamic equilibrium, the state with maximum entropy" [Entropy]. The software entropy metaphor names the condition of a software system where change is inevitable, and that change will cause increasing uncontrolled complexity unless a vigorous effort is made to prevent it [Jacobson].

---

3. It's difficult to comprehend that some are unfamiliar with the 2008 financial crisis that extended years into the future. This (ultimately global) crisis was triggered by subprime lending to unqualified borrowers for home purchases. Some early readers of the manuscript for this book asked, "What is a subprime loan?" Learning about that history could save those readers from a lot of financial grief.

4. Other analogs besides entropy also paint a vivid picture of the problem, such as software rot, software erosion, and software decay. The authors mostly use entropy.

Big Ball of Mud

An application or system like the one previously described has become known as a *Big Ball of Mud*. In terms of architecture, it has been further described as haphazardly structured; sprawling; sloppy; duct-taped-and-baling-wired; jungle; unregulated growth; repeated, expedient repair. "Information is shared promiscuously among distant elements of the system, often to the point where nearly all the important information becomes global or duplicated. The overall structure of the system may never have been well defined. If it was, it may have eroded beyond recognition" [BBoM].

It seems appropriate to describe the Big Ball of Mud "architecture" as the *un*architecture.

Throughout the remainder of this chapter, as well as in this book in general, we will key in on a few of these characteristics: haphazardly structured; unregulated growth; repeated, expedient repair; information shared promiscuously; all important information global or duplicated.

An enterprise norm of the Big Ball of Mud results in organizations experiencing competitive paralysis, which has spread across business industries. It is quite common for large enterprises, which once enjoyed competitive distinction, to become hamstrung by systems with deep debt and nearly complete entropy.

You can easily contrast the Big Ball of Mud system in Figure 1.2 to that depicted in Figure 1.1. Of course, the segment of the system in Figure 1.1 doesn't represent the number of features that are supported by the system in Figure 1.2, but clearly the architecture of the first system brings order, whereas the lack thereof in the second offers chaos.

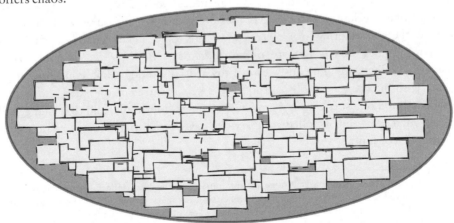

Figure 1.2 *The Big Ball of Mud might be classified as the unarchitecture.*

These chaotic conditions prevent more than a few software releases per year, which result in even worse problems than the software releases of previous years. Individuals and the teams to which they belong tend to become indifferent and complacent because they know they can't produce the change they see as necessary to turn things around. The next level from there is becoming disillusioned and demoralized. Businesses facing this situation cannot innovate in software and continue to compete under such conditions. Eventually they fall victim to a nimble startup that can make significant strides forward, to the point where within a few months to a few years, it can displace previous market leaders.

Running Example

From this point forward, we present a case study using an existing Big Ball of Mud and describe a situation where the affected business struggles to innovate as it faces the realities of the associated deep debt and entropy. Because you might already be tired of reading bad news, here's a spoiler: The situation improves over time.

There is no better way to explain the issues every company has to face with software development than with examples borrowed from the real world. The example offered here as a case study in dealing with an existing Big Ball of Mud comes from the insurance industry.

At some point in life, just about everyone has to deal with an insurance company. There are various reasons why people seek to obtain diverse insurance policies. Some are to address legal requirements, and some provide security measures for the future. These policies include protection for health, personal lines such as life, automobile, home, mortgage, financial products investments, international travel, and even the loss of a favorite set of golf clubs. Policy product innovation in the field of insurance seems endless, where almost any risk imaginable can be covered. If there is a potential risk, you're likely to find an insurance company that will provide coverage for it.

The basic idea behind insurance is that some person or thing is at risk of loss, and for a fee, the calculated financial value of the insured person or thing may be recovered when such loss occurs. Insurance is a successful business proposition due to the law of large numbers. This law says that given a large number of persons and things being covered for risks, the overall risk of loss among all of those covered persons and things is quite small, so the fees paid by all will be far greater than the actual payments made for losses. Also, the greater the probability of loss, the greater the fee that the insurance company will receive to provide coverage.

Imagine the complexity of the insurance domain. Is coverage for automobiles and homes the same? Does adjusting a few business rules that apply to automobiles make covering homes possible? Even if automobile and home policies might be considered "close enough" to hold a lot in common, think of the different risks involved in these two policy types.

Consider some example scenarios. There is a much higher possibility of an automobile striking another automobile than there is of a part of a house striking another house and causing damage. The likelihood of a fire occurring in a kitchen due to normal everyday use is greater than the likelihood of the car's engine catching fire due to normal everyday use. As we can see, the difference between the two kinds of insurance isn't subtle. When considering the variety of possible kinds of coverage, it requires substantial investment to provide policies that have value to those facing risk and that won't be a losing proposition to the insurance company.

Thus, it's understandable that the complexity among insurance firms in terms of business strategy, operations, and software development is considerable. That is why insurance companies tend to specialize in a small subset of insurable products. It's not that they wouldn't want to be a larger player in the market, but rather that costs could easily outweigh the benefits of competing in all possible segments. It's not surprising, then, that insurance companies more often attempt to lead in insurance products in which they have already earned expertise. Even so, adjusting business strategies, accepting unfamiliar yet measured risks, and developing new products might be too lucrative an opportunity to pass up.

It is time to introduce NuCoverage Insurance. This fictitious company is based on real-world scenarios previously experienced by the authors. NuCoverage has become the leader in low-cost auto insurance in the United States. The company was founded in 2001 with a business plan to focus on providing lower-cost premiums for safe drivers. It saw a clear opportunity in focusing on this specific market, and it succeeded. The success came from the company's ability to assess risks and premiums very accurately and offer the lowest-cost policies on the market. Almost 20 years later, the company is insuring 23% of the overall US market, but nearly 70% in the specialized lower-cost safe-driver market.

Current Business Context

Although NuCoverage is a leader in auto insurance, it would like to expand its business to other kinds of insurance products. The company has recently added home insurance and is working on adding personal lines of insurance. However, adding new insurance products became more complex than was originally perceived.

While the development process of personal lines of insurance was ongoing, management had an opportunity to sign a partnership with one of the largest US banks, WellBank. The deal involves enabling WellBank to sell auto insurance under its own brand. WellBank sees great potential in selling auto insurance along with its familiar auto loans. Behind the WellBank auto insurance policies is NuCoverage.

Of course, there are differences between NuCoverage auto insurance products and the ones to be sold by WellBank. The most prominent differences relate to the following areas:

- Premiums and coverages
- Rules and premium price calculation
- Risk assessment

Although NuCoverage has never before experienced this kind of partnership, the business leaders immediately saw the potential to expand their reach, and possibly even introduce a completely new and innovative business strategy. But in what form?

Business Opportunity

NuCoverage's board of directors and executives recognized an even larger strategic opportunity than the WellBank partnership: They could introduce a *white-label*[5] insurance platform that would support any number of fledgling insurers. Many types of businesses might potentially support selling insurance products under the business's own brand. Each business best knows its customers and grasps what insurance products could be offered. The recently inked partnership with WellBank is just one example. NuCoverage can certainly identify other forward-thinking partners that would share the vision of selling insurance products under a white label.

For example, NuCoverage could establish partnerships with car makers that offer their own financing. When a customer purchases a car, the dealer could offer both financing and manufacturer-branded insurance. The possibilities are endless, due to the fact that any random company cannot easily become an insurance company, but can still benefit from the margins gained through insurance sales. In the long run, NuCoverage considered diversifying with new insurance products such as motorcycle, yacht, and even pet insurance.

This possibility seems very exciting to the board and executives, but when the software management team learned about the plans, a few of them had to swallow hard. The original auto insurance application was built quickly under a lot of pressure to deliver, which quickly led to a Big Ball of Mud Monolith. As Figure 1.3 illustrates, with more than 20 years of changes and deep unpaid debt, and the ongoing development of the system for the personal lines of insurance, the teams have reached a point of stifling unplanned complexity. The existing software will absolutely not support current business goals. All the same, development needs to answer the call.

---

5. A white-label product is a product or service produced by one company (the producer) that other companies (the marketers) rebrand to make it appear as if they had made it.

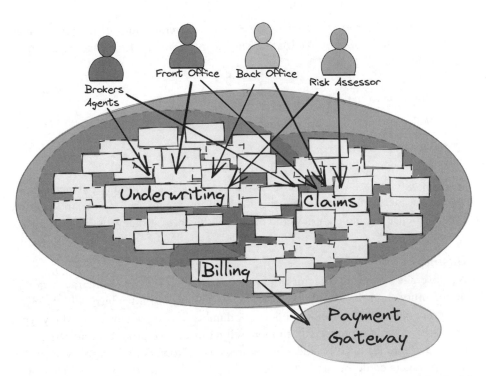

Figure 1.3 *The NuCoverage Big Ball of Mud. All business activities are intertwined with tangled software components that are in deep debt and near maximum entropy.*

What NuCoverage must understand is that its business is no longer insurance alone. It was always a product company, but its products were insurance policies. Its digital transformation is leading the firm to become a technology company, and its products now include software. To that end, NuCoverage must start thinking like a technology product company and making decisions that support that positioning—not only as a quick patch, but for the long term. This is a very important shift in the company mindset. NuCoverage's digital transformation cannot be successful if it is driven only by technology choices. Company executives will need to focus on changing the mindset of the organization's members as well as the organizational culture and processes before they decide what digital tools to use and how to use them.

Your Enterprise and Conway's Law

A long time ago (well, in 1967), in a galaxy not far away (our own), another really smart software developer presented an unavoidable reality of system development.

It's so unavoidable that it has become known as a law. The really smart developer is Mel Conway, and the unavoidable reality is known as Conway's Law.

> Conway's Law: "Organizations which design systems are constrained to produce designs which are copies of the communication structures of these organizations" [Conway].

The correlation to the preceding description of Big Ball of Mud is fairly obvious. It's generally a matter of broken communication that causes the "haphazardly structured; unregulated growth; repeated, expedient repair."

Still, there is another big communication component that's almost always missing: the business stakeholders and the technical stakeholders having productive communication that leads to deep learning, which in turn leads to innovation.

> Assertion: Those who want to build good software that innovates must get this communication–learning–innovation pathway right before trying anything else.

Funny things, these laws. Is it possible to "get better" at a law? For example, humans can't really "get better" at the law of gravity. We know that if we jump, we will land. The law and our earth's gravitational influence even enable us to calculate how much hang time anyone who jumps can possibly have. Some people can jump higher and farther, but they are still subject to the same law of gravity as everyone else on earth.

Just as we don't get better at the law of gravity, we don't really get better at Conway's Law. We are subject to it. So how do we get Conway's Law, right? By training ourselves to be better at dealing with the unavoidable realities of this law. Consider the challenges and the possibilities.

Communication Is about Knowledge

Knowledge is the most important asset in every company. An organization cannot excel at everything, so it must choose its core competencies. The specific knowledge a company acquires within its domain of expertise enables building competitive advantage.

Although a company's knowledge can be materialized in physical artifacts such as documentation, and in models and algorithms by means of source code implementations, these are not comparable to the collective knowledge of its workers. The greater part of the knowledge is carried by individuals in their minds. The knowledge that has not been externalized is known as *tacit knowledge*. It can be collective, such as the routines of unwritten procedures within the business, or the personal preferred ways of working that every individual possesses. Personal knowledge is about skills and crafts—the undocumented trade secrets and historical and contextual knowledge that a company has collected since its founding.

People inside the organization exchange knowledge through effective communication. The better their communication is, the better the company's knowledge sharing will be. Yet, knowledge is not just shared statically as if feeding encyclopedic input with no other gain. Sharing knowledge with an achievement goal in mind results in learning, and the experience of collective learning can result in breakthrough innovation.

Knowledge Is Not an Artifact

Because knowledge is not something that one person passes to another in the same way that a physical object is exchanged, the knowledge transfer takes place as a combination of *sense-giving* and *sense-reading*, as illustrated in Figure 1.4 [Polanyi].

Sense-giving occurs when a person communicates knowledge. The knowledge is structured into information and externalized [LAMSADE]. The person on the receiving side undergoes the process of sense-reading. This individual extracts data from the information received, creating personal knowledge and internalizing it. The probability that two people will give the same meaning to the same information is determined not just by the accuracy of the communication that has occurred between those individuals, but also by past experiences and the specific contexts in which the receiver places it.

It is not guaranteed that the piece of information that someone receives is exactly what another person wants to communicate. This is illustrated with a concrete example.

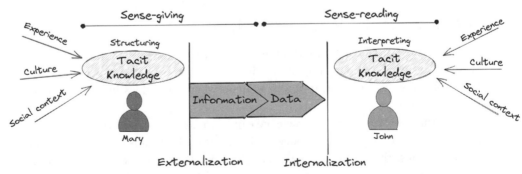

Figure 1.4 *Tacit knowledge transfer through the process of sense-giving and sense-reading.*

The Telephone Game

The Telephone Game illustrates the trouble with certain communication structures. You might know this game by another name, but the rules are the same. People form a line, and at one end of the line a person whispers a message to the next person in line, which is then repeated to the next person, and so forth, until the message reaches the last person in the line. Finally, the last message receiver tells everyone the message that they received, and the person at the beginning of the line discloses the original message. Of course, the fun comes from the repeated message becoming badly distorted by the time it reaches the end.

What's most interesting about this game and the effects on communication is that the distortion occurs at every separate point of communication. Everyone in the line, even those closest to the message's origin, will be told something that they can't repeat accurately. The more points of relay, the more distorted the message becomes.

In essence, every point of relayed communication creates a new translation. This highlights the reality that even communication between just two people is difficult. It's not unfeasible to reach clarity and agreement, but it can be challenging to get there.

When this happens in business, it's not a game, and it isn't fun. And, of course, the more complex the message, the more likely it is for greater degrees of inaccuracy to occur. As Figure 1.5 shows, there are often many points of relay. In very large

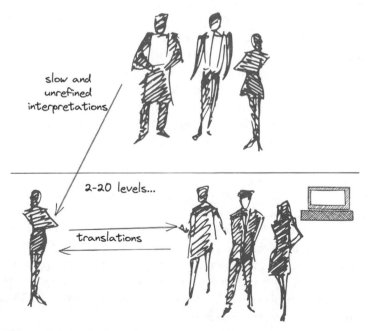

Figure 1.5 *Typical communication structure from C-level to project managers to developers.*

organizations, there might be even more than 20 levels. The authors often hear of so much hierarchy that it seems insuperably difficult for anything in the organization to be accomplished with any degree of accuracy, and the software developers near the end of the line marvel at it.

Reaching Agreement Is Hard

The negative feelings of team members, such as indifference, complacency, disillusionment, and demoralization, can be overcome. It's done by helping the team create reachable goals and providing new, lightweight techniques, such as shaping the team for better communication and engaging in stepwise, value-driven restructuring of the software.

Yet, the separations between points of communication and even the style of communication at each level of hierarchy can cause a widening gap in business and technical stakeholders. When the communication gap is broad in the face of big changes, agreement is hard to achieve.

A noxious problem exists when technical leadership see themselves and their teams as threatened by criticism of their work and hints that big change is imminent. After all, the distorted message being heard intimates that what has existed for a long time isn't sustainable. As has been noted more than a few times throughout history, humans have egos and more often than not are heavily invested in what they have produced as a result of hard work. This strong attachment is often referred to as being "married." When an institution as tightly connected as marriage seems breakable, the involved parties often adopt a defensive posture that not only tightly grips *what* has been done, but also clings to *how* things have been done. Moving beyond that hardened stance isn't easy.

There are also those from outside who strongly recommend the kind of changes that are incompatible with business as usual. This apparent adversary hasn't gone through the decades of hard work under conflicting time forces that are blamed for the deep software debt and entropy that today throbs like two sore thumbs. All of these uncomfortable perceptions accumulate into a pressure cooker of emotions and shouts of "Executive betrayal!" in the conscious thoughts of technical leadership. It's obvious that the responsible parties have been singled out and will now be repaid for ongoing delivery under unrelenting impossible circumstances with a swift shove under a speeding bus.

When technical leadership has these misgivings, they typically multiply their doubts by confiding in at least a few members of their teams who will support their concerns. Naturally those supportive team members themselves confide in others, and the fear leads to widespread resistance.

But Not Impossible

This whole problem is most often perpetuated by a company culture known as "us versus them." This happens, once again, because of deficient communication structures. Glancing back at Figure 1.5, do you see a big problem? It's the hierarchy, which breeds an "us versus them" mentality. Edicts come down from on high and subordinates carry out the orders. If this hierarchy is retained, executives shouldn't expect outcomes that lead to cooperative change.

Cooperative change must emanate from leadership, which begins at the executive level. When executive leadership can see the untenable result of hierarchical command and control, the answer is not to replace the old controlled with the newly controlled.

In every endeavor, teams are by far more successful at large undertakings than are individuals. Mature sports teams succeed by crafting innovative playbooks and communicating each play to the whole team with tedious precision.

Acting like a team requires being a team. In teams, communication is not one way. Any one team member can have enough experience to suggest that something was overlooked in the playbook, or that a given play could be better with this or that additional move or removal of an inefficiency. When every team member is respected for their competency and experienced viewpoint, it serves to make communication that much more effective (Figure 1.6).

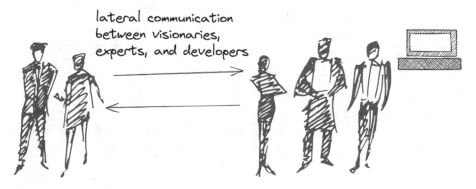

Figure 1.6 *Optimal communication structures are the result of team play.*

Consider these keys to optimal communication:

- It's us, not us and them.
- Servant leadership must not be beneath anyone.
- Realize the power in building strategic organizational structures.

- No one should feel threatened for communicating their constructive viewpoints.

- Positive influence is critical in motivating people toward constructive action.

- Forming business–technical partnerships based on mutual respect is essential.

- Deep communication, critical thinking, and cooperation are indispensable to achieve disruptive, transformational, software systems.

These strategic behavioral patterns are not new and novel. They are centuries old and are the practices of successful organizations.

Conway's Law doesn't leave anyone guessing about how to make organizational communication structures work for the greater good. As the conclusion of Conway's paper states:

> We have found a criterion for the structuring of design organizations: a design effort should be *organized according to the need for communication.*
>
> Because the design which occurs first is almost never the best possible solution, the prevailing system concept may need to change. Therefore, *flexibility of organization is important to effective design.*
>
> Ways must be found to reward design managers for keeping their organizations lean and flexible. [Conway]

These ideas are reflected in Figure 1.5 and are woven throughout this book.

(Re)Thinking Software Strategy

Focusing on thinking and rethinking before the more technical bits is advisable. Until we understand what strategic business goals must be pursued, we shouldn't try to specify system technical characteristics. After some thoughts on thinking and rethinking, introducing system-level planning will have meaning and purpose.

Thinking

Known as the source of many quotable quotes, (George) Bernard Shaw made this statement with regard to thinking:

> I suppose that you seldom think. Few people think more than two or three times a year. I have made an international reputation for myself by thinking once or twice a week.

Of course, we all think every day. Life would be impossible without thought. Yet, Shaw's entertaining statement exposes an interesting fact about people in general. Much of life is conducted in routine function and regularly employs a kind of auto-pilot. The less people need to think about specifics, the less they will tend to think consciously about what they do. This is why older people tend to lose cognition unless they remain mentally engaged into their later years. Shaw shows that *deep thought* by even the most notable among thinkers may not occur that often. Rightly, then, a lack of deep thought is a concern even among knowledge workers.

The problem with knowledge workers going on autopilot is that software has little tolerance for mistakes, and especially mistakes left unaddressed for long periods of time. If individual software developers aren't careful, they will become lax in paying debt in their software and transition into the mode of allowing unregulated growth and using repeated, expedient repair.

There is also a concern that developers will begin to increasingly rely on what product companies want to sell them, rather than thinking for themselves in the context of their business focus. New technology buzz and hype are pumped in from outside with much more frequency than is possible from internal business channels. However, the constant drumbeats are missing the context of what matters most locally. Developers who have become complacent may wish for technology to solve the problems. Others will simply long for new toys to engage their minds. Likewise, the dynamic underlying the Fear of Missing Out (FOMO) is not driven by deep, critical thought.

As Figure 1.7 highlights, thinking a lot about everything involved in system specification is essential in making proper business decisions, and later the necessary supporting technical decisions. Here are some motivation checkers:

- *What are we doing?* Perhaps poor-quality software is being released as a means to meet a deadline. This doesn't put the teams in a good position to refactor later, and chances are strong that refactoring is not planned. It's possible that the team is pushing for a big reimplementation using a newer, more popular architecture as a solution. Don't overlook the fact that those involved have already failed to introduce a helpful architecture into existing systems or allowed a lapse in maintaining the architecture that was already in place.

- *Why are we doing it?* External messages based on selling products as solutions may sound more attractive than taking sensible steps to shore up existing software that has lost its reason for existing in exchange for simply keeping it operational. FOMO and CV-driven development can become a stronger motivator rather than practicing good development techniques. Be certain that a particular architecture or technology is justified by actual business and technical needs.

- *Think about all the things.* Every single learning must be examined with critical thought, both for and against. Having a strong opinion and talking the loudest is proof of nothing. Thinking in an informed manner, clearly, broadly, deeply, and critically are all extremely important. These can lead to deep learning.

Seeking deep thought kicks off our real mission, which is rethinking our approach to software development that leads to strategic differentiation.

Figure 1.7 *Be a leader in thought. Think a lot and discuss.*

Rethinking

The ancient Hippocratic Oath[6] is said to have included the statement "First do no harm." This seems relevant not only in medicine but in other fields, including software engineering. A legacy system is just that—a legacy. Legacy implies value,

---

6. Whether the Hippocratic Oath is still considered relevant and applicable today, or at what point the specific statement "First do no harm" originated, is beside the point being made. Many physicians still perceive the oath and the highlighted statement as important.

something that is inherited. After all, if it didn't have value, it wouldn't be a legacy; it would be unplugged. The system's continued and broad use is what makes it irreplaceable at present. As much as software professionals often think that the business doesn't get it, the business totally gets that decades of investment into a system that has supported and still supports revenues must not be harmed.

Of course, the deep debt and entropy might not be the fault of those currently responsible for keeping a system operational, or those who highly recommend its ultimate replacement. Frankly, many legacy systems do need some help into retirement. This is especially the case when these systems are implemented with one or more archaic programming languages, technologies, and hardware created by people with great-grandchildren, or who are no longer with us. If this sounds like COBOL using an old database and running on mainframe computers, the authors won't deny the similarities.

Still, there are other systems matching this description, such as the many business systems built on C/C++. At the time the work was done, C/C++ was admittedly a better choice than COBOL. One big advantage was the low memory footprint required by C programs, and the fact that a lot of software was being built for PCs and their 256K–640K RAM limits. There are also systems built on completely obsolete and unsupported languages and technologies such as FoxPro, marginalized Delphi, and the only-mostly-dead Visual Basic language.

The major problem with replacing a legacy system is related to losing features in the replacement process or just plain breaking things that previously worked. Replacement also happens in the face of continued legacy change—perhaps slow change, but change nonetheless. Change doesn't necessarily mean new features. It can mean daily patches of code and persisted data. Trying to replace a moving target is like, well, trying to replace a moving target. It's hard. This is not to mention the fact that the software is already in the condition it's in because it hasn't received the care it has both deserved and needed. So suddenly introducing great care as the target moves and as people are actively firing rounds at it seems iffy at best.

That a system is to be justifiably replaced using modern architectures, programming languages, and technologies doesn't make the task any less precarious. Many conclude that jumping in and getting it over with by ripping apart the current implementation and coding up a new one is the only way to go. It is common for those championing such efforts to request several months to accomplish this feat, undisturbed by change. That request translates into halting the moving target for a number of months, and as has already been noted, the system will very likely require patches to code and data. Shall those be put on hold for an unknown length of time?

When There's No Choice

One of the authors was involved in such an effort when platforms shifted out from under an implementation. For example, think of moving a large system with a graphical user interface implemented on MS-DOS to the Microsoft Windows API. One really tricky thing, among many that you never think about until you are deep into the problem, is that two APIs may transpose parameters. For example, in the different APIs, the GUI X,Y coordinate system changed. Missing even one of those translations can cause untold problems that are extremely difficult to track down. In this case, "extremely difficult" involved months of investigation. The overarching reason for the complexity was the unsafe memory space with C/C++ programs, where incorrect memory references not only overwrite memory in invalid ways, but sometimes end up overwriting memory in different ways every time. Thus, the bizarre memory access violations occurred in many mysterious ways.

Of course, that's not a typical problem faced in today's modernizations—modern programming languages mostly prevent that specific kind of error. In any case, there are potential gotchas that are completely unpredictable. Dealing with these kinds of unplanned complications can eat up much of the "number of months" that were presumably reserved for "jumping in, ripping apart, and coding up a new one." It's always harder and takes longer than you think.

Where is the rethinking in all this? In blowing the common legacy escape hatch, it appears likely that a lot of harm will be done. It's a knee-jerk reaction to vast problems that leads to a high probability of replacing them with immense problems or ending up with two sets of enormous problems. The Big Ball of Mud being the enterprise norm leads to competitive paralysis—but to first cause no harm, the patient must still be able to breathe if there can be any hope to perform health-restoring treatments. We need to find a way to jump into a reimplementation, but not by doing one of those cannonball dives that makes a huge splash. This requires some special anti-splash measures and maneuvers.

What hasn't been considered is the creation of new learning opportunities. If we merely rewrite in C# a large system that was originally implemented in Visual Basic, from a strategic point of view nothing at all has been learned. One client, for example, observed in a replacement effort of a COBOL legacy system that 70% of the business rules developed over 40 years had become obsolete. These still lived in the COBOL code and required cognitive load to deal with them. Now, imagine not learning this information, but instead spending the time and the effort to translate all of these business rules from COBOL to a modern architecture, programming language, and technology set. The transformation was already a complex multiyear program without including a very large body of unnecessary rework.

Expanding our previous motivation checkers, the following questions highlight the need for vital strategic learnings:

- *What are the business goals and strategies?* Every software feature within a strategic initiative should have direct traceability to a core business goal. To accomplish this, state (1) the business goal, (2) the target market segment (persons and/or groups) that must be influenced to reach that goal, and (3) the impact that must be made on the target market segment. Until the necessary impacts are understood, there is no way to identify the software functionality that is needed or a range of specific requirements. The tools for uncovering the strategic goals and impacts are described later in this book.

- *Why aren't we doing it?* There's another important term in technology that needs to be taken into account when making strategic decisions: You Aren't Gonna Need It (YAGNI). This term was meant to help teams avoid the development of currently unnecessary business features, and there are good reasons to do so. Spending time and money, and taking risks, on delivering unnecessary software is a poor choice. Unfortunately, declaring YAGNI has become a general way to cast any opposing viewpoint in a bad light. Using YAGNI as a trump card won't win team loyalty or create breakthrough learning opportunities. Sometimes not implementing some features that "aren't needed" is a mistake of enormous proportions. If a breakthrough that can lead to innovative differentiation is shot down immediately, it's likely more a problem with the shooters' ability to think deeply and recognize an opportunity or the loss thereof. In fact, absolutely refusing to make room for subsequent discussions will reveal the weakest thinkers in the mix.

- *Can we try new things?* Teams might agree or disagree about what might work in their target market. It is mostly impossible to absolutely foresee the market's reaction to a given expression of strategy. Gauging the market's response accurately requires giving the market the opportunity to try out the business ideas. Using the science of experimentation may provide the only true way to understand the real possibilities and limitations of strategies; however, to try new things, it's not always easy to think outside of the established mental model. "It is tremendously difficult for people to realize when they are chained to a model, especially if it is subconscious or so woven into the culture or their expectations that they can no longer see how much it is holding them back" [Brabandère].

- *What are the service-level requirements?* Once a reasonable set of strategic business goals is understood, the teams involved can start to identify the necessary architectural decisions that must be made. The candidate architectural decisions will depend on the service-level requirements. Teams should not settle on solutions too quickly because there are often advantages in delaying decisions about some details of the architecture. For example, even if the teams are convinced that a Microservices architecture is necessary, delaying the introduction of services separated by the computing network can help the team focus on actual business drivers rather than trying to cope with the distributed computing overhead too early. (See the section "Deployment Last," in Chapter 2, "Essential Strategic Learning Tools.")

Rethinking is a critical step, and it feels right. There is a benefit from thinking multidimensionally and critically, and rethinking from a position of ordinary to a fresh strategic vantage point.

We need not conclude, however, that all legacy Monoliths are necessarily the Big Ball of Mud variety. While the vast majority are definitely Big Ball of Mud systems, we must think carefully before making this judgment. The point being made follows next.

Are Monoliths Bad?

Over the past several years, the words *Monolith* and *Monolithic* as applied to software have come to have very negative connotations. Even so, just because the vast majority of Monolithic legacy systems have arrived at the Big Ball of Mud zone, that doesn't mean it is a necessary destination. It's not the Monolith that's the problem—it's the mud.

The term *Monolith* can simply mean that the software of an entire application or whole system is housed in a container that is designed to hold more than one subsystem. The Monolith container often holds all or most of the subsystems of an entire application or system. Because every part of the system is held in one container, it is described as *self-contained*.

The internal architecture of a Monolith can be designed to keep the components of different subsystems isolated from each other, but can also provide the means for communication and information exchange between subsystems. Figure 1.8 shows the same two subsystems from Figure 1.1, but with both subsystems inside a Monolithic container.

In Figure 1.1, we assumed that the two subsystems were physically separated from each other in two processes, and that they communicated via a network. That diagram implies a distributed system. In Figure 1.8, the same two subsystems are physically together in the same process and perform their information exchange through simple in-process mechanisms such as programming language methods or functions.

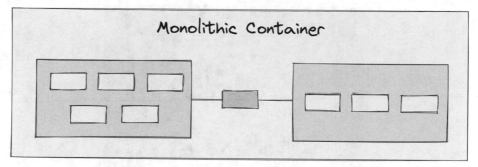

Figure 1.8 *A Monolithic container showing a portion of a whole system. Only two of possibly several subsystems that make up the whole are shown here.*

Even if the ultimate system architecture is to be Microservices, there are advantages to the system starting out life as a Monolith. Not having a network between subsystems can prevent a lot of problems that are unnecessary to contend with early on and are quite counterproductive. Also, using a Monolith is a good way to demonstrate commitment to loose coupling between subsystems when it is easier to allow tight coupling. If transforming to a Microservices architecture is the plan, you will ultimately find out how loose the coupling actually is.

Although some oppose the approach of using a Monolithic architecture for early development where a distributed Microservices architecture is the target, please reserve judgment until this topic is discussed in Parts II and III of this book.

Are Microservices Good?

The term *Microservice* has come to mean many different things. One definition is that a Microservice should be no more than 100 lines of code. Another claims that it's not 100 lines, but 400. Yet another asserts that it's 1,000 lines. There are at least a few problems with all of these attempted definitions, which probably reflect more on the name itself. The term "micro" is often seen to imply size—but what does "micro" mean?

When using "micro" to describe computer CPUs, the full term is *microprocessors*. The basic idea behind a microprocessor is that it packs all the functionality of a CPU onto one or a few integrated circuits. Before the design and availability of microprocessors, computers typically relied on a number of circuit boards with many integrated circuits.

Note, however, that the term *microprocessor* doesn't carry the idea of size, as if some arbitrary specific number of integrated circuits or transistors is either appropriate or not. Figure 1.9 shows a case in point—that one of the most powerful CPUs

Figure 1.9 *The Intel Xeon is one of the most powerful modern microprocessors. No one has said it is not a microprocessor because it has "too many circuits and transistors."*

available is still a microprocessor. For example, the 28-core Xeon Platinum 8180 sports 8 billion transistors. The Intel 4004 had 2,250 transistors (year 1971). Both are microprocessors.

Microprocessor limits are generally set based on purpose; that is, some microprocessor types simply don't need to provide the power of others. They can be used for small devices that have limited power resources, and thus should require less draws on power. Also, when the power of a single microprocessor—even one of outstanding proportions—is not enough for the computing circumstances, computers are supplied with multiple microprocessors.

Another problem with putting some arbitrary limit on the number of lines of code in a Microservice is the fact that a programming language has a lot to do with the number of lines of code required to support some specific system functionality. Saying that this limit is 100 lines of code for Java is different than saying it is 100 lines of code for Ruby, because Java tends to require 33% more code than Ruby. In a matchup of Java versus Clojure, Java requires around 360% more lines of code.

Furthermore, and even more germane to the point, creating tiny-tiny Microservices has been shown to result in a number of disadvantages:

- The sheer number of Microservices can grow beyond hundreds, to thousands, and even tens of thousands.

- Lack of dependency comprehension leads to unpredictability of changes.

- Unpredictability of change results in no changes or decommissioning.

- More Microservices are created with similar (copy-paste) functionality.

- The expense of ever-growing yet often obsolete Microservices increases.

These major disadvantages suggest that the result is unlikely to be the hoped-for cleaner distributed system solution and autonomy. With the background given in this chapter, the problem should be apparent. In essence, the many tiny-tiny Microservices have created the same situation as the Monolithic Big Ball of Mud, as seen in Figure 1.10. No one understands the system, which falls prey to the same issues that are experienced with a Monolithic Big Ball of Mud: haphazard structure; unregulated growth; repeated, expedient repair; information shared promiscuously; all important information global or duplicated.

Some solutions and additional efforts may be made to move beyond these outcomes, but they generally do not use a completely separate container deployment per Microservice.

The best way to think about a Microservice is not by defining the size, but rather by determining the purpose. A Microservice is smallish in comparison to a Monolith, but the guidance we provide is to avoid implementing tiny-tiny Microservices. These points are discussed in detail later, in Part II of this book.

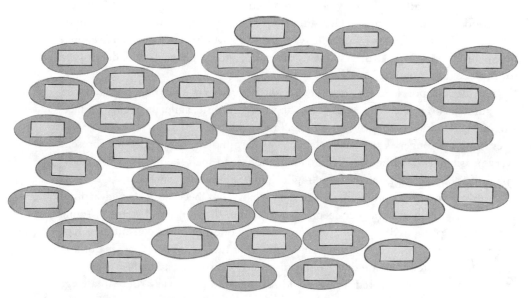

Figure 1.10 *Many tiny-tiny Microservices result in a distributed Big Ball of Mud.*

Don't Blame Agile

In the 1969 film *If It's Tuesday, This Must Be Belgium*, a tour guide leads groups of Americans on fast-paced sightseeing tours through Europe. As far as touring is concerned, this is a classic example of travelers going through the motions.

The same kind of tour can happen with agile software development. "It's 10:00 a.m. and we're standing. We must be doing agile." With reference to daily standups, going through the motions turns otherwise valuable project communications into mere ceremony. Reading Scrum.org on the topic "Agile: Methodology or Framework or Philosophy" is a real eye-opener. At the time of writing, there were approximately 20 replies to this post, and about as many different answers.[7] A reasonable question regarding this concern is, why should that matter?

Recently, agile software development has drawn a lot of criticism. Perhaps most of the criticism is directed toward a specific project management methodology for which mastery certifications can be obtained after a few days of training, because the two are often conflated. This is a sad state, given what agile software development should represent. Much of the industry claiming to use agile methodology or to be agile can't really define it, as noted in the previous Scrum.org experience.

The original agile philosophy never promised to turn poor software developers into good software developers. Has agile made any promises at all? There's a mindset to developing software in an agile way (the Agile Manifesto), and there is a history behind that [Cockburn]. As already observed, agile can't even cause developers to embrace that mindset.

Consider one problem. The ideas of agile software development have been reduced to arguments over whether to refer to this approach as Agile, agile, or "Agile." In fact, we could even draw fire for referring to it as an "approach." So, from here on, we will refer to "it" no longer as "it" but as #agile. This terminology is intended to represent every possible use. However each individual chooses to spell #agile, software developers must demand to get more from #agile than #agile takes from them.

Consider a second problem. A vast complexity has become wrapped around some rather straightforward concepts. For example, the terms and steps of #agile are actually presented as subway maps. At least one high-end consultancy represents its #agile approach in the form of a map of the New York City or London subway/tube system. Although traveling anywhere on an extensive subway network is not extremely complicated, most wouldn't choose to take every route in a large system on a daily or weekly basis just to reach a necessary destination, such as the workplace in the morning and home in the evening.

---

7. Given that the number of permutations in three options is six, somehow ending with 20 answers seems odder than the fact that there are even 20 answers at all.

This is all very unfortunate. Many have hijacked #agile and moved it far away from its origins, or simply travel in naivety. Usage should be far simpler. Working in #agile should boil down to these four things: collaborate, deliver, reflect, and improve [Cockburn-Forgiveness].

Before accepting any extraneous and elaborate routes, teams should learn how to get to work and back home in these four basic steps:

1. *Identify goals.* Goals are larger than individual work tasks. They require collaboration to find the impacts that your software must make on the consumer. These kinds of impacts change the consumers' behaviors in positive ways. They are recognized by consumers as what they need, but before they even realized their need.

2. *Define short iterations and implement.* An iteration is a procedure in which repetition of a sequence of operations yields results successively closer to a desired result. A team collaborates to identify these. Given project pressures, unavoidable interruptions, and other distractions, including the end of day and week, teams should limit work items to a number that can be readily remembered and grasped.

3. *Deploy increments when legitimate value is achieved.* An increment is the action or process of increasing, especially in quantity or value; something gained or added; or the amount or degree by which something changes. If delivery of value is not possible by means of one day's work, then at least an increment toward value can be reached. Teams should be able to string together one or two additional days of iterations and reach value delivery.

4. *Review the outcome, record debt, goto 1.* Now reflect on what was accomplished (or not), with the intention of improving. Has the increment achieved an intended and vital impact? If not, the team may shift toward another set of iterations with increments of different value. If so, note what the team sees as reasons for success. Even when reaching delivery of some critical value, it is normal that an incremental result doesn't leave the team feeling entirely successful. Implementation leads to increased learning and a clearer understanding of the problem space. The iteration is time boxed and doesn't leave enough time to immediately remodel or refactor current results. Record it as debt. The debt can be addressed in the next iterations, leading to an increment of improved value that gets delivered.

Planning too far ahead will lead to conflicts in goals and execution. Going too far too fast can lead to purposely overlooking debt or forgetting to record it. When under heavy pressure, the team might fail to care for debt sooner than later.

The few steps identified in this brief overview of essential #agile can take teams a long way forward. This is the mindset that experimentation affords, and what #agile should primarily be about. It's possible to get more out of #agile than #agile takes.

Getting Unstuck

Any company that has gotten stuck in a Big Ball of Mud and taken complex detours with technologies and techniques needs to get unstuck and find its way out. There isn't one single answer; there are no silver bullets. At the same time, there are means that can serve companies well.

A software system that has become deeply in debt and possibly reached the maximum entropy level took years or even decades for its sterling qualities to erode and digress that far. It's going to take time to make progress out of this mess. Even so, effecting big change is not a waste of time or money. Consider two reasons for this assertion, both based on the poor decision to continue to invest in a losing proposition:

- *Escalation of commitment.* This is a human behavior pattern in which an individual or group facing increasingly negative outcomes from a decision, action, or investment nevertheless continues the behavior instead of altering course. The actor maintains behaviors that are irrational, but align with previous decisions and actions [EoC].

- *Sunk cost fallacy.* A sunk cost is a sum paid in the past that is no longer relevant to decisions about the future. "Sunk costs do, in fact, influence people's decisions, with people believing that investments (e.g., sunk costs) justify further expenditures. People demonstrate 'a greater tendency to continue an endeavor once an investment in money, effort, or time has been made.' Such behavior may be described as 'throwing good money after bad,' while refusing to succumb to what may be described as 'cutting one's losses'" [SunkCost].

This does not mean that saving any part of the preexisting system always equates to chasing the sunk cost fallacy. The point is that continuing to maintain the existing system as is, with its deep debt and near maximum entropy, is a losing proposition from both an emotional standpoint and a financial position.

Time won't stand still and change won't cease while teams heroically defeat the great brown blob. Moving onward as time ticks away while surrounded by mud and inevitable change, and without sinking deeper, is an absolute necessity. Succeeding under those conditions depends more on attitude than on distributed computing. Positive attitude is developed through confidence, and the remainder of this book delivers a number of tools and techniques to build the confidence needed to make strides to achieve strategic innovation.

Summary

This chapter discussed the importance of *innovation* as a means to achieve software differentiation as a primary business goal. To aim for relentless improvement in digital transformation is the strongest play in the age of "software is eating the world." Software architecture was introduced, along with the role that it plays inside every company. The chapter explored how the effects of Conway's Law shape the communication paths inside organizations and teams, and the ways it impacts the software produced by organizations and teams. Discussing the importance of communication brought the topic of *knowledge* to the fore. Knowledge is one of the most important assets in every company. To obtain the best results with software, knowledge must be raised from tacit to shared. Knowledge cannot be shared without proper communication paths, and competitive advantage can't be achieved without either. Ultimately, bad communication leads to incomplete knowledge and poorly modeled software—and then to the Big Ball of Mud as the best possible outcome. Finally, we focused on the original #agile mindset and how it can help teams to get unstuck and focus on the right goals.

The principal points made in this chapter are as follows:

- Innovation is the most important aspect of digital transformation. Innovation leads to profitable differentiation from competitors, and should therefore be a strategic goal of every company.

- Software architecture must support the inevitable change without extreme cost and effort. Without good architecture, the best alternative is bad architecture, which eventually leads to unarchitecture.

- The Big Bull of Mud is often the outcome of broken communication that can't possibly lead to deep learning and shared knowledge.

- The people in organizations must exchange knowledge through open and nuanced communication that can lead to breakthroughs in innovation.

- Monoliths are not necessarily bad and Microservices are not necessarily good. Choosing one over the other based on purpose is a result of an informed decision.

Chapter 2 introduces strategic learning tools that can help mitigate poor communication and set the bar higher for enterprise culture. By applying these tools, you can learn how to make informed decisions based on experimentation, and how they can affect the resulting software and its architecture.

References

[ANW] A. N. Whitehead. "Technical Education and Its Relation to Science and Literature." *Mathematical Gazette* 9, no. 128 (1917): 20–33.

[a16z-CloudCostParadox] https://a16z.com/2021/05/27/cost-of-cloud-paradox-market-cap-cloud-lifecycle-scale-growth-repatriation-optimization/

[BBoM] https://en.wikipedia.org/wiki/Big_ball_of_mud

[Brabandère] Luc de Brabandère and Alan Iny. *Thinking in New Boxes: A New Paradigm for Business Creativity.* New York: Random House, 2013.

[Cockburn] https://web.archive.org/web/20170626102447/http://alistair.cockburn.us/How+I+saved+Agile+and+the+Rest+of+the+World

[Cockburn-Forgiveness] https://www.youtube.com/watch?v=pq1EXK_yL04 (presented in French, English, and Spanish)

[Conway] http://melconway.com/Home/Committees_Paper.html

[Cunningham] http://wiki.c2.com/?WardExplainsDebtMetaphor

[Entropy] https://en.wikipedia.org/wiki/Entropy

[EoC] https://en.wikipedia.org/wiki/Escalation_of_commitment

[Jacobson] https://en.wikipedia.org/wiki/Software_entropy

[LAMSADE] Pierre-Emmanuel Arduin, Michel Grundstein, Elsa Negre, and Camille Rosenthal-Sabroux. "Formalizing an Empirical Model: A Way to Enhance the Communication between Users and Designers." *IEEE 7th International Conference on Research Challenges in Information Science* (2013): 1–10. doi: 10.1109/RCIS.2013.6577697.

[Manifesto] https://agilemanifesto.org/

[Polanyi] M. Polanyi. "Sense-Giving and Sense-Reading." *Philosophy: Journal of the Royal Institute of Philosophy* 42, no. 162 (1967): 301–323.

[SunkCost] https://en.wikipedia.org/wiki/Sunk_cost

Chapter 2

Essential Strategic Learning Tools

A strategy is the *what* aspect of business creation, leading to new initiatives that are intentionally unique and produce a combination of profit sources. It asks, what must our business do to differentiate, or extend and increase its uniqueness, from other businesses? This makes strategic planning a means to attain innovation, but there must actually be innovation in recognizing a valuable, differentiated strategy.

> So you can't go out and ask people, you know, what the next big thing is. There's a great quote by Henry Ford, right? He said, "If I'd have asked my customers what they wanted, they would have told me 'A faster horse.'"
>
> —Steve Jobs

This doesn't mean that it would be fruitless to ask a customer what they think is the next big thing. Actually "a faster horse" can be a great hint that "faster travel" is the critical takeaway. It is important to talk with customers and the public in general. Still, the business should have the talent to gain a keen understanding of the *what* part of business. It's a requisite for success. It must be sought after, and the dig-and-find happens through learning. Note the earlier part of the quote from Jobs, speaking of Apple's own internal talent with regard to the iPod.

> We did iTunes because we all love music. We made what we thought was the best juke-box in iTunes. Then we all wanted to carry our whole music libraries around with us. The team worked really hard. And the reason that they worked so hard is because we all wanted one. You know? I mean, the first few hundred customers were us.
>
> It's not about pop culture, and it's not about fooling people, and it's not about convincing people that they want something they don't. We figure out what we want. And I think we're pretty good at having the right discipline to think through whether a lot of other people are going to want it, too. That's what we get paid to do.
>
> —Steve Jobs

To learn well, it sure helps to have good tools for digging to unearth knowledge from people and facts. This chapter provides strategic discovery tools and demonstrates how they can be used. Some of the best tools are more inside than outside.

Making Decisions Early and Late, Right and Wrong

Decisions can be paralyzing if you don't learn how to thrive on making timely, as well as right and wrong, decisions. Both can work to our advantage. Don't fear decision making. Understand when decisions should be made. Some decisions are best made as early as possible; others are best made as late as possible. Some decisions will be right; some will be wrong. Gain the fortitude and acquire the techniques required to celebrate hard decisions, right and wrong.

A common principle of #agile is that all decisions should be made at the last responsible moment [Cohn]. How do we know when we have reached this "last responsible moment" decision point at any given time? Advice is provided by Mary and Tom Poppendieck:

> Concurrent software development means starting development when only partial requirements are known and developing in short iterations that provide the feedback that causes the system to emerge. Concurrent development makes it possible to delay commitment until the last responsible moment, that is, the moment at which failing to make a decision eliminates an important alternative. If commitments are delayed beyond the last responsible moment, then decisions are made by default, which is generally not a good approach to making decisions. [Poppendieck]

More concisely, it can be said that decisions should not be made irresponsibly, whether they are made early or late [LeanArch]. Irresponsible decision making occurs when there is not enough insight to support any given decision, which is likely an occasion of making decisions too early. Yet, gaining necessary insight is possible if there is currently enough information to support a decision. If information is available but unvetted, the next steps should be obvious.

As time advances, avoiding necessary decisions is even worse than making the wrong decisions. Self-motivated workers don't sit around waiting for things to happen. Early on, writing some initial code or defining general-purpose modeling abstractions is common behavior, and usually involves at least a few opinionated developers going in different directions. These arbitrary actions lead to commitments but exclude the team from the decision-making process. That pattern sets a definite structure for the application or the underlying architecture that can last for the entire software life cycle.

Ask yourself, is it really desirable to commit to uncontrolled structure, form, and abstraction based on unconfirmed assumptions? Obviously, it is best to consciously decide on the direction that application architecture should take. Even so, it's possible for a team to drag its collective feet for fear of creating the wrong architecture.

Decisions can be made if the team has enough information to get started. This might involve several practitioners providing different viewpoints, but kicking the can down the road can't go on indefinitely. Moreover, if we make some poor decisions, they are not necessarily written in stone. Assuming a team can be honest about the negative impacts of accepting poor decisions and not allowing them to go unaddressed, they will take corrective action as quickly as possible. Refactoring an architectural structure early on is not a large time sink. Later on, that cost increases. Making course corrections is all part of learning, and learning should lead to changes.

Yet, if we waited a long time to start structuring the application before we made the wrong decision, what would be gained? Would delaying have brought about the same decision that was made when corrective action was taken? Or was experiencing the ill effects of a wrong decision what led to the better decision? Experience has shown that the latter tends to prevail. This is why we record debt and pay it as soon as possible. That is actually mature decision making at the last responsible moment.

This points back to attitude: Don't be paralyzed by decision making or by making a decision that proves to be wrong. As a computer scientist—a purposeful juxtaposition to a software developer—almost everything done can be treated as an experiment. We are confident that some experiments are only confirmations that our assumptions were correct. Other experiments are undertaken to determine if anything we thought stands up to the test.

In the end, making some decisions early on is irresponsible. For example, settling upfront on architecture, such as using Microservices, or trying to create generalized solutions and modeling abstractions, is wrong. These decisions should be postponed until we prove that those choices are justified and necessary.

The difference between experts and amateurs has much to do with timing.

In his essay "Delaying Commitment" (*IEEE Software*, May/June 1988), leading British computer scientist and professor Harold Thimbleby observes that the difference between amateurs and experts is that experts know how to delay commitments and conceal their errors for as long as possible, repairing flaws before they cause problems. Amateurs try to get everything right the first time, so overloading their problem-solving capacity that they end up committing early to wrong decisions [DrDobbs].

What Thimbleby didn't say is that the expert continuously records debt and pays it, even if it is done informally in their isolated thoughts.

The outcome of making decisions is the learning process it triggers. Decision leads to actions, which cause new requirements and knowledge to emerge. At the same time, progress is made in solving core application challenges. Don't neglect this aspect of decision making, because in the end it comes down to learning and knowledge acquisition. As described in Chapter 1, "Business Goals and Digital Transformation," knowledge is the most important asset in any business. Knowledge changes everything.

There is still the risk that our uncertainties will influence us in other ways. Cognitive biases regularly lead people to make irresponsible decisions. We may also fall for fallacies such as the Fear of Missing Out, among others [LogFal]. Consider some influences in the context of irresponsibly choosing Microservices:

- *Appeal to authority.* An appeal to authority is an argument stemming from a person judged to be an authority and affirming a proposition to the claim that the proposition is true. For example, if someone recognized as an expert claims that Microservices are good and Monoliths are bad, the listener can make decisions that are harmful and inappropriate for their own context.

- *Appeal to novelty.* Appeals to novelty assume that the newness of an idea is evidence of its truth. If Microservices are the newest fad, adoption is a must.

- *Bandwagon fallacy.* Similar to Fear of Missing Out. The bandwagon fallacy occurs when arguments appeal to the growing popularity of an idea as a reason for accepting it as true. People take the mere fact that an idea suddenly attracts adherents as a reason to join in with the trend and become adherents of the idea themselves. Microservices are growing in popularity so we have to adopt them very quickly as well.

Tools are available that can help fight all kinds of fallacies and confirmation biases. One of them is to use critical thinking.

Critical thinking is a type of thinking pattern that requires people to be reflective, and pay attention to decision-making which guides their beliefs and actions. Critical thinking allows people to deduct with more logic, to process sophisticated information and to look at various sides of issues, so that they can produce more solid conclusions. [CT]

Software development involves a considerable amount of decision making, whether or not a specific decision has a large impact. It's rarely straightforward to trace the roads taken, and the roads not taken, through the software life cycle. This is especially the case for the project newcomer. Yet, it's even difficult for long-time team members to recall every past decision. Perhaps a given team member wasn't directly involved in a specific decision. More often, the sheer number of decisions made by a team, combined with the fact that the memories of those decisions aren't strengthened by frequent travel through the hippocampus, impedes instant recall. Under these conditions, a team is often left with only the result of a decision, without a way of tracing why it was made.

Although commonly neglected or completely unconsidered, decision tracking should be one of the most important activities in software development. Tools such as Architecture Decision Record (ADR) help teams maintain a decision log, which is very helpful in tracking the team's decision journey, including what happened and why. ADR helps connect the initial subject of the decision to the expected and ultimate outcome of that decision. The section "Strategic Architecture," later in this chapter, describes ADR and other techniques in more detail.

A wealth of software development techniques exist that can help teams in deferring binding long-term decisions and tracing the decisions being made in the life cycle of a software development project. These are described later in this book. One such tool is the Ports and Adapters Architecture, which is discussed in Chapter 8, "Foundation Architecture." In addition, cognitive frameworks such as Cynefin, which is described later in this chapter, may be used to aid in decision making.

Culture and Teams

Creating an #agile culture that uses experimentation and learning requires that people be rewarded for being wrong as long as that process eventually leads to being right, whatever "right" ends up being. Businesses that want to succeed at digital transformation must change their culture from a perspective of software as support to the view of software as product. Culture is a big deal, and so is how teams are formed and supported.

Engineering Model versus Contractor Model

This is a good place to introduce the idea of using an engineering model approach to software development as opposed to the contractor model. First consider the typical contractor model. Under this model, whether used by employees or actual contractors, developers must be given accurate tasks to work on, and they must not fail in even small ways. The engineering model uses hypothesis-based experimentation to explore multiple options in an effort to learn and improve.

SpaceX and Tesla use the engineering model. In contrast, the vast majority of software projects operate within the contractor model. In the face-off between these two approaches, which leads to the greatest innovation per capita across the software industry is clear.

"SpaceX reached their key goals—dramatically reduce the cost to launch payload into space, and recover and reuse booster rockets—on a greatly reduced timeline. How? What SpaceX did not do was to work under contract to the government, which was the only funding mechanism for space exploration until recent years. Instead, they were willing to crash rockets to reach their goals. The strategy of integrating events (in this case, test booster launches) is how multiple engineering teams rapidly try out their latest version of components with those developed by all the other teams. The government would never have tolerated the crashes that SpaceX suffered, meaning that government contractors had no choice but to be correct the first time. Yet, SpaceX speeded up the development of a reliable, cheap, booster rocket by perhaps a factor of five simply by trying things out to discover the unknown unknowns, instead of trying to think everything through in excruciating detail. This is a classic engineering approach, but would generally not be allowed in a contractor model. The SpaceX engineering teams found that it was far cheaper to have crashes in order to find the problems rather than to wait 'forever' until there was no risk" [Mary Poppendieck].

The culture of a business encompasses values and behaviors that contribute to its unique physical, social, and psychological environment. Culture influences the way teams interact, the context within which knowledge is created, the acceptance or resistance they will have toward certain changes, and ultimately the way they share knowledge or withhold it. Culture represents the collective values, beliefs, and principles of organizational members [Org-Culture].

Organizations should strive for what is considered a *healthy culture*. The aim is to derive cultural benefits, such as a better alignment with achieving the organization's vision, mission, and goals. Other benefits include increased team cohesiveness among the company's various departments and divisions, higher employee motivation, and greater efficiency.

Culture is not set in stone. It can be improved or damaged depending on the actions of leadership and employees. If the culture is currently unhealthy, it needs to be altered to yield sound, healthy benefits.

The building of a healthy organizational culture should be set in motion before attempts are made to build anything else. Businesses that don't take healthy cultural aspects far enough risk losing their workforce, and consequently a part of their knowledge base. This failure also undermines productivity and innovation in the long term, which leads to the business becoming less successful.

A culture that focuses on facilitating innovation is valued by leaders and employees alike. Although leaders claim to understand what building a culture for innovation entails, creating and sustaining it is hard. An impediment to building cultures that are innovative is, obviously, not understanding what such a culture is and how to cultivate it.

Failure Is Not Fatal

An organization's viewpoint on failure is one of the most important cultural factors, for good or for ill. Why are so many teams afraid to fail? The fear of failure determines the way that the team members make decisions, or completely avoid making them. More accurately, the fear of making the *wrong* decision, which then leads to failure, is often the reason that decisions are perpetually deferred or never made.

Recall from earlier in this chapter that the engineering model trumps the contractor model by allowing for failure so that the organization can learn. Failure is not the objective. Instead, the point is to challenge assumptions enough that some failure is inevitable. All experimental failure is a means to an end, to learn what works. It's said that if a team doesn't fail at all, they are not exploring. Instead, the team is resting their decisions on what they already know as best, and that's very likely ordinary.

Is the fear of failure worse than failure itself? Which is worse, failing or never trying? The Wright brothers began aeronautical research and experimentation in 1899, with many failures following their initial efforts. It is said that they owed much of their success to the many failures of others before them. Most people remember only their first successful powered airplane flight of 1903. That is, in fact, the way it should be—celebrate the arrival and the route taken.

Building an #agile, failure-tolerant culture that fosters willingness to experiment and provides people with psychological safety can only increase business success and competitive advantage. However, it has to be counterbalanced by some exacting behaviors. While an organization's culture should be tolerant to failures, it should be intolerant toward incompetence and complacency [Pisano]. This attitude is especially very important in software development, as it is fraught with uncertainty. The large number of Big Ball of Mud (see Chapter 1, "Business Goals and Digital Transformation") systems, and the fact that these are the norm throughout the world, proves that failure in the midst of some success is quite common. This problem ends up being recursive, however, which leads to strategic demise.

1. Creating a Big Ball of Mud from the outset is a failure in terms of software development principles (this doesn't imply that it was intentional).

2. The fact that the Big Ball of Mud system actually functions to the extent that it is useful is an initial success for the business.

3. Given no effort to change the long-term impacts of 1, the Big Ball of Mud system codebase will only become worse, which will have a greater effect later.

4. The Big Ball of Mud system's ability to respond to change decreases to the point of inertia, which ultimately produces failure in terms of providing for the business's long-term needs.

Failures can lead to interesting learning opportunities. Important lessons learned can also be a result of poor model designs, brittle code, deficient architectures, flawed analysis, and general incompetence. Recognizing these situations before point 3, and certainly before point 4, is critical.

Therefore, the distinction has to be made between positive and negative failures. Positive failure yields information and knowledge, while negative failure can be expensive and harmful to businesses. The rewards of failure should only be realized in the face of tangible learning outcomes and knowledge that ultimately result in success. The Wright brothers failed many times, but they also eventually succeeded in flight.

Failure Culture Is Not Blame Culture

The relationship between failure and blame culture is often not well understood. Blame culture is negative, as it is based on punishment of failures, whether those failures eventually lead to positive or negative results. In a blame culture, learning outcomes are not celebrated, and often not taken into account as truly critical to ultimate success. Instead, they are discarded.

Blame culture also hinders any initiatives in experimentation. The result is that things continue to be done in the same, pedestrian, ordinary way. Everybody is afraid to try something new, because if they fail, they will be blamed. In organizations with a blame culture, successes are at best passed over, as if there was no possibility of a failure, and failures are punishable. No one wants to take risks. This smells like the contractor model.

As a result, instead of innovating, businesses attempt to increase profit through operational efficiencies. A few of the most popular approaches are the use of mergers and acquisitions. These account for numerous personnel consolidations, which do lead to greater profits. This route does not often attempt business innovation as a profitable pursuit. Instead, operational efficiencies are seen as the easiest way to continue producing favorable annual reports to shareholders. Although this strategy can work for a time, it can't produce endless gains. In fact, it's just a different path to diminishing returns. Without another merger or acquisition, profits edge toward zero.

Life and Death Decisions: COVID-19 Vaccines and Mining Rescue

During the pandemic, the US government funded numerous vaccine research and development projects. Some failed. Some succeeded. The government knew that some would fail, but it was willing to take that risk in anticipation that some would succeed.

The mining disaster in Chile and subsequent rescue is another example of experimentation. The operation was headed up by probably the top mining engineer in the country, who tried 4 or 5 approaches at the same time to rescue the miners. Some failed; others did not reach the miners as quickly as the one that was successful, and just in time. What mattered is that lives were saved.

The use of multiple options is always the proper engineering approach when the challenge is a matter of life and death. Even if that's not the case, exploring multiple options is usually the fastest, most efficient way to solve tough problems. [Mary Poppendieck]

To say the least, a business focused on operational efficiencies is a breeding ground for blame culture. This flawed culture uses (passive-)aggressive management, micromanagement inside of teams, invasive time tracking of a team's work, and pushing team members to work late hours as a way to meet deadlines. Blame plays a major role when performance is so critically scrutinized that the only way to avoid looking bad is to make others look bad.

Experimentation need not be more expensive than the lack of it. The same goes for communication that leads to effective learning through knowledge sharing. Consider both in the face of Conway's Law.

Getting Conway's Law Right

As stated in Chapter 1, "Business Goals and Digital Transformation," we cannot "get better" at Conway's Law, just as we cannot "get better" at the law of gravity. Laws are unavoidable. With gravity on the earth scale, there is no alternation in a normal setting. If you stand somewhere in France or in the United States, the force of gravity is the same. However, at the universe scale, gravity is not the same. Depending on whether a person is on the earth or the moon, they will not experience gravity in the same way. This holds as well for Conway's Law.[1]

Each organization experiences Conway's Law differently because each one is structured and organized differently. Making organizational changes will either reduce or

---

1. Until we experience software development on the moon, we'll state only that different conditions can change the influence of Conway's Law for teams on earth.

intensify the influence of Conway's Law. As highlighted in Team Topologies [TT], if the desired theoretical system architecture doesn't fit the organizational model, then one of the two will need to change.

Yet, it is a mistake to think that any reorganization should be undertaken only for technical architecture purposes. Technical architecture is a supporting requirement for business strategic architecture. The individual team organization must facilitate the necessary contextual conversations between the business experts and the software development experts. "Domain expert engagement is to architecture as end user engagement is to feature development. You should find that end users and domain experts are your most treasured contacts in Lean and Agile projects" [LA].

> There is the organizational pattern "Inverse Conway Maneuver" coined in 2015 by people from ThoughtWorks. It was codified when Microservices became very popular. The pattern advises to organize teams according to the desired architecture structure, rather than expecting existing teams to match up to the architectural goals. By reconfiguring teams for the optimal inter-team communication, the desired architecture is more likely due to the optimized communications structure. [TW-ICM]

Mel Conway's original paper addresses this very "maneuver" in the conclusion. Pertinent quotes from that paper are listed here for context:

> "We have found a criterion for the structuring of design organizations: a design effort should be organized according to the need for communication."

> "Flexibility of organization is important to effective design."

> "Reward design managers for keeping their organizations lean and flexible."

Conway deserves credit for having the insight to codify the solution to the law that he observed so long ago in 1967 (and published in 1968).

The question remains, how can teams be organized effectively to improve the communication between teams? We list some opportunities here:

- *Keep the team together.* According to Bruce Tuckman [Tuckman], the team must undergo the steps of *forming* and *norming*, before it reaches the *performing* stage. It takes time for team members to find ways of effectively working with each other. Many exchanges are informal and a matter of habit. Teams build a tacit knowledge that enables them to perform[2]—but that takes time.

---

2. When a team is working in project mode and the project is considered complete, the team is often disbanded and the software is handed over to the maintenance team. The tacit knowledge of the former team doesn't survive the transition.

- *Limit the team size.* You should build the smallest possible team, but no smaller, to work on a given software domain solution. Coordination and communication costs inside big teams become worse asymptotically as the team grows. Moreover, the team size factor is dictated not only by the first Conway's Law ("Communication dictates design"); that is, communication paths can also be estimated by applying Fred Brooks's *intercommunication formula*: $n(n-1)/2$ [Brooks]. The more people who compose a team, the worse communication will be. There will be too many communication paths. For example, with 10 people there will be 45 communication paths,[3] and with 50 people there will be 1,225 paths. Teams of 5 to 10 people are considered optimal.

- *Make independent teams.* Effective coordination between teams that are dependent on each other requires much time and effort. Minimizing code dependencies, coordination of releases, and deployments can have positive impacts on both delivery times and quality.

- *Organize teams around business capabilities.* Software development is a very complex process requiring a wide variety of skills. Therefore, encourage diversity of skills inside the team. If the team is composed of people having different skills, such as business expert, software architect, developer, tester, DevOps, and even an end user, they can be equal to the task. Such a range of skills not only affords autonomy for decision making and accountability, but also, according to Conway's Law, enables the building of a healthier structure (not focused on siloed skills). With this approach, it won't be necessary to have a lot of communication outside of the team to carry out daily responsibilities.

- *Define communication gateways for teams.* A team with a broad skill set and vital autonomy can optimize in-team communication, but must still shape inter-team communication through gateways. The result might be a similar shape as the communication between architecture components. Consider inter-team discussions to require protocols, along with mapping and translation between teams. The protocols should establish boundaries to protect against interfering with team goals, distractions, and possibly even unauthorized exchanges. These should reflect a one-to-one relationship with the integrating software architectures. The topic of context mapping is discussed in Chapter 6, "Mapping, Failing, and Succeeding—Choose Two."

- *Assign a single responsibility to the team.* Requiring a single team to manage too many tasks and contexts in the same architecture, or worse, assigning multiple projects in parallel, will not end well. Unless these mistakes are

---

3. $10 * (10 - 1) / 2 = 45$.

avoided, communication complexity will increase and overlap, with the risk of mixing together and confusing contextual concepts. Yet, single responsibility doesn't necessarily mean a single context, because the team may decide that solving a single problem space may require multiple contexts.

- *Eliminate multitasking from the team.* Although not directly related to Conway's Law, human brains don't multitask very effectively, and especially not in complex problem-solving situations. Multitasking requires context switching. Humans are bad at this because we require *context-dependent memory*. Each context switch can require several or even dozens of minutes to complete. Multitasking is not just a productivity killer—it also breaks down effective communication channels. The misperception that multitasking works for humans is remedied by observing the large number of errors produced by a person who tries it, such as completely overlooking steps that are basic to anyone giving due focus. It's amazing how below-average very intelligent people become under such circumstances.

Figure 2.1 depicts different team organizations yielding different architecture structures that match the respective team organizations. On the left, teams are silos of skills. Often, the team at the communication cross-roads—the backed team in Figure 2.1—has all the burden of communication and coordination between the others—DBA teams and UI teams. What makes the teams even less efficient is that they work in multiple business contexts—here, it's Claims, Underwriting, and Insurance Products—which is an additional source of complexity to take into account. The interdependencies and highly coordinated communications complicate value delivery to the business.

On the right side of Figure 2.1, teams are cross-functional and aligned with business capabilities. Note that these teams are autonomous and responsible for the whole life cycle of the subsystem architecture that they own. Their day-to-day responsibility is not just the software development; the team also has insight into how software they developed behaves in production. This leads to better contact with end users, as the team members have to assist them as part of their support work. It is a kind of virtuous circle, because the new insights from customers and users help teams to enhance the business capability for which they are responsible.

A point not to be overlooked is the criticality of creating teams primarily for the sake of in-team contextual communication between business experts and software development experts. If a given team can talk across to other teams with great ease but can't have deep communication with business experts in support of building their own strategic deliverables, the fundamental communication problem has not been solved, and is possibly even worse than before the reorganization.

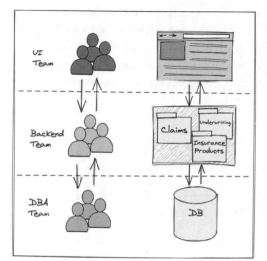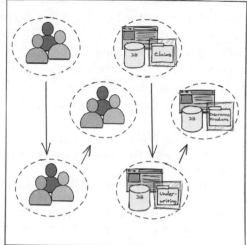

Figure 2.1 *Conway's Law. Left: Skill silos. Right: Cross-functional skills, business capabilities.*

Enabling Safe Experimentations

Acknowledging the difference between blame and failure culture is the first step toward building a better and healthy culture. The next step is to enable safe experimentation for businesses—which doesn't mean an organization simply allows its teams to throw in random architectural choices or technologies.

Safe experimentation means discipline, and discipline means carefully selecting ideas that will potentially yield great learning results and knowledge. There are different interpretations of "safety," but as Erik Hollnagel states, "Safety is a freedom from unacceptable risk" [Hollnagel]. In other words, this process must allow for the prevention of unwanted events and protection against unwanted outcomes.

While the safe experimentation is ongoing, the learning process is evaluated, and the information gathered is inspected, which enables the organization to decide whether the experimentation should be moved forward or canceled. What counts is increasing safety by reducing failures and, therefore, the risk for the business. Killing a safe experimentation is less risky than trying out new things blindly and calling it experimentation; otherwise, everything can be called experimentation.

Modules First

So, we're going from "essential strategic learning tools," including a discussion of a culture of failure as necessary to succeed, directly into some techie topic of "modules"? First of all, this topic is really not very technical. Everyone understands that containers of various kinds are made to hold items inside (e.g., kitchen drawers and drawers for storing food in a refrigerator). How the containers are labeled and what is put inside of each should be logical. Otherwise, when it comes time to retrieve the desired items from a container, they will be hard to find. For software development, teams must get this right before trying to do much else. Wasn't the same assertion made in Chapter 1 regarding Conway's Law? Yes, exactly.

Conway's Law continues [Conway]:

> Why do large systems disintegrate? The process seems to occur in three steps, the first two of which are controllable and the third of which is a direct result of our homomorphism.
>
> First, the realization by the initial designers that the system will be large, together with certain pressures in their organization, make irresistible the temptation to assign too many people to a design effort.
>
> Second, application of the conventional wisdom of management to a large design organization causes its communication structure to disintegrate.
>
> Third, the homomorphism insures that the structure of the system will reflect the disintegration which has occurred in the design organization.

Considering modules only a "techie topic" is to sell short one of the most valuable tools that supports strategic learning.

Modularity is also the solution to how humans deal with very complex problems that must be solved. No one person is able to keep in mind the whole business problem space and deal efficiently with it. Before solving a big problem, humans tend to decompose what they know into smaller sets of problems. The smaller problems are easier to reason about. Of course, solutions to smaller problems are then combined to address the big problem; otherwise, modularity would be useless.

This way of solving problems has deep roots in psychology and reflects the limitations of the human mind. The human brain can keep a very limited set of concepts in focus at one time. This is described in George A. Miller's paper from 1956, "The Magical Number Seven, Plus or Minus Two: Some Limits on Our Capacity for Processing Information" [Miller]. Miller's Law says that humans can keep 7 ± 2 "chunks" or pieces of information in short-term memory. The exact number can vary from person to person, but what is sure is that this capacity is very limited. Due to this limitation, humans work out a hierarchical decomposition of information into smaller chunks, until they are about the right size to feed our mental model without causing stress on cognitive load, which would prevent processing of the information.

Now, back to the point of modules. Applying these components to complex problem solving helps manage chunks of information that have undergone the process of decomposition. This makes complex problem solving possible because humans can use stepwise processing to create successful outcomes.

Modularity is an indispensable foundation for Conway's Law as well. That's because *modules are where we should capture critical communication and what is learned from it.* At the same time, modules can save teams from smearing mud all over their solution space. Modules are used both as conceptual boundaries and as physical compartments.

Don't worry. It will all make sense in a moment. Consider how modules support learning through communication.

Figure 2.2 shows three modules: Insurance Products, Underwriting, and Claims. Each of the three is the home of a separate business capability.

A team consists of both business and software development stakeholders. For the sake of this example, one team is assumed to work on only one of the three business capabilities. The team that will be discussed here is responsible for delivering a solution for Underwriting.

For this team, Underwriting is considered the primary context for their conversations. To provide an Underwriting solution, however, the team will also likely need to discuss Insurance Products and Claims, and even other capabilities of the business. Yet, they have no responsibility or authority in those other conversational contexts.

Because their conversations will take various paths through the entire business domain, team members must recognize when their discussions "exit" their own context, "enter" another context, and possibly still others, and then "return" to their own context. When in conversation, if the team learns something relative to their own context, they should record some words or expressions in their contextual module that they consider to be keepers—that is, ones that will definitely help drive their further discussions and the ultimate solution.

A conceptual module doesn't have a location, so where are the conversations literally recorded? For now this could be on a whiteboard, in a wiki, or in another kind of document. Certainly, the issue of not losing this information from an erased whiteboard should influence how it's captured more permanently.

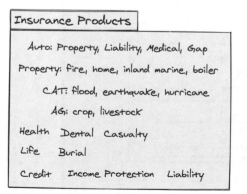
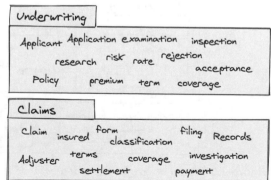

Figure 2.2 *A module is both a conceptual boundary and a physical compartment.*

If it helps for the sake of their communication, the team can also record any part of their conversation that applies to another module, but the team doesn't have the authority to make firm, lasting decisions about those other contexts. In fact, if the team requires any official details about the other contexts, they will have to communicate with the respective teams. So, any terms or expressions they come up with for foreign contexts are only proxies for the real things for which the other teams are responsible. Also, whether proxy or official, the terms and expressions recorded for other contexts are placed in the respective contextual module, not in the team's module.

As the team's conversations progress, they lead to more learning, and the team continues to identify additional business concepts. Figure 2.3 reflects the progress, including the notion that creating additional modules inside the main Underwriting module helps to further organize their conversations as they become more specific.

A fair question is, would it make sense to promote the internal modules—Intake, Processing, Policy, and Renewals—to top-level modules of their own? That's a possibility to consider in time, and there are advantages to doing so. But where exactly? At this time, the team should fall back on the earlier advice that in essence asserts, "The team doesn't yet have enough information to accept that decision." It would be irresponsible to go there now. Future conversations might lead in that direction, but jumping to that conclusion now doesn't make sense. At this time, calling this a (non-)decision based on the currently identified concepts, and the team's understanding of the cohesiveness of each concept relative to the others, makes them less likely to be separated.

This is pretty cool. It's like the team is trying to keep everything all tidy inside their own conceptual boundary. But they're not just trying—they're succeeding. This is a major step in the right direction for avoiding the Big Ball of Mud. Considering that good communication and making decisions are the primary strengths behind software development, the team is definitely on the right track.

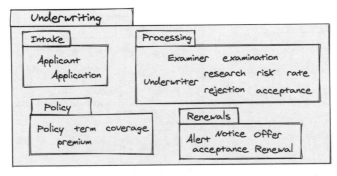

Figure 2.3 *A module compartment of other module compartments used to organize source code.*

It's essential to also reflect these measures in the software implementation. The team must prevent the reflection of order in their conversational design into a software model from being undermined over time. This leads to the second use of modules: A module is also a physical compartment. The team should create a physical module in which to place their source code. Using what's exemplified in Figure 2.3, Table 2.1 lists examples of corresponding software modules.

Table 2.1 *Modules of Underwriting Provide Explicit Compartments for the Implementation*

Module Name	Description
NuCoverage.Underwriting	The Underwriting root module
NuCoverage.Underwriting.Model	The module where the Underwriting Model is kept
NuCoverage.Underwriting.Model.Intake	The module of the Model of Intake
NuCoverage.Underwriting.Model.Policy	The module of the Model of a Policy
NuCoverage.Underwriting.Model.Processing	The module of the Model of Processing
NuCoverage.Underwriting.Model.Renewals	The module of the Model of Renewals

Depending on the actual programming language in use, these modules can be declared a bit differently, but that's not important now. What is important is that the team can create compartments with very explicit names that clearly identify where things belong. Given their basic sensibility, there's no way for confusion or disorderliness to exist at this point in time.

Another advantage of this approach is that if at any future time the team does decide to promote any of the models to become a top-level module on its own, the refactoring of what exists is quite straightforward. Considering this point, it's clear that modularity trumps knee-jerk deployment decisions every single time.

Deployment Last

Choosing Microservices first is dangerous. Choosing Monoliths for the long term is also dangerous. As with any decision making in #agile, these decisions should be made at the last responsible moment. The following are two principles from the Agile Manifesto:

- Our highest priority is to satisfy the customer through early and continuous delivery of valuable software.

- Deliver working software frequently, at intervals ranging from a couple of weeks to a couple of months, with a preference for the shorter timescale.

Today, "a preference to the shorter timescale" can mean days, hours, or even minutes. In summary, this translates to *deliver early and deliver often*.

Under such conditions, how can deployment decisions be delayed for as long as possible? Think *type* rather than *inception and frequency*. Deployment type is a choice, and there are multiple deployment options from which to choose. Choices can change. Delivery inception and ongoing frequency are mandatory, regardless of the deployment choices.[4]

Early on, it is best to choose a deployment option that supports fast experimentation, implementation, and delivery. This specifically points to using a Monolithic architecture in the early stages, because trying to solve distributed computing problems before the business problems are understood is an act of futility.

To get this right out in the open, many software developers love the ideas behind distributed computing. It's cool, thrilling even, to consider the prospects. For those who have never attempted this at all, or have little experience, it's exciting to think in terms of getting elbow deep into distributed computing as soon as possible.

It's a bit like anything new, such as driving. When you're young, the opportunity to drive is generally a highly anticipated adventure. After the challenge of driving is no longer new, driving fast might be a new thrill to seek. After a high-cost speeding citation or a bad accident (plus a high-cost citation!) curtails the allure of high-speed driving on public roads, the realization sets in that driving is for the most part a means to an end. Still, the idea of getting an incredible sports car and having access to a racetrack elicits new thrilling thoughts. Even so, in time the appeal of traveling safely from one point to another is hard to deny. Especially when you have a family, it's top priority.

Those who have done distributed computing find it challenging, and there is undeniable pleasure in getting it to work well. At the same time, distributed computing is not a thrill sport. And it's hard. Any experienced software developer who is capable of being both realistic and responsible will admit that distributed computing is a means to an end. It should be the business drivers that lead to considering any computing infrastructure that will produce good customer outcomes.

If delivering software to the cloud is a means to the end of producing business-driven customer satisfaction, it's likely that at least some distributed computing will be required. All the same, finding ways to reduce the total distribution of computing resources or reducing the complexities as much as possible should be the top priority. If still in doubt about this, please return to Chapter 1 and reread the section, "Digital Transformation: What Is the Goal?"

We're not advocating for Monoliths over Microservices. We're advocating for the best possible decision for the business circumstances. Avoiding the problems

---

4. Chapter 9, "Message- and Event-Driven Architectures," covers how this may be different for the serverless architecture, which may include function as a service (FaaS).

inherent to distributed computing—inter-subsystem software communication that involves a network connection—best supports early delivery and sustained delivery. Early on, there is no need to face the scale and performance challenges because they simply don't exist.

When the business decides at the last responsible moment that opening up greater access to the system is in sight, the team must be prepared to measure how the system handles the increasing load. When performance and scale indicators are trending toward the need to address these issues, extracting one or more modules from a Monolith into Microservices is likely a reasonable way forward. Admittedly, this requires a style of development using architecture and design techniques that reflect the loose coupling of Microservices but work seamlessly inside a Monolith, and without the failure conditions common to distributed computing.

When the team has decided on modules first, and when deployment options start out as simple as possible, that approach puts them on solid ground to make decisions based on empirical information at the most responsible time.

Everything in Between

After modules, but before advanced deployment decisions, there is considerable work to be done. The work involves the following tasks:

- Identifying which business capabilities will be hosted in a given part of the system

- Pinpointing impactful strategic functionality

- Understanding software development complexity and risk

- Collaborating to understand the overall business process

- Reasoning out the assertions employed to prove all this works correctly.

The sections that follow cover the first three of these tasks. Chapter 3, "Events-First Experimentation and Discovery," covers collaborative learning around business processes, and reasoning on software correctness assertions.

Business Capabilities, Business Processes, and Strategic Goals

A business capability is a function of the business that exists to generate revenues. Some functions are core business capabilities, while others are not. A core business capability is one at which the business must excel and differentiate within. The business must innovate in its core capabilities. A supporting business capability is one that is needed to make one or more of the core capabilities work, but not one in which the business should attempt to innovate. Yet, a supporting capability might not be available for off-the-shelf purchase, in which case it must likely be built. There are also generic business capabilities, such as those that keep the business functioning but don't directly support the business core capabilities. These generic business capabilities should be purchased (licensed, subscription, etc.) wherever possible.

Note that a business capability is a *what* of the business, not the *how*. Consider that Underwriting is a NuCoverage business capability. *How* the company performs this capability could be by humans using snail mail and telephones, or it could be with fully automated digital workflow processing. The *what* and the *how* are two different things. *How* being an implementation detail is important, but one that could change over time. Even so, the *what*—Underwriting—will likely exist into the foreseeable future.

NuCoverage must innovate to offer insurance products at competitive discounts and still drive gains that are at least as good as those realized by the competition. Additionally, NuCoverage will now innovate by offering its insurance products with white labels. These are clearly direct revenue generators. Yet, which are the core business capabilities and which are supporting business capabilities? Consider the reasoning illustrated in Figure 2.4 and described in the list that follows.

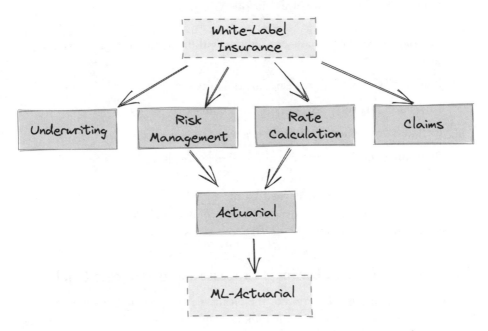

Figure 2.4 *Some NuCoverage business capabilities. Solid boxes are present business capabilities; dashed boxes are future business capabilities.*

- Underwriting is the capability that produces a decision on whether a given insurable risk is worth issuing a policy or whether a policy must be denied. The business capability is implemented with digital workflow processing, but how the workflow processing is accomplished is not a business capability.

- Because Underwriting doesn't occur in a vacuum, assume that some form of risk management is necessary to distinguish what's a good business investment from what's bad for the business. In insurance, this risk management centers on actuarial concerns and is complex enough to hold the status of being a science. The current Actuarial business capability is based on industry data and experience, but will be enhanced with larger datasets and fast machine learning (ML) algorithms in the future that can determine good risks versus bad risks. The future algorithms will be the implementation, but are not the business capability.

- Every insurance company must handle claims filed against policies, and NuCoverage is no exception. Fair loss recovery is the deal that insurance companies make with insureds. For a digital-first insurance company, deeply understanding a policyholder loss and the applicable coverage is a core business capability. It's a matter of not overpaying on the replacement value, but also not taking a reputation hit due to unfair settlements. How would Claims work? That's a necessary question to answer, but the *how* is different from the *what* that is the business capability.

- NuCoverage grew to the point where using an enterprise resource planning (ERP) system helps the operational side of the business be efficient, and this is not by any means unimportant. Operational efficiencies should benefit NuCoverage as much as possible. Yet, as previously noted, thriving on operational efficiencies alone is not a sustainable business model. Because the ERP is not core to revenue generation, it is generic with respect to the core capabilities of the business. Not to oversimplify matters, but to highlight the distinction between core and other capabilities, selecting an ERP was in essence a matter of choosing between multiple products that checked all the same boxes on the features and benefits list.

- NuCoverage is now on the cusp of entering the white-label insurance platform market. Although it might be considered only a change to a different technology set, it's even more of a mindset adjustment. NuCoverage must shift into a software-as-a-product mode rather than viewing software as support. Just getting this up and running is core. It will move away from being core in time, after it's a well-oiled machine, but presently it's critically important to make the WellBank deal successful.

The preceding points prompt the need to answer a few questions. Is Underwriting a core business capability? Is Actuarial a supporting business capability? Are there details under Claims that might reveal more business capabilities? How will NuCoverage succeed in taking such a big leap to incorporate a completely new business model without harming its current one? These questions are answered later when we examine them more closely against strategic design.

For now, let's focus on the business processes—the *hows* of a business and their relationship to the *what*, a Business capability. Business processes are a succession of activities that define and support business capabilities and, therefore, the strategic business goals. Most processes involve multiple business capabilities that work together, as represented in Figure 2.5.

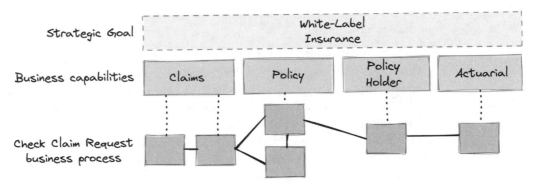

Figure 2.5 *Business processes involve multiple business capabilities to support a strategic goal.*

For example, the Claims business capability involves many business processes, such as *Check Claim Request* and *Settle Claim*, that support the capability. The *Check Claim Request* business process existed before NuCoverage defined a new strategic goal—namely, supporting white-label insurance—but it must certainly be adapted to the new goal as seen in Figure 2.5. Consider how the *Check Claim Request* business process currently works:

1. It kicks in when a new claim against a policy is recorded. Checking a claim request might require coordination of multiple business capabilities aside from Claims. For instance, the Policy business capability would be needed to check whether the policy is still active. It might happen that a claim is recorded toward an inactive or just expired policy. Obviously, the request could be dropped most of the time, but not necessarily always. There are always corner cases in any business that have to be addressed.

2. Once the check is done, the Policy business capability provides the coverage information, which determines how the claim should be handled.

3. Next, the Policy Holder Management business capability provides the current and historical views of the policy holder information. It might be useful to check any information related to the driver involved in a claim if there are any issues recorded against the driver's driving license, such as suspension or a cancellation, or to check the current policyholder's postal address for the claim follow-up process.

4. A check with the Actuarial business capability is done to discard any fraudulent claim request.

To support the white-label business strategic goal, NuCoverage might decide to implement a parallel *Check Claim Request* for mobile devices. This could become an enabler for making more deals with agent customers, such as WellBank. It is important to note that more business capabilities would be involved in this process, all operating at the same time. The Claims business capability might also be part of wider business processes at the organization level.

An important question remains unanswered. How can teams discuss and discover business capabilities and business processes without conflating or confusing the two, leading the session astray? Here are some rules of thumb:

- The best way to differentiate a business capability from a business process is with a naming style. Generally, business capabilities should be named with a noun–verb combination, such as *Subscription Billing*[5] or *Claims Processing*.[6] In contrast, business processes should be named with a verb–noun combination, such as *Check Claim Request*.

- A business process demonstrates that a company is interested in *how* to get things done, and the corresponding process models are an excellent depiction of how the business flows. Thus, the business capabilities capture the structure, whereas the business processes capture the flow.

- Business processes can change frequently due to technology advances, regulation, internal policies, channel preferences, and other factors, so they are considered volatile. Business capabilities capture the essence of *what* a business does and focus on the outcomes; thus, they change far less often.

---

5. The name *Billing* was chosen for this business capability because it is a verb, and it demonstrates how it could be mistaken for a business process. Note that the whole name is *Subscription Billing*, which adheres to the rules of business capability naming. Elsewhere in the book, *Billing* might be used for brevity.

6. Elsewhere in the book, *Claims* might be used for brevity instead of the full name *Claims Processing*.

A business capability facilitates strategic-level communication. The benefits of using business capabilities for strategic discussions include their higher-level, conceptual, and more abstract notions and intentions. Yet, attempting to identify business capabilities in discussions with business stakeholders can become sidetracked by process. Many business people are process-driven and results-focused, so they naturally prefer to talk about business processes rather than business capabilities.

For all these reasons, it is important to understand and to recognize the difference between a business capability and a business process. This is a subtle but very important distinction. The process creates coupling between business capabilities. Wrongly designed model boundaries mistakenly based on processes instead of business capabilities, and vice versa, could cripple business activities and operations, and they work against natural communication channels in the organization. Chapter 5, "Contextual Expertise," explores how business capabilities are realized as software models.

The important takeaways are simply stated: Business processes underpin business capabilities, and business capabilities underpin business strategy.

Strategic Delivery on Purpose

One of the biggest problems in software development is developing functionality and features within software that have little to no value to the business. Yes, this is the classic reason for asserting You Aren't Gonna Need It (YAGNI)—but even so, calling YAGNI in such cases mostly fails to happen or fails to be heard.

Oftentimes, this waste happens because software developers don't have well-established communication channels and collaboration with business stakeholders. This naturally leads to creating software that never should have existed. It's not so much that some teams thought a feature was a good idea in their own opinion and delivered it on the fly. Instead, it's more often the case that the developers don't understand the requirements as expressed by business stakeholders. If they don't know that their implementation is wrong and won't be used until some future time, it will remain unused and lurking as a distant problem in waiting.

Just as common is the problem in which business stakeholders and influential customers/users demand some functionality, or sales and marketing perceive a need due to becoming aware of the potential for closing a big deal, and that demand drives the addition. Then, after the imagined value is delivered, the demand may evaporate for any number of reasons: The customer/user finds a workaround, or loses zeal, and the sales team closes the deal on a promise, or even loses the deal altogether. At some point, the imagined value is forgotten after the hard and risky work of bringing it to fruition is complete.

Another reason for implementing unnecessary features is even more basic—plain old bad decisions. Of course, this problem can be chalked up to failing to learn, but going so far as to fully implement such features can be too high a price to pay if that cost could be avoided by undertaking less expensive experimentation.

All of these situations are a major source of frustration for both the business stakeholders and the software development team. To add to this morass, when decision logs are not kept, there is little to no traceability other than a reliance on tacit knowledge. At the same time, although decision logs tell a team why something happened, they are of little help in the case of backing out wrong features. Some will argue that source code versioning can point to the means to remove the unused code—and that's true if the versioning decisions were made with the assumption that the feature could be wrong. Frankly, using source code versioning for backing out features that were not suspected as being wrong, that have lurked for a long time, and on which other features are now dependent, is an iffy proposition at best.

In all of the aforementioned cases, the problem isn't the weakness of source code versioning. It's generally one of two problems:

- It's a matter of failed communications, a warning that has already been sounded with a consistent drumbeat in this book.

- An opinion and obsession forced a decision, rather than clearly identified goal-based business drivers.

In the first case, please return to the drums section. In the second case, there's a clear need to surface actual business goals.

A decision-making tool named Impact Mapping [Impact] was built for facilitating such decisions and can help distinguish strategic functionality investments from mere imaginary value. To pinpoint the impacts that must be made to achieve strategic goals, consider the following questions:

1. **Why?** List a number of business goals. A complete list of goals is not necessary because goals can be named one at a time. Yet, listing a few or several might help pinpoint the more strategic ones, and indicate how they differ from the lesser important ones. "Make Mary Happy" is not a business goal, and neither is "Make WellBank Happy." "Bundle Home and Auto Insurance" is a business goal, as are "Quote Home and Auto Bundle Rate by Home Address" and "White-Label Auto Insurance."

2. **Who?** For a given goal, identify one or more *actors* that must be influenced to change their behaviors to make the business goals successful. For the purpose

of this tool, an "actor" is a person, a group, an organization, a system, or something similar that must be influenced to achieve the stated goal. Any actor identified can be positive, neutral, or negative. In other words, the influence made must change the behavior of an actor that is already positive with respect to the business. Alternatively, the actor might currently be indifferent or even negative to the business. This could be a user of another solution or the business offering that solution, and in both cases our business must influence a change in behavior.

3. *How?* Define the impacts that must be made on each actor to achieve the goal. This is not a grab bag of every possible feature that an actor might need, but rather a select set of business activities focused on achieving the strategic goal by changing a very specific behavior, or lack thereof, to an improved one. It's important to include impacts that address not just positive actors, but also neutral and negative ones. For negative actors, state impacts that could impede this business's positive impacts, and how the impedances can be combated and removed.

4. *What?* Name the deliverables necessary to realize each impact. In the context of strategic software, deliverables are generally the software features that implement the means to cause a specific impact. Note, however, that in identifying deliverables, it is possible that software is not the best answer. Or it could be that an interim measure should be taken until the software can be implemented. For example, until NuCoverage can implement a highly automated Actuarial system that is based on fast data analyzed using machine learning algorithms, the company might choose to bootstrap its Underwriting business capability using highly skilled human underwriters. The underwriters can also help, along with actuaries as business experts, in specifying the Actuarial system. In time, the human underwriters can transition to work full-time as experts in a software innovation capacity.

Most software initiatives will start with step 4 and probably never identify steps 3, 2, or 1. In terms of strategic business, steps 1–4 are not only the correct order, but also offer a clear way forward. These steps are used to find even nontechnical or other means of gap filling to achieve a business goal. In doing so, they can also point out ways to decrease financial expenditures because the best deliverables may be more obvious when all answers are not required to look like software.

As pointed out in Impact Mapping [Impact], a mind map is a good way to put this technique to work. Figure 2.6 provides a template and example.

Of the impacts shown in Figure 2.6, some are necessary supporting ones, and others are strategic. For example, a supporting impact is that a new Agent, such

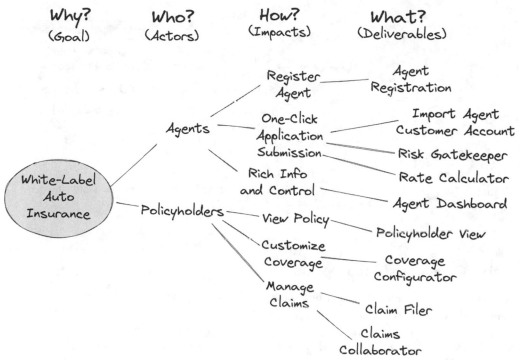

Figure 2.6 *Impact map for White-Label Auto Insurance.*

as WellBank, must be able to register.[7] Once registered, supplying the Agent with a means to quickly submit a new, valid application is accomplished by means of a strategic impact: *One-Click Application Submission.*

Connected with the *One-Click Application Submission* impact are three deliverables: *Import Agent Customer Account, Risk Gatekeeper,* and *Rate Calculator.* The first one, *Import Agent Customer Account,* does not currently exist in any form. The other two exist to some degree, because they are already being used in support of the current core business. Undoubtedly, a new deliverable will be needed that ties these together. This means that the mappers should identify some controlling component, such as an *Underwriting Processor,* to manage the background workflow. This discovery is seen in Figure 2.7. Chapter 3 covers these components in more detail.

---

7. This is not open to anyone. Becoming an insurance agent has a qualifying process. NuCoverage helps with onboarding new agents through a franchise arrangement, but leaves registration details to the new agent.

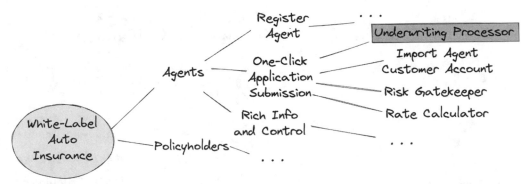

Figure 2.7 *Further discovery within One-Click Application Submission reveals a controlling component named Underwriting Processor.*

Using Cynefin to Make Decisions

Software development activities would be far easier if every requirement of the system was known upfront and in precise detail. But, no: Requirements are envisioned and then changed, and changed again, and changed again. Experimentation outcomes, new knowledge acquisition, production usage feedback, external factors such as competitor activity, and market disruptions cannot be factored into the development plan months or even weeks in advance.

Many businesses are convinced that making a few tweaks to the original plan will be enough. NuCoverage will pursue a new market opportunity by means of white-label products. Naturally, this will ripple through its business strategy, through the organization, and all the way to software development. How can the business inform itself to a fuller degree of the effort needed to effect this change?

The Cynefin framework is a tool that can be used for this purpose. It was created by Dave Snowden in 1999 and has been applied with success to many fields, including industry, research, politics, and software development. It helps decision makers identify how they perceive situations and how they make sense of their own behaviors and those of others.

As illustrated in Figure 2.8, the Cynefin framework includes four domains: *Clear*, *Complicated*, *Complex*, and *Chaotic*. A fifth domain, *Disorder*, is in the center.

In the list that follows, business drivers are used as examples. However, the Cynefin domains could also be explained using technical drivers.

Figure 2.8 *Cynefin framework with its five domains.*

- *Clear.* Also known as Obvious or Simple, *Clear* means that the relationship between cause and effect is known to all, is predictable in advance, and is self-evident for any reasonable person. Common practices are applied and the approach is to *sense*—see what's coming in; *categorize*—make it fit to pre-defined categories; and *respond*—decide what to do. Everyone already knows the right answer. NuCoverage's software development team already knows how to process electronic documents, and it's obvious to them how it is done.

- *Complicated.* The relationship between cause and effect needs further analysis. In this kind of scenario, a business expert's knowledge is used to ensure previously successful practices are applied. While there might be multiple solutions to the problem, an expert's knowledge is used to determine what should be done. The approach is to *sense*—see what's coming in; *analyze*—investigate or analyze using expert knowledge; and *respond*—decide what to do. Although underwriting is a common process in the insurance industry, software developers would be unable to correctly implement an underwriting solution without relying on expert knowledge to guide them.

- *Complex.* The relationship between cause and effect is clear only in hindsight. Complex problems have more unpredictable results. Although there may be expectations regarding how to reach a correct solution, attempting to implement those solutions may not bring good or even acceptable results. The organization is more likely to reach a good solution only after making mistakes or through observations that lead to hindsight realizations. This is the place where safe experimentations have to take place. Knowledge must be acquired from failures, and the new understanding must be used to drive change in practices, environments, and digital assets. In this domain, the outcome keeps changing such that expert knowledge and common practices cannot be applied with ensured success. Rather, it's through the result of innovation and emergent practices. The approach is to *probe*—gather experimental input; *sense*—observe failure or success; and then *respond*—decide what to do. Fully automated digital actuarial analysis in multiple lines of insurance is a complex domain.

- *Chaotic.* There is no relationship between cause and effect at the system level. This kind of scenario requires a solution right away. When a crisis is experienced, there is a need to address it before it causes further harm. First, a state of order must be restored. Chaos is caused by an accident that leads to uncontrolled outcomes, and that requires emergency measures to bring the situation under control. The approach is to *act*—attempt to stabilize; *sense*—observe failure or success; and *respond*—decide what to do next. This is the situation where a system failure in one area cascades into other areas and leads to major service disruptions. The system must be first stabilized before any corrective action can be made.

- *Disorder.* This is the domain when you are uncertain of what stage you are in and whether any plans are working. Disorder is the most dangerous situation, one that must be exited as soon as possible. To do so, the situation must be quickly decomposed; the components must be analyzed; the organization must determine to which of the other four domains a given component belongs; and it must choose the proper approach to solve each component of the problem. Planned progress can be made only after order is restored. It's clear now that *Disorder* is centralized because the components of the situation are pushed out into one of the other four domains.

With both the *Chaotic* and *Disorder* domains, after stabilizing the situation, attention must be given to producing a thorough retrospective and to a prevention plan to avoid the exact or similar future disruptions. Naturally, the prevention plan, including well-informed changes to flawed digital assets, must be carried out very soon, and requires improved monitoring and observation of the affected areas and the overall system.

A key component of the Cynefin framework is *knowledge*. Understanding each situation helps make both the problem and the solution more obvious. Using the recommended approach of each domain (sense–categorize–respond, etc.) helps one better understand the problem and to transition each to the lower level of complexity. The transitions between domains are made clockwise. It's important to note that the *Clear* domain solutions can cause complacency and move to *Chaos* very quickly. That can happen when tacit knowledge is lost (a key person leaves the company without knowledge transfer), when such knowledge is applied incorrectly, or if a common successful practice becomes obsolete but its use continues.

According to Snowden, using agile project management is a way to transition from the *Complex* domain into the *Complicated* domain. Breaking down a large and complex domain into many smaller problems decreases the complexity of the problems that must be solved.

The takeaway is that new software development is at least in the *Complicated* domain, often in the *Complex* one, and sometimes in the *Chaos* domain. Many customers and developers see software development as a *Complicated* undertaking, but rarely view it as *Complex*. In general, everyone involved in software-development is very good at underestimating complexity, but is surprised when it becomes obvious, and often this ends up in producing solutions that can even lead to chaos, or at least deep debt and entropy.

When a *Complex* domain is recognized—or worse, when it is not—if the team is neither naive nor intellectually dishonest, they will admit that there is no obvious way to get from problem to solution. Once *Complex* is understood to be the case, an interactive approach using safe experimentation is a must.

Further, in a *Complex* domain, the best source of information for decision makers is not prediction, but rather observing what has already happened. Observation provides an empirical model on which iterative experimentation is based. Adapting to frequently changing states helps the team achieve a better understanding of the problem, which makes possible informed decisions in support of correct solutions. The section "Applying the Tools," later in this chapter, demonstrates how NuCoverage uses the Cynefin framework to determine whether it should use Microservices.

Where Is Your Spaghetti and How Fast Does It Cook?

So far, this book has invested two chapters in ways to strategically innovate with software development so as to seek unique business value through differentiation. The next two chapters take this exploration further, with deep dives into collaborative communication, learning, and improved software organization. The reason? Innovating toward strategic, competitive advantage is hard.

Whatever an individual's food preferences, pasta and other noodle dishes are generally among the favorites of most. If that's not the case for a few, it certainly is true for the majority. Just imagining a pile of spaghetti or Asian noodles with a delicious sauce sends people in pursuit of an appetite fix.

With that in mind, it's hard to imagine the sight of pasta sending our appetites off a cliff. And yet, the term "spaghetti code" was introduced decades ago to describe the sickening source code of a really poor-tasting software system. It makes people want to pursue an altogether different kind of fix. The saddest thing about badly written software is that business complexity is challenging enough without adding implementation complexity.

Spaghetti business always exists before software, and spaghetti code is the bane of a system's existence. Ad hoc architecture, progressive distortion of the software model, wrongly chosen abstractions, seeking opportunities for code reuse before use is even achieved, and unskilled developers are some of the reasons that software complexity prevents business from tackling business complexity to an innovative degree. Fight software complexity. Achieve by cooking business complexity.

Is taking a small step of cooking spaghetti a giant leap to rocket science? It's said that "choose-some-noun isn't rocket science." In this case, replace "choose-some-noun" with software development: "software development isn't rocket science." Yet, business innovation with software continues to solve increasingly difficult problems with regularity.

The tools provided in Chapters 1 and 2, and in the next few chapters, are meant to help cook business spaghetti in 10–12 minutes—that is, more rapidly than this feat would be achieved without the tools. Sometimes it's not the tools themselves that make for faster cooking. The key is often unlocking human thinking to reach a higher efficiency than is possible without the tools.

Strategic Architecture

Software architecture is commonly seen as a set of decisions to be made by technology-minded professionals. The architecture of a software component, subsystem, and whole-system solution generally belongs to those professionals known as *software architects*. The term *architect* has a number of different meanings and implications, and that meaning is generally tied to a business culture. The authors know architects with deep technical qualifications who still work on programming tasks on a regular basis; at the opposite extreme, some architects have only briefly or never implemented software in their careers. In truth, neither end of this spectrum qualifies or disqualifies those serving in the capacity of architect from filling an important role. Qualifications are always based on aptitude, attitude, adaptability, and agility.

Software architects must possess the ability to create a flexible architecture that can readily adapt to strategic changes in support of just-in-time decision making. The worst failings in software architecture are found where architects make architectural decisions that fall outside common practices with proven success, and those lacking real-world constraints—sometimes referred to as ivory tower architects and architectures—and those that are ad hoc with no attempt at manifesting communication-based structures. These failures can be classified into two categories: bad architecture and no architecture. (The first chapter used the term *unarchitecture*.)

Clearly, software architects should not be the only professionals responsible for architecture. The architecture supports the value chain delivery that is being developed by several different stakeholders. Because architecture is a place that supports communication among the people who have specified a solution, as well as contains a flexible structure to support the current and future decisions around the solution, it really belongs to every stakeholder, including business experts and developers. This leads to a critical point: A software architect must possess the skills to openly facilitate the collaboration that leads to a sound architecture.

Plain and simple, this book promotes a very simple and versatile architecture style. It is known by a few different names. Two of the most common names for this style are *Ports and Adapters* and *Hexagonal*. It is also known as *Clean Architecture,* and a less common name is *Onion Architecture*. These are all different monikers for the same thing. By any name, this architecture style supports flexibility and adaptability at every point of implementation and change, as you will learn in more detail in Chapter 8, "Foundation Architecture."

A key perspective on strategic software architecture is how it evolved through time, and for what reasons. It can be difficult to track the motivation behind certain decisions through the life cycle of an application, subsystem, and whole system. Decisions must be explained to those new to a team. It's also important for long-standing team members to be able to refresh their own memories about, and explain to business stakeholders, why things are the way they are.

Thankfully, there is a simple, agile tool, known as the Architectural Decision Record (ADR), that can assist in this process. ADRs help teams track software decisions made over the long haul. An ADR provides a document template that is used to capture each important architectural decision made, along with its context and consequences.

Each ADR should be stored along with the source code to which it applies, so they are easily accessible for any team member. You might protest that #agile doesn't require any documentation, and that the current code should be self-explanatory. That viewpoint is not entirely accurate. The #agile approach avoids *useless* documentation, but allows for any documentation that helps technical and business stakeholders understand the current context. More to the point, ADRs are very lightweight.

A number of ADR templates are available, but Michael Nygard proposed a particularly simple, yet powerful, one [Nygard-ADR]. His point of view is that an ADR should be a collection of records for "architecturally significant" decisions—those that affect the structure, nonfunctional characteristics, dependencies, interfaces, or construction techniques. Let's examine the structure of this template:

- *Title:* The self-explanatory title of the decision.
- *Status:* The status of the decision, such as proposed, accepted, rejected, deprecated, superseded, etc.
- *Context:* Describe the observed issue that has motivated this decision or change.
- *Decision:* Describe the solution that was chosen and why.
- *Consequences:* Describe what is easier or more difficult due to this change.

The next section provides an example of the ADR of a team within NuCoverage.

Applying the Tools

NuCoverage must determine whether it should continue to run its business with the existing Monolithic application, or to use a different architecture to support their new white-label strategy. Its senior architects recommend using a Microservices architecture. It's unwise to make such a decision hastily. The business and technical stakeholders decided to use the Cynefin framework to gain a better understanding of the situation by means of a decision-making tool that fosters thorough analysis. Table 2.2 summarizes what they came up with.

Table 2.2 *Cynefin at Work to Determine the Risks and Complexities of Migrating from a Monolithic Architecture to a Microservices Architecture*

	Current Context	Dangers to Migration	Response to Dangers
Clear Known Knowns	Monolith is well modularized.	Complacency and comfort.	Recognize the value and limitations of "common practices."
	Splitting modules from in-process to network calls is not a problem.	Team has a strong desire to dig into the distributed systems.	Don't assume it's just a simple transition to Microservices.
	Microservices common practices are well known to every member of the team.	No deep analysis made of the current state. Universal common practices don't exist.	Don't oversimplify the solution.
Complicated Known Unknowns	Monolith may not be well modularized, but it's currently unknown for the whole scope of application.	New approaches to migration are ignored by experts.	Encourage external and internal stakeholders to challenge experts' opinions.
	Common practices for Microservices aren't established in the community.	Experts are overconfident in their own solutions or in the efficiency of past solutions.	Use experiments and scenarios-based analysis to force people to think differently and in a different way about the response.
	The team has no experience in the migration from Monoliths to Microservices.	Views of experts are conflicting and they cannot agree on a common approach to migration.	
Complex Unknown Unknowns	Monolith is not well modularized, and certainly it won't be easy to replace in-process communication by means of the network.	Desire for accelerated resolution of the migration problem from stakeholders.	Be patient and allow the patterns to emerge through experimentation.
	No one agrees on best practices for migrating from the Monolith to Microservices.	Temptation to force a given decision on the rest of the stakeholders.	Learn from failures and see which practices work and which don't work.
	The team has no experience in the migration to Microservices, and it is difficult to identify real experts for the task.	Authoritarian response model to migration.	
Chaotic Unknowables	Monolithic application is difficult to deploy and to restart on a daily basis.	Relying too long on local practices that were discovered through use.	Set up parallel teams to work on the same domain problem.
	Many production bugs cause teams to take extra emergency support time to make the business run.	No innovation.	Challenge the current point of view and encourage innovation.
		Relying too much on the "cult of the leader" architect to keep the business system running.	Shift from this context to a complex one.

After significant analysis, all stakeholders involved agree that NuCoverage is in the *Complex* domain, because no one is confident that the current Monolithic application can be easily transformed to a Microservices-based distributed architecture. There appears to be no broad agreement on the common practices either in the community or among known Microservices experts.

One implication of using a Microservices architecture is that messages must be exchanged between each of the services. To make an architectural decision around this requirement, discussions around various mechanisms are held, which lead to the decision to initially use REST-based messaging. This decision is captured in the ADR shown in Listing 2.1.

Listing 2.1 *ADR That Captures the REST Message Exchange Decision*

```
Title: ADR 001: REST Message Exchange

Status: Experimental; Accepted

Context: Feed event messages to collaborating subsystems

Decision: Remain technology agnostic by using Web standards

Consequences:
Advantages: HTTP; Scale; Inexpensive for experiments
Disadvantages: Performance (but unlikely)
```

The current thought for the best way forward is found in the following points:

- Ensure an environment of experimentation with the option to fail, free from reprisals.
- Limit the experimentation scope to the current Monolithic application.
- Engage two experts from whom the team can learn, and to help avoid the likelihood of failure.

There is a sense of urgency in regard to establishing software architecture and design patterns that can be used by NuCoverage for the safe transformation of its Monolith to a Microservices architecture style, all in support of the new white-label insurance strategic initiative. Even so, the teams are making good progress and look forward to the journey ahead.

Summary

This chapter presented multiple strategic learning tools, including culture as a success enabler. Consider these essential for any business to achieve its strategic goal through differentiation and innovation. Making informed decisions is vital because the outcomes of ad hoc decisions are completely unreliable. Applying context to and forming insights into decisions is essential. To reinforce this, culturally safe experimentation and controlled failure are critical to better decision making, because Conway's Law is unforgiving of the inferior. As such, partitioning a problem space into smaller chunks feeds understanding, and using well-formed modules is essential to that effort. The recognition of business capabilities as modular divisions within and across which operations occur is core to every business that is expected to lead in revenue generation. Goal-based decisions are better than feature-based decisions, and Impact Mapping helps teams make strategic decisions on purpose. Some tools, such as the Cynefin framework, help with decision making. Others, such as ADRs, enable decisions along with long-term tracing.

The most salient points of this chapter are as follows:

- Understanding when decisions are most appropriate is essential to responsible decision making.

- The results of experimentation are an important source of knowledge for informed decision making.

- Beware of organizational culture and how it affects the safe use of experimentation and controlled failure as a decision-making tool.

- Recognizing business capabilities leads to applying modularity for better understanding and problem solving.

- Tools such as Cynefin and ADRs can help with decision making and long-term traceability.

The next chapter peers into events-first experimentation and discovery tools, which enables rapid learning and exploration that leads to innovations.

References

[Brooks] Frederick P. Brooks, Jr. *The Mythical Man-Month.* Reading, MA: Addison-Wesley, 1975.

[**Cohn**] Mike Cohn. *User Stories Applied: For Agile Software Development.* Boston, MA: Addison-Wesley, 2004.

[**Conway**] http://melconway.com/Home/Committees_Paper.html

[**CT**] "Book Reviews and Notes: *Teaching Thinking Skills: Theory and Practice.* Joan Baron and Robert Sternberg. 1987. W. H. Freeman, & Co., New York. 275 pages. Index. ISBN 0-7167-1791-3. Paperback." *Bulletin of Science, Technology & Society* 8, no. 1 (1988): 101. doi:10.1177/0270467688008001113. ISSN 0270-4676.

[**DrDobbs**] Mary Poppendieck. "Morphing the Mold." August 1, 2003. https://www.drdobbs.com/morphing-the-mold/184415014.

[**Hollnagel**] Erik Hollnagel. "The ETTO Principle: Efficiency–Thoroughness Trade-Off or Why Things That Go Right Sometimes Go Wrong." https://skybrary.aero/bookshelf/books/4836.pdf.

[**Impact**] Gojko Adzic. *Impact Mapping: Making a Big Impact with Software Products and Projects.* https://www.impactmapping.org/.

[**LA**] James O. Coplien and Gertrud Bjornvig. *Lean Architecture: for Agile Software Development.* Hoboken, NJ: Wiley, 2010.

[**LogFal**] https://www.logicalfallacies.info

[**Miller**] "The Magical Number Seven, Plus or Minus Two: Some Limits on Our Capacity for Processing Information." https://en.wikipedia.org/wiki/The_Magical_Number_Seven,_Plus_or_Minus_Two.

[**Nygard-ADR**] https://github.com/joelparkerhenderson/architecture_decision_record/blob/master/adr_template_by_michael_nygard.md

[**Org-Culture**] "Organizational Culture." https://en.wikipedia.org/wiki/Organizational_culture.

[**Pisano**] Gary P. Pisano. "The Hard Truth about Innovative Cultures." https://hbr.org/2019/01/the-hard-truth-about-innovative-cultures.

[**Poppendieck**] Mary Poppendieck and Tom Poppendieck. *Lean Software Development: An Agile Toolkit.* Boston, MA: Addison-Wesley, 2003.

[**TT**] Matthew Skelton and Manuel Pais. *Team Topologies.* Portland, OR: IT Revolution, 2019.

[**Tuckman**] Bruce W. Tuckman. "Developmental Sequence in Small Groups." *Psychological Bulletin* 63 (1965): 384–399.

[**TW-ICM**] https://www.thoughtworks.com/radar/techniques/inverse-conway-maneuver

Chapter 3

Events-First Experimentation and Discovery

Extroverts thrive on communication, and many business executives, sales and marketing people, and personnel with other customer-facing roles match that description. They tend to be energized and reinvigorated by social interactions. Many extroverts find that their best insights are the result of unreserved expression and active listening. Software developers and programmers are often the extreme opposites—introverts with a strong impulse for silence and solitude, while also welcoming of the opportunity to work through challenging puzzles. For these professionals, large numbers of people, noisy conversations, and social requirements to participate can be draining.

Yet contrary to popular opinion, neither of these stereotypes is necessarily accurate. In fact, a few decades ago, it was estimated that among 450 CEOs, 70% of those top executives were introverts. That didn't often help those leaders in articulating their business visions and models in environments where "communicating is the staff of life" [Fortune-Campbell]. Whatever personality characteristics are considered strengths or weaknesses, individuals are what they are, and most are capable of rising above to meet complex tasks head-on. The ability to overcome weaknesses, even those that are born from strengths—extroversion that leads to impatience and overbearing dominance while engaged in knowledge sharing—lies within nearly everyone [Inverted-U]. It is imperative to do so because collaborative communication among distinctively intelligent and respectful people is an undeniable agency in strategic innovation and differentiation, which distinguishes one business from all others.

The question is, how can the broad range of personality types overcome communication challenges to achieve deep dives into collaborative communication, learning, and improved software construction? That's the topic tackled in this chapter.

In software development, some fundamental concepts underlie the way that components work well together. We introduce these concepts first, so that we can quickly build up to the full use of tools that assist in active learning, and that can open the way to accelerated knowledge acquisition.

Commands and Events

Much of what we as humans do each day is in response to commands and events. We tend to capture human thinking in terms of intent of action (command) and the result of that action (event). Consider work-related human-to-human communication.

Sometimes what we do is in reaction to a command, such as "deliver a vision statement to the board of directors by the close of business." This statement might not be thought of as a command, but when boiled down, that's exactly what it is. It is *an imperative that requires follow-through to do something.*

A second kind of communication in which we engage daily is reacting to events. When the vision statement is completed and delivered to the board of directors, the members of the board might react to the fact that the vision document is available. Part of their reaction will be to read the vision statement and prepare comments to be made about it when the board next meets. In this case, the event is *the vision document was delivered to the board of directors.*

Perhaps one or more members of the board won't be able to read the document immediately, or even at all, due to other priorities or personal circumstances. This means that the event might have three outcomes:

- Accept the event-carried fact. Then, by human thought, the board member receiver translates this fact into a few self-commands: read the vision document and prepare comments to be made on the vision document.

- Postpone the handling of the event-carried fact until later, at which point it might be possible to, in the future, deal with the fact that the event happened.

- Ignore the handling of the event-carried fact altogether, knowing that someone else is in a better position to comment on it.

With this understanding, consider how these communication concepts apply to software: first with commands, and then with events.

In discussing "events first," why lead off with commands? This is a horse-and-cart dilemma. An event is primarily the result of a command. But wait—we don't yet have definitions. In software, what *is* a command and what *is* an event?

In software, a command is an imperative record—that is, a set of data named as *an explicit request to do something*. Looking back to when graphical user interfaces arrived on the scene en masse some 30 years ago, consider the typical **OK** button and **Cancel** buttons that populated their windows. Users clicked these buttons to cause the software to perform some action. These buttons are known as *command buttons*, because when the button is clicked, it causes a command to occur. The button labeled **OK**, when clicked, causes an action that generally means *complete this dialog box window by applying it*. Clicking the **Cancel** button means *cancel this dialog box window from being applied*. Hence, often a software command action is carried out as the result of a user clicking a specific button that causes the command to be executed, and the set of data entered in the dialog window is included as part of the command.

From a software perspective, an event *captures a record of the fact that a command was executed*. It's a set of data that is named in such a way that it expresses an action that occurred in the past. To clarify, an event is *typically* caused by a command. To the business, the occurrence is important enough to make a record of the incident. Now couple this understanding with the dialog window **OK** command: Once it is executed, an event is recorded, and that event might contain some or all of the data from the command.

Consider an example of using the command and event combination. An applicant wants to apply for an insurance policy. To do so, the applicant fills out an online policy application form with the required data. To cause the data to be submitted, the user interface has a command button named **Apply Now**. Clicking the **Apply Now** button submits the form to a service as part of the **Apply Now** command data. Upon receiving the form data, the service validates it, and assuming that the data is complete and correct, the service starts the policy approval process by recording an event named *Policy Application Submitted*, which holds pertinent data from the command. Figure 3.1 illustrates this process.

Note how the **Apply Now** command is stated in the imperative, as in *do this now*. A command may be rejected, and in this case it's possible that the rejection will occur due to the application being invalid.

Assuming that the **Apply Now** command is carried out to completion, the fact is recorded in an event that is named as a noun–verb expression in past tense, *Policy Application Submitted*. As a rule, the event is persisted into a database to fully preserve the recorded fact for guaranteed subsequent use.

In some cases, an event occurs without a command to cause it. For example, an event might occur when the clock reaches a specific time, such as 23:59:59 on 31 August. To a specific business, it might be important that the month has ended. If this is an important occasion to NuCoverage, our fictional example company, it can be captured as a factual event. A name such as *Month Ended* might work well if it is

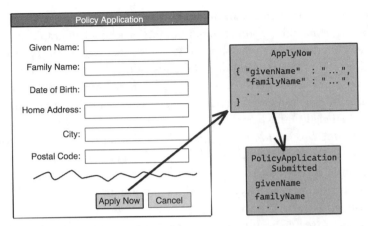

Figure 3.1 *The Apply Now command causes the Policy Application Submitted event.*

captured within the context of sales. Yet, in a financial context such as accounting, a month's end means something different. For example, *Ledger Period Closed* could work well as an event for a book of record. Figure 3.2 depicts this model of time-based events.

This speaks further to a thought that was introduced in Chapter 2, "Essential Strategic Learning Tools." It's vital to honor the context of communication when naming concepts. Chapter 2 focused on contexts named Claims, Underwriting, and Insurance Products. This chapter introduces Sales and Accounting as two additional contexts, each housed in a unique module. This example underscores that

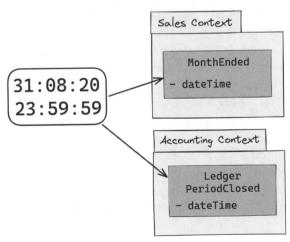

Figure 3.2 *Events caused by a date–time change; no command involved.*

many different contexts might exist within a given business, and that to have effective communication, these contexts must be clear and in the forefront of team members' minds during software design conversations.

Using Software Models

What might not be apparent is that the preceding examples are expressions of software models. Software modeling is a big part of making sense of businesses' complexities. Furthermore, the models produced are used to relate everyday business procedures and processes to software components. The names used for software models make sense when they are not arbitrarily chosen, but rather thoughtfully selected and in harmony with the context of team communications.

From here forward, this book draws heavily on software modeling as a practice that leads to deep learning and breakthrough insights resulting in differentiating innovation. Events are at the heart of a tool used by teams to help them make constructive and rapid strides toward deep learning. In addition, both commands and several software modeling concepts play important roles.

Rapid Learning with EventStorming

Thomas Edison, a known inventor and innovator, commented on his many attempts to succeed. In the wake of a large number of what would normally be called "failures," Edison said, "I have not failed. I've just found 10,000 ways that won't work."

Edison didn't actually invent the lightbulb. By the time he was working on this problem, lightbulbs had already become common in street lamps, factories, and shops. But they had limitations. What Edison invented was the first practical and affordable lightbulb [Time-Edison]. He also didn't invent this device on his own. To accomplish this feat, Edison's team tested 6,000 different filaments before finding the one that met with the goal [Edison-Museum].

Alexander Graham Bell invented the telephone—sort of. It was argued by several others that they had created the original invention. In any case, Bell arrived at his patented telephone in 1876 after centuries of experimentation and discoveries by others, including the acoustic string phone in 1667, attributed to British physicist and polymath Robert Hooke. Edison also contributed to the success of the telephone by inventing the carbon microphone, which produced a strong telephone signal. Yet telephone use was originally underwhelming because it ran over telegraph exchanges, to the benefit of very few consumers. Without the ultimate invention of telephone exchanges, the widespread use of the telephone would never have been possible [Phone-History].

The point being made here is that it is often shortsighted vision or lack of knowledge that brings about lesser innovations, and then others envision improvements on those predecessor inventions. The key point: Teams will often start out to solve one set of problems, but discover greater opportunities to innovate through experimentation and collaboration. Don't prevent this from happening because it might be pointing out that the initial aim was only obvious and ordinary, or at best an interim step. This process is led by communication, and that's what leads to innovation.

Experimentation within a failure-tolerant culture is key to creating an environment of innovation. Yet what stands in the way of such an environment is the following question: How many times must failure be faced before innovation is reached, and how long, and how much funding will that require?

Admittedly, having 6,000 to 10,000 failures is rarely part of the business plan, timeline, and budget. Then again, neither was the early lightbulb or the early telephone.

> In short, exceptional organizations are those that go beyond detecting and analyzing failures and try to generate intelligent ones for the express purpose of learning and innovating. It's not that managers in these organizations enjoy failure. But they recognize it as a necessary by-product of experimentation. They also realize that they don't have to do dramatic experiments with large budgets. Often a small pilot, a dry run of a new technique, or a simulation will suffice. [HBR-Failure]

In actuality, these sorts of great inventions, such as the broad availability of true quantum computing, are sorely needed to truly advance technological progression. In turn, those who seek invention must be prepared to invest heavily in experimentation and to learn at least 10,000 ways that won't work. For everyone else, building incremental innovations as a means to generate revenues, which are then reinvested in building more incremental innovations, is the key. Learning rapidly and inexpensively is a necessity.

As a best-in-class approach to communication, collaboration, and discovery-based learning, the modeling tool and set of techniques known as EventStorming [EventStorming], conceptualized and developed by Alberto Brandolini, offers these benefits with low overhead. The cost of this approach derives from the inclusion of all the knowledge workers necessary to participate in creative sessions, with these sessions being constrained only by their collective imagination. Sessions exclude neither business experts nor software development experts. To the contrary, Event-Storming requires the participation of everyone with vision, a vital stake, questions, answers, a willingness to discuss the known knowns and the known unknowns, and the tenacity to unearth the unknown unknowns. It calls on all of them to leverage this knowledge to achieve something beyond the ordinary.

Note

Vaughn Vernon, one of the authors, highlighted EventStorming in his 2016 book, *Domain-Driven Design Distilled* [DDD-Distilled]. It was during one of Vaughn's 2013 IDDD Workshop events in Europe, in which Alberto Brandolini was invited to participate as an instructor, that EventStorming was first introduced. That's also where domain-driven design (DDD) was introduced to large numbers of professionals and gained a strong foothold, and where the authors of this book first met in person. That workshop was a bright moment in software development history. Vaughn and several students in that workshop have used and championed EventStorming ever since.

Achieving beyond-ordinary software delivery demands that all business silos that are generally uncommunicative (the cause of unpleasant communication), or that even make cross-divisional cooperation prohibitive, must be overcome. Both non-communication and various competitive and adversarial behaviors stand in the way of innovation. The business ultimately suffers even more than the people blocked from making progress. Everyone has a choice, and two choices should be provided: collaborate or step out of the way.

The basic idea behind EventStorming is to model a time-ordered series of descriptive happenings in a system. The fact-based happenings, which are recorded on sticky notes as model elements of past occasions, are supplemented by other kinds of model elements that capture supporting details about the dynamic environment. Time order is recorded from left to right. The orange-colored elements (if rendered in color) in the model in Figure 3.3 are events, and the other colors indicate supplemental, supporting elements. From the number of orange elements consistently used across the timeline, it should be clear that this is a tool for *events-first modeling*.

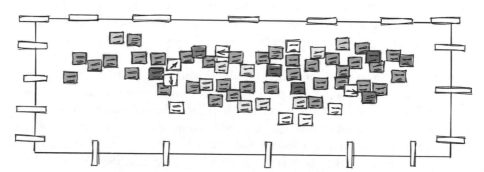

Figure 3.3 *EventStorming produces insights and awareness of business opportunities.*

When Remote Sessions Are Demanded

EventStorming is primarily facilitated as an in-person activity. However, it can be approximated using online collaborative tooling such as with voice and video calls, as well as by using a virtual whiteboard with drawing capabilities. The authors have both experienced and discussed the advantages and disadvantages of holding storming sessions in a virtual environment.

The advantage of using remote sessions is that teams can be composed of remote workers who are still required to collaborate to get creative work done. In the era of virtual-everything due to health threats created by in-person collaboration, this is not only an advantage but an imperative. Even assuming that in-person collaboration becomes generally viable again, remote sessions will continue to be a necessity—even if it wasn't an option due to businesses' policies before the COVID-19 pandemic. Remote is here to stay.

The major impediment commonly encountered with remote EventStorming sessions is that the communication channels are stifled. Most have by now witnessed that conversation between just two people, given a few seconds in delay of body motion and voice reception, is often choppy. When attempting to involve a large number of people in such a discussion, this problem becomes even worse. With in-person sessions, conversations tend to fork and rejoin—but if that starts to happen with a greater number of people participating virtually, it's going to be far worse than what happens when only two individuals are talking. This might be handled by establishing conversation protocols such as hand raising and virtual breakout rooms, but none of these can facilitate the kind of interactions that in-person sessions afford. As with any collaborative setting, we get what we get to the extent of the platform's limitations.

There is also a physical space limitation in many remote encounters, given that a video call and the virtual whiteboard both require computer display real estate. When participants have at least two displays or one very large display, this is not really an issue. Hosting the video call within a smaller display area and the virtual whiteboard in a larger area can generally make the experience better; however, it is less common for business executives and other management to possess such large viewing spaces. You should strongly consider this as a cost of doing business. You can overcome the display real estate limitations by purchasing enough large external displays for everyone who is needed to participate. Such displays can usually be acquired for a few hundred dollars/euros each, and most notebook computers have the capacity to drive both the onboard and external displays simultaneously. Those currently unfamiliar with these large displays will soon find them indispensable even beyond remote EventStorming.

Some practitioners—including the originator of EventStorming, Alberto Brandolini—conclude that it is impossible to use this technique properly with online collaboration tools [Remote-Bad]. Others prefer the virtual approach over in-person sessions and are quite comfortable with it. Such facilitators tend to have a very limited number of participants not by intention, but rather based on need.

The widespread existence of remote teams, as well as the desperate times that have forced remoteness upon us even when it is not desired, have created a clear need for virtual EventStorming sessions. This is something that even Alberto has acknowledged [Remote-Demanded].

Facilitating Sessions

This section of the chapter discusses EventStorming as facilitated *in-person*. Using the previous advice and common sense, apply the best practices outlined in the sections that follow as much as possible when you have no other choice than *remote facilitation*. The physical modeling tools are discussed first, followed by a description of the efforts needed from individuals.

Modeling Surface

EventStorming requires a virtually unlimited modeling surface, which can be created by attaching a long strip of paper on a wide wall, say 10 meters/yards.[1] This width is obviously not unlimited, but for a lot of cases it will be enough, and thus as good as unlimited. If it's not enough, teams must find a wider wall or continue on an adjacent wall. Depending on purchasing options, rolls of compatible paper (914 mm/36 inch wide) might be available—for example, 3M Masking Paper [3M-Paper], 3M Scotch Banner and Sign Paper [Scotch-Paper], Pacon Colored Kraft Duo-Finish Paper [Pacon-Paper], and various plotter paper options. Figure 3.4 illustrates this setup.

Markers

Participants must do handwriting, so you should get these awesome pens: Sharpie Fine Point Permanent Marker [Sharpie] (not Sharpie Ultra Fine!), shown in Figure 3.5. This is not a joke; the pens make a noticeable difference. If they're using pencils, ballpoint pens, or ultra-fine-point pens, participants won't be able to see the handwriting well from even a short distance away. If they're using very thick markers, the handwriting will be illegible due to ink bleed and limited writing space. Also

---

1. Yes, the authors are well aware that meters and yards are not the same length. But for those who understand metric and those who understand standard, the measurements have meaning.

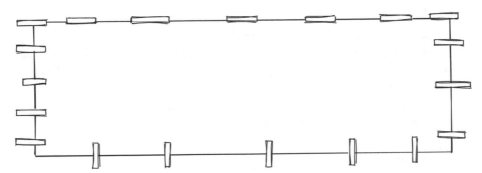

Figure 3.4 *Use a wide wall and a long strip of paper for the modeling surface.*

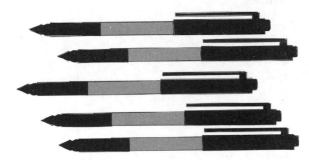

Figure 3.5 *The right marker makes everyone smarter. Promise.*

not to be overlooked is that the authors insist the Sharpie Fine Point pens make all participants smarter. Just Right™ is not just for "Goldilocks and the Three Bears" [Goldilocks].

Sticky Notes

A plentiful amount of sticky notes of a specific set of colors are used as model element types. Every color represents a different kind of concept within a specific modeling perspective. Even so, an important consideration is to avoid turning storming sessions into a science. Keep the modeling experience simple, remembering that the business itself is complex enough without adding an extra burden of modeling complexity. The most important aspect of storming is to engender open communication leading to discovery-based learning. Correcting newcomers in an effort to create the "perfectly defined model" will backfire, because that will chase away people critical to success from sharing in vital communication. If everyone understands one another and contributes to breakthrough learning, call it a successful experience.

Consider using the element colors and types shown in Figure 3.6 and described in the following list.

Figure 3.6 *The sticky note modeling elements by color and type name. (Note: For print-book readers, colors have been denoted with patterns.)*

- **Commands are light blue.** A command is an imperative, an explicit request to do something. Generally, commands are the result of a user gesture to perform some action on data.

- **Events are orange.** An event records a fact that something important happened in a given model context, and is frequently the outcome of a user successfully executing a command. An event is named as a noun–verb in the past tense. For example, our model includes events named *Policy Application Submitted*, *Month Ended*, and *Ledger Period Closed*. Given that this tool is named Event-Storming, it is expected that the greater number of stickies will be events, at least early on, because it is events that drive the modeling experience.

- **Policies are purple.** A policy is a named business rule or set of rules that must be met, or a set of guidelines available for use upon an outcome. For example, after a command is executed, an event is emitted and there might be a decision on how this event impacts the downstream model. (Purple is a generic color that might actually be named lilac or mulberry by the manufacturer.)

- **Aggregates/entities are pale yellow.** This is where data is held, commands are applied and affect the data, and events are the resulting outcomes that describe what happened. These elements are the nouns of a model, such as *Application*, *Risk*, *Policy*, *Claim*, and *Coverage*.

- **User roles are bright yellow.** This is a user who plays a role in the model, such as an *Underwriter* or *Adjuster*. It might also be the name of a persona chosen for the purpose of representing someone with enumerated characteristics. These elements are useful for walking through specific scenarios, stories, and use cases. The personas can be used to predict how the imaginary individuals will think and what they will do or want to do under a given set of circumstances.

- **Views/queries are forest green.** To render a view for a user, a query must be executed on a datastore to retrieve the view's data. This element can also represent when an event occurrence must be projected into the datastore to update the view data for subsequent querying and rendering to the user interface.

- **Processes are purple.** A process is similar to a policy but is responsible for carrying out a series of steps to cause an ultimate outcome. The routing rules for executing the series of steps are basically a policy that specifies the process. (Purple is a generic color that might actually be named lilac or mulberry.)

- **Contexts and external systems are light pink.** It's possible that your business process will receive a stimulus from an external system, or that an external system will be affected by the process being modeled. The external systems and subsystems are contextual regarding the teams and conversations within them. Additionally, as the storming activity increases, it might become clearer which areas of the system belong in specific communication contexts. If so, place a pink sticky above the area of the model and name the context.

- **Opportunities are lime green.** Mark areas of the model that represent opportunities to explore and experiment within to exploit new competitive advantage. Those familiar with strengths, weaknesses, opportunities, threats (SWOT) analysis might consider these to be similar to opportunities.

- **Problems are red.** These stickies mark spots in the model where problems in a specific area of the business process require further exploration and experimentation. The additional efforts should lead to improvement, with possible innovation. Those familiar with SWOT analysis might consider these to be similar to threats.

- **Voting arrows are dark blue.** After a productive storming session, modelers are each given two dark-blue stickies on which to draw arrows and point them to opportunities and/or problems in the model. The opportunities and/or problems that have the most arrows pointing to them should be our next areas of focus.

- **Notes are white.** Notes can be written directly on any of the applicable model elements if there is room to do so. Writing a note might be a sign that a policy should be defined instead. Sometimes notes crosscut multiple model elements but don't call for policies. Also, drawing directional/flow arrows can be useful, especially when the flow turns back upstream. Both types of notes can be put on white stickies or another-color note that is clearly not a model element. *Don't write directly on the paper modeling surface.* Model element stickies get moved around, and notes on stickies can move with them. Notes and symbols written on the paper modeling surface cannot be moved, so they end up as distracting scratch-outs all over the place.

Since the inception of the EventStorming technique, sticky notes with the "standard colors" have become increasingly more difficult to find, so you might need to adjust your color palette to whatever is available. In such cases, be sure to provide a template similar to that illustrated in Figure 3.6. It's quite important to use distinct colors for each model element type to keep all collaborators in sync with each other.

In addition, you should create a unique icon for each of the model element types. The main reason for the icon is to indicate the element type for participants who are colorblind. When conducting workshops, the authors regularly encounter students who have some form of colorblindness. For some people, the difference between colors shows up distinctly as shades of gray or as a darker hue. Even so, the icons can help them distinguish element types at a quick glance, and can even be advantageous for new participants not familiar with the color palette.

Big-Picture Modeling

When using EventStorming, big-picture modeling is an exercise in discovering the overall flow of the system under exploration. Typically a commercial transcontinental flight cruises at 35,000 feet/10,700 meters, give or take. With clear skies, from that altitude the human eye can see 240 miles/386 kilometers, and possibly farther. Relatively speaking, that's the kind of system vision of process and flow desired from big-picture storming. Standing on the ground, the human eye can see approximately 3.3 miles/5.3 kilometers. That might be the desired relative distance, but probably even less, when using design-level storming.

> **Note**
>
> Using EventStorming for *big-picture modeling* is the topic of this book. Detailed discussions and examples of *design-level modeling* are found in our follow-on implementation book, *Implementing Strategic Monoliths and Microservices* (Vernon & Jaskuła, Addison-Wesley, forthcoming).

To use EventStorming effectively, it's important to understand how the modeling elements work together. Depending on the scope (either big picture or design level), there will tend to be fewer or more—or at least different—numbers and combinations of model element types in use. Consider creating a cheatsheet based on the common use of big-picture model elements.

Cheatsheet

The tool name *EventStorming* gives a pretty good clue of the priority within the model element types. Even so, other elements will be quite helpful. Nine are discussed in this book, and can be employed in various combinations depending on the modeling situation at hand. Figure 3.7 provides a view of the cheatsheet modeling elements, and the following bullet points give ideas on how to use them.

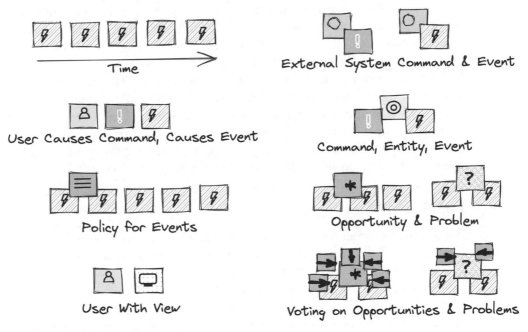

Figure 3.7 *The big-picture EventStorming cheatsheet.*

- **Events.** Create a timeline from left to right using any number of event elements that are needed to express the ideas within the process. More details on this process appear later in the section "Applying the Tools," but for now think in terms of flooding the modeling surface with events. To begin with, the order is less important than the existence of events, and the more the better.

- **Commands.** An event is generally caused by a command, but not always. A command is typically the result of some user action. Thus, if showing the command that causes an event is useful, place the command element to the left of the event that it causes. That's because the command occurs in time order prior to the event.

- **Policies.** Because some previous unknowns will be discovered during storming, the session participants will naturally be unfamiliar with some of the ideas in the making. Rather than taking a significant amount of time to try to dig into the details that nobody currently knows in depth, use a policy sticky to name the area of ambiguity and then move on. It will be better to undertake detailed specification at a point when more research can be done. Sometimes the people experiencing disagreement won't readily think of moving on, so the storming facilitator is responsible for marking the spot and keeping the team focused.

- **User role/persona.** Whether or not it is decided to show a command that causes an event in a specific area of the model, it might be useful to show the kind of user who will be involved in the scenario being realized. Put a bright-yellow user/persona sticky note before (to the left of) the elements that are the result of the action they make.

- **Context/external system.** As the storming activity reveals which areas of the system belong in specific communication contexts, place a pink sticky above each area of the model that is identifiable and name the context. When a command or event from an external source enters the model currently under design, the source of the stimulus can be shown with a pink sticky note. This draws attention to the fact that consideration must be given to accepting the external stimulus, and possibly even how it will be emitted from the external system.

- **View/query.** When it is useful to draw careful attention to an important user experience, place a green sticky on the modeling surface with the name of the view and/or query that provides the user interface and/or the data. In such cases, it's often useful to show the user role/persona that will interact with the view. A view/query can also be used to show that the data that will eventually be used for this purpose must be explicitly collected and possibly even pre-assembled and formatted.

- **Aggregate/entity.** This kind of element might be less commonly needed in the big-picture model, but it can still be helpful to show an important data holder and behavior component known as an aggregate or entity. This component is a noun. Commands are executed on this component, and events are emitted from it. Thus, whenever an aggregate/entity is used, it can be paired with a command to its left (what it is told to do) and one or more events to its right (the outcome emitted due to executing the command).

- **Opportunity and problem.** Mark areas of the model where opportunities can be exploited and where problems must be resolved. Note that a problem is different from a policy that marks model ambiguity and/or disagreement. A problem is something that the team understands well enough to determine that it is currently wrong and will cause issues in the future. Those familiar with SWOT analysis might consider these to be similar to opportunities and threats.

- **Voting.** After going far into the modeling exercise and identifying some opportunities and/or problems, have the team vote on the opportunities and/or problems that need the most attention. The opportunities and/or problems that receive the most votes will be addressed; the others can be backlogged for later or dismissed as unimportant.

In time, the modeling surface will be flooded not only with orange events, but also with other types of elements and colors. When there seem to be too many, move them into time order, and tear off the redundant ones and those that don't belong. Now look at the floor. If it's colorful with many stickies, that means success. It's cheap to make these kinds of "mistakes" and learn from them. Removing a lot of unnecessary stickies is far better than imagining too few.

Applying the Tools

Those invited to participate in this high-altitude modeling experience must include both business and technical experts, either with preexisting knowledge of the system under development or a stakeholder interest in what is to follow. Most likely those two groups will overlap.

Include everyone . . .

- Originating and responsible for carrying the vision forward

- With a vital business and/or technical stake

- Who has questions and answers about the system under exploration

- Who understands known knowns and the known unknowns

- Possessing the tenacity to unearth the unknown unknowns

- Driven to leverage acquired knowledge to achieve beyond the ordinary

Everyone should have a marker and access to sticky notes, especially the orange variety used to model events. All involved should speak openly.

Consider a party or lunch catered in the office. What happens? Unless there's a plan in place to get things moving, most people sit or stand around waiting for someone to make the first move toward the food. One or a few people who are really hungry and less shy swoop right in, grab a plate, get some food, find a place conducive to eating the type of food served, and start eating. These first movers are sometimes called *icebreakers*. A planned icebreaker makes it easier for anyone to be more open to getting some food. It might be as simple as assigning a few people to hand out plates to others and then escort them up to the food.

In a similar manner, start an EventStorming session by asking one or a few participants to be prepared to break the ice. The icebreaker(s) should start the storming process by thinking of and writing on an orange sticky note the name of some event in the timeline. Place it on the modeling surface relative to where it happens in the timeline, either closer to the beginning, in the middle, or toward the end. These icebreaker events are based on something that is already well known or at least a common assumption about how the system does or will function. Figure 3.8 shows the early placement of a few icebreaker events.

One of the worst problems with an EventStorming session occurs when the team starts off seeking a high degree of agreement and desire for consensus and team approval. That is actually the way to shut down creativity. Agility emphasizes individual expression and spontaneity over consensus and approval. Because everyone has a marker and sticky notes, spontaneity is promoted. Encourage everyone to write down what they know and what they think would be an improvement over what exists or what is assumed.

Conversations will ebb and flow. The timeline can be sorted out after ideas flow for a while and an ebb occurs. Some participants will detach from the main group and then rejoin. This is all-natural and should not be discouraged.

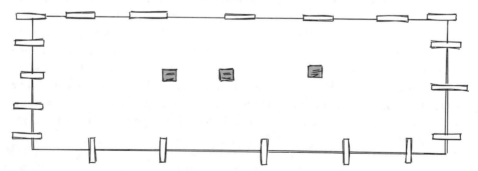

Figure 3.8 *Icebreaker events get the storming under way and promote spontaneity.*

Sometimes there will be uncertainty and even disagreements over how things currently are or how they should be. These ambiguities might be resolved if the right business experts are present, but sometimes there's simply not enough understanding of the existing or proposed business process rules. The wrong way to handle this issue is to allow the disagreements to continue, because it's an indication that the right questions and the right answers aren't available. In such cases, the facilitator should wield the purple policy sticky, slap it on the modeling surface at the point of confusion, and name it. Consider this a placeholder for a future conversation that will probably require interviews with those better acquainted with the subject matter. It might also require research to learn more about standards that must be followed, and probably experimentation around the specific sphere of knowledge, or current lack thereof.

Figure 3.9 demonstrates how a policy can be used to mark the unknowns around the events in question. Refer back to Figure 2.6 and Figure 2.7 in Chapter 2, which show discoveries around the impact named *One-Click Application Submission*. The events in Figure 3.9 correspond to the deliverables surfaced there. This EventStorming session may have occurred before or after the Impact Mapping session, or simultaneously. These are tools that can easily be used together at just the right time.

The point of the *Agent Underwriting Policy* in Figure 3.9 is that the storming team is uncertain about the details around the submission of the full array of data required for agent customer import and of the same customer's application for coverage. The idea from Figures 2.6 and 2.7 is that the *One-Click Application Submission* must carry the full payload of customer account and application information, but the team doesn't yet know what that must be or how it will be provided by the agent (e.g., WellBank). So, they mark this area with a policy that must receive attention from at least a few different NuCoverage subject-matter experts. Using the policy allows the storming session to move on without getting bogged down in details that cannot be disambiguated at the present time.

Figure 3.9 also indicates how a command is the cause of one or more events. The command *Submit Agent Customer Application* is incoming from the external Agent System (e.g., WellBank). The team decided to show this command in the big-picture model because it helped illustrate the full context of the usage and process scenario. Indicating that the external Agent System is responsible for issuing the command calls out the need for considerable work to be done in that area. The external system will no doubt be the objective of ongoing EventStorming sessions that involve another group. That group will likely have some overlap of members from this effort.

Figure 3.9 *The Agent Underwriting Policy marks a place where the model needs more details.*

Reviewing Figure 3.10, both an opportunity and a problem have been discovered. When an Insured user views their policy information, they should be prompted to enhance their coverage. For example, a user who has a good driving record might be offered multi-car discounts. Further, when NuCoverage begins to offer home insurance through the white-label channel, the Insured might also be offered more favorable home insurance coverage and pricing. The team discusses how this can be done, and is certain it will require additional data from the agent—for example, WellBank. This process should include proactive email and campaigns as well as offers shared in customers' monthly bank statements.

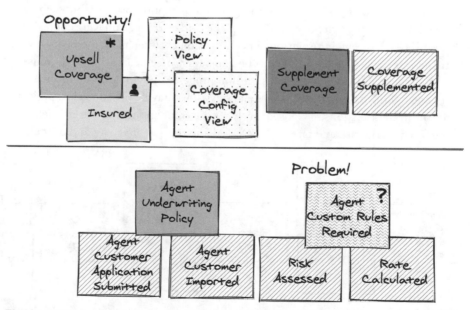

Figure 3.10. *An opportunity and a problem have been identified.*

Figure 3.10 also highlights a problem. Although agents such as WellBank are satisfied with the risk and rate rules, as well as the premiums and coverages that NuCoverage offers to its customers, the team anticipates that some agents will want to specify custom rules for all these items, and possibly more. In addition, NuCoverage might need to provide customizable user interface components, even beyond styling with rebranding.

When the team reaches the point of voting on opportunities and problems, the consensus is that the *Upsell Coverage* opportunity should definitely be pursued immediately. However, because WellBank is the first agent that will go live and it is currently happy to offer the standard NuCoverage risk and rate rules, as well as premiums and coverages, the team has voted that now is not the last responsible moment to make decisions on *Agent Custom Rules Required*. This specific problem will be backlogged and addressed at the appropriate future time. The section "Applying the Tools" in Chapter 6, "Mapping, Failing, and Succeeding—Choose Two," explains what happens at that future time.

Another issue that the NuCoverage team would like to address is why so many applicants drop out of the application process before completion, which NuCoverage observed from available data. Compared to those users who start out applying, the full application submission rate is very low, which means significant numbers of potential new policies aren't being issued. NuCoverage decides to use EventStorming to discover the current subscription process.

Figure 3.11 shows just the beginning of the subscription process, but very early on, an interesting pattern can be observed. The *Underwriting* and *Rate* contexts are constantly exchanging information. The discussion between team members reveals that the rate according to risk has to be constantly assessed and the rate must be repeatedly calculated while the subscription process is ongoing. Based on the current assessed risk, a number of additional questions may be posed to the applicant, who fills in their responses. Consequently, as different application forms' fields are being filled in, the risk and rate are reassessed and recalculated over and over again.

Figure 3.11 *Current subscription process.*

The team has quickly identified that the *Rate* context must have very detailed data to calculate the fairest price and assess the correct risk, and this has a very direct impact on the user experience. To get the final rate, applicants must respond to many questions that sometimes they cannot answer without having very specific documents in front of them. And if it happens that the estimated risk is high, the subscription process is stopped, leaving the applicant frustrated and without the ability to apply for a policy or even see the calculated premium prices. The team concludes that the subscription process is too cumbersome and that the risk assessment and rate calculation must be done differently. They throw out the current EventStorming model and start a new one.

It happens that for some time, the *Rate* team has been doing controlled and safe experiments with machine learning algorithms in an effort to replace the old method of rate calculation and risk assessment. They didn't want to follow the hype and play around with machine learning algorithms, but rather wanted to make practical use of this approach. Thus, experimentation afforded the team the opportunity to learn how the software could benefit from machine learning. They were experiencing real pain in maintaining the current risk assessment and rate calculation models. The rules were really complicated, it was very difficult to include the new rules into the model, and adjusting calculations of prices was very error prone. The *Rate* team was spending part of their time fixing production bugs based on wrongly calculated prices and poorly assessed risks. Figure 3.12 highlights the results of their work.

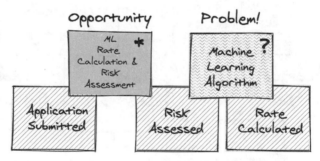

Figure 3.12 *Discovery of the machine learning opportunity.*

The impact on the business was sizable. Machine learning seemed to be a really promising technology, given that the company already had a lot of historical data. Additionally, more data can be readily purchased[2] from data providers, so as to

---

2. This reference does not mean private personal information sold without the consent of the owners, but rather non-identifiable information that can be purchased in some countries. Such information includes data about vehicles and the risks associated with them: accidents, number of stolen units, etc.

enrich the machine learning algorithms. Given even minimal input from the application form, the team could then use the new algorithms to assess risk and calculate a rate. Even if the team expects some number of false positives, the risk of the business insuring too many bad drivers is not that high. Over time, the machine learning algorithms will be fine-tuned and the results should be better. Also, the team will experiment with the new implementation through A/B testing to further limit the risk of delivering financially damaging implementations. The discovery of this opportunity has boosted the team's enthusiasm, and the fact that the application process can be simplified has led to another discovery.

NuCoverage's business people, hearing that the application process can be simplified, came up with another idea. They had for some time considered how they could use social media channels to drive sales, but knew it would be nearly impossible because of the complicated application form. Now, though, they could envision a chatbot on Facebook that would allow users to apply for a policy with only a few clicks. Not only would the business leverage social media recommendation engines, but it could also determine the best risk and price based on the contextualized and historical data available to the machine learning algorithm. This was captured in the model shown in Figure 3.13.

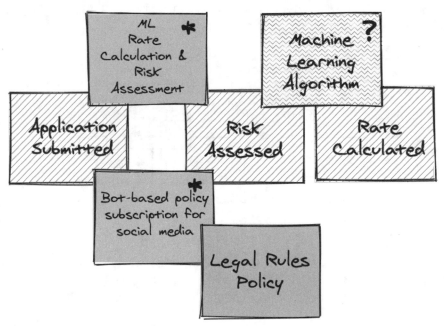

Figure 3.13 *EventStorming led to another interesting discovery.*

The business knows that most young people are solely using social media and mobile phones as their view out to the world. Opening this policy application channel would be a key enabler in NuCoverage's quest to expand to new markets. Winning over young people, by demonstrating that the business understands them, has the potential to build loyalty for life.

Yet, the business must also demonstrate its ability to leap forward and grow with its policyholders and ongoing social trends, no matter what changes life brings. The business must address the next stages in the life of every policyholder, because most will involve new insurable risks. This means more experimentation and discovery-based learning to uncover deep knowledge as facilitated by the domain-driven approaches you will learn about in Part II of this book.

Summary

You should embrace tools that help teams overcome communication challenges and achieve deep dives into collaborative communication, learning, and improved software construction. Enabling safe and rapid experimentation within a failure-tolerant culture is key to creating an environment supportive of innovation. EventStorming captures the expression of human thinking. It includes ways to record intentions expressed as actionable commands, and the result of such actions as events are key to exploration. In addition, a number of modeling elements are available for deeper learning: policies, data and behavioral entities, user roles, views, contextual boundaries, as well as ways to mark opportunities and problems, and which ones to pursue.

The most prominent points of this chapter are as follows:

- Events-first modeling bridges the communication gap between all stakeholders and enables human-oriented productivity and discovery.

- Driving experimentation with events-first models assists with active learning, and accelerates knowledge acquisition at a low cost, in terms of both people's time and tooling.

- EventStorming enables cross-divisional cooperation by overcoming the challenges of existing business silos that hinder essential communication.

- Beginning modeling efforts by examining events helps teams leverage constructive feedback and achieve rapid strides toward deep learning by making sense of business software complexities.

So far, this book has heavily emphasized the realization of business software strategy through learning and discovery to bring about differentiating innovation. In Part II, we note how businesses can reach domain-driven results by building on the approaches already discussed. Employing a knowledge-driven perspective unveils a steady stream of improvements to software products, leading to strategic differentiation with competitive advantage.

References

[3M-Paper] https://www.3m.com/3M/en_US/company-us/all-3m-products/~/3M-White-Masking-Paper/?N=5002385+3293242382&rt=rud

[DDD-Distilled] Vaugh Vernon. *Domain-Driven Design Distilled*. Boston: Addison-Wesley, 2016.

[Edison-Museum] http://edisonmuseum.org/content3399.html

[EventStorming] https://leanpub.com/introducing_eventstorming

[Fortune-Campbell] https://archive.fortune.com/magazines/fortune/fortune_archive/1996/05/13/212382/index.htm

[Goldilocks] https://en.wikipedia.org/wiki/Goldilocks_and_the_Three_Bears

[HBR-Failure] https://hbr.org/2011/04/strategies-for-learning-from-failure

[Inverted-U] https://www.researchgate.net/publication/258180060_Too_Much_of_a_Good_Thing_The_Challenge_and_Opportunity_of_the_Inverted_U

[Pacon-Paper] https://pacon.com/dual-light/rainbow-colored-kraft-duo-finish-rolls-36-x-1000-white.html

[Phone-History] https://en.wikipedia.org/wiki/History_of_the_telephone

[Remote-Bad] https://blog.avanscoperta.it/2020/03/26/remote-eventstorming/

[Remote-Demanded] https://blog.avanscoperta.it/2020/03/26/eventstorming-in-covid-19-times

[Sharpie] https://www.sharpie.com/all-markers/classic/super/SHSuperBlackFine

[Time-Edison] https://time.com/3517011/thomas-edison/

Part II

Driving Business Innovation

Executive Summary

In Part I, we established the goals of pursuing digital transformation as a revenue-generating business strategy, and applying the proper mindset, culture, and learning tools to facilitate this effort. Now it's time to delve into a software development technique that promotes and upholds the value-generating goals. It helps businesses understand where strategic investments should be made, and where they should not.

The technique and practices advanced in this part of the book are readily adoptable. To provide a brief summary, this approach acknowledges that differences in perceptions and viewpoints within business capabilities and processes are not only common, but necessary. That is, depending on the context of an area of business expertise and the specific communication that occurs there, what might appear to be equivalent concepts may, in fact, be vastly different or have a critical nuance of difference from other viewpoints. As an example, consider the concept of policy inside NuCoverage. There are various meanings for this term, because in reality policy is not a single concept, but many. To understand the differing concepts with the same name, the term *policy* must be surrounded by the context in which it has a given meaning and set of business rules.

Admittedly, when you're introducing a "new way" of approaching software development, there's a danger in it being viewed as yet another shiny object. With that being said, it's notable that this technique is not at all new. The concepts are more than two decades old, and the proposed technique codifies the essence of several worthwhile practices that have been used for additional decades. The authors have decided to promote not the name, but rather the practices used with this approach. That's because names can be misused to describe the use of poor practices, and sadly that has been the case with this technique for a while now. Like anything, people want to be associated with success, but often don't want to put in the effort necessary to understand and practice the technique as intended. Throwing together some words is meant to elevate them to the "club," whatever that is supposed to mean. Yet, if the practices are the focus of this book, then chances are better that the practices will be adopted rather than a name only.

The other choice is to do what most software teams are prone to do: attempt to merge the clearly recognizable differences between one term used in multiple contexts of human thought and communication into a single unified thing. That kind of merger has proven problematic and even damaging time and again, and it most often leads to the large, gnarly, mud-like software that such great effort is being spent to defeat. Intake of an application to obtain a policy, calculating the risk and premium rate of a potential policy, underwriting a policy, filing a claim against a policy, and renewing a policy are all very different concepts, and they should be modeled differently in separate software contexts. The technique and practice offered in Part II uses separate module-based software contexts to host the range of different uses.

Chapter 4: Reaching Domain-Driven Results

The word *domain*, as used in this book, refers to a sphere of knowledge. As already established, knowledge is one of the most valuable assets of any business.

- Existing knowledge is important and valuable, but a business that rests on its current knowledge risks that it is ordinary, or that even new, breakthrough knowledge can become ordinary if and when the competition catches up. Continuous knowledge acquisition must be at the top of the software requirements list.

- When a sphere of knowledge is identified by a name, this domain has preexisting knowledge. The trick is not just to continue to acquire knowledge in the preexisting subsystems, but also to gain new breakthrough knowledge in the areas of anticipated innovation.

- A domain names and encompasses a problem space—that is, an area of the enterprise where new software concepts will deliver competitive advantage. Each of the subparts of the problem space domain are logically known as subdomains, and two or more of these will be used to establish industry leadership for the innovator.

- A single subdomain is a contextual division where a given area of business expertise can be explored and developed. Multiple subdomains each reflect a different context of expertise.

- Consider the abstractions in Chapter 4 as being the opposite of plug-in, all-too-familiar business capabilities. Concrete examples follow in Chapter 5.

Chapter 5: Contextual Expertise

There are generally multiple perspectives in a single problem space domain. Different business experts view the problem space from different angles. The differences in perspectives are where the contextual divisions are likely to be established.

- A contextual division of expertise forms a perimeter around the project and team responsible for it. The boundary is established to keep terms, meanings, and business rules consistent within and to prevent any other terms, meanings, and business rules from infiltrating and causing corruption by outside forces.

- Within a contextual boundary of expertise, the terms, meanings, and business rules used by the single responsible team working in that area form a special team language. This language is ubiquitous inside the boundary because it is regularly expressed orally by the team, written in documents, and drawn in diagrams, and the source code of the software model reflects the language.

- A contextual division that is formed around an area of highest strategic importance and investment is known as the *core*. To make known the difference between the core and those contexts deemed worthy of lesser investment, the names *supporting* and *generic* are used for the latter. Generally, supporting subdomains must be developed internally or outsourced, but will not receive deep intellectual investment. Generic subdomains may be purchased or downloaded from open source venues.

- Business capabilities are a good place to look when establishing contextual boundaries. Although there can be finer divisions of expertise, the contexts can be first chosen as business capabilities. When finer-grained areas of expertise are recognized, those can be extracted from an initial business capability context. This points to the importance of understanding the organization-specific business capabilities.

Chapter 6: Mapping, Failing, and Succeeding— Choose Two

Because there will always be multiple business capabilities, and related contextual areas of expertise, it's critical to understand how to interact and integrate with the software models found in other context boundaries. This requires a clear understanding of the team dynamics between any two teams, as well as which facilities are available for integration. One set of techniques to support such efforts is known as *mappings*. It's important to use these and other domain-driven techniques properly, or negative outcomes can occur.

- Maps are drawings that represent reality.

- Drawing lines between any two contextual boundaries to indicate a relationship between them creates a map. Maps are good choices for displaying directions, flow, and any travel complexities.

- The lines drawn between any two context boundaries represent the existing inter-team relationship, direction of dependencies, and a means of integration.

- There are eight different ways that two contexts can be mapped, which are not mutually exclusive.

- An additional topographical mapping tool is provided in Chapter 6, which helps show specific integration points and concrete examples between any two or more contexts.

- Existing inter-team relationships that are not ideal might be changed if the status quo causes unworkable circumstances. The existing situation must first be understood and identified to recognize how it must change for the better.

- Fair warnings are provided to use the given tools properly, as opposed to circulating a technique name in an attempt to become a club member. Before any team jumps in, make sure they understand these points of potentially unrecoverable failure, and how to avoid them.

Chapter 7: Modeling Domain Concepts

When it comes to actual software implementation, a few powerful tools can be applied to implement domain models.

- Entities model unique things and generally support other software components making changes to their data. Because of their uniqueness, one entity can be easily distinguished from another.

- Value objects are like currency. Paper money contains a number of images, numbers, and other qualities, such as the type of paper and ink, but in the end most people only care about its purchasing value. Furthermore, most people couldn't care less about which paper note with a value of 5 that they have, and would willingly exchange one 5 note for another. In other words, a value is a value is a value. Many things in software can be modeled as values, and far more should be than actually are in practice.

- Aggregates are entities that have a special purpose—namely, representing a set of data that per business rules must remain consistent at all times. The consistency rules are maintained both when in operation on a computer and when stored in a database.

- Domain services provide business logic that operates on entities, aggregates, and value objects, but are not directly associated with any one of the types on which they work.

- Functional behavior provides the kind of software operations that are like mathematical functions. These operations are meant to take one or more input parameters and produce an answer that is consistent with its mathematical properties.

That was neither mysterious nor intimidating. This knowledge-driven software development approach is straightforward and highlights differences in perspectives between multiple business experts who might be describing what appear to be the same concepts but which are actually different. It also helps businesses understand where strategic investments should be made, and where they should not.

Chapter 4

Reaching Domain-Driven Results

Domain-driven is a curious term. The Merriam-Webster dictionary gives ten definitions for the word *domain*. The first three might be among the ideas that come to mind when thinking of this word:

1. Complete and absolute ownership of land

2. A territory over which dominion is exercised

3. A region distinctively marked by some physical feature

This book discusses business software strategy and innovation. Because every business is unique, it could well be that "domain" draws attention to the "dominion" of the business ownership of properties and operations, and perhaps even the distinctive features among these. While not wrong, none of these is the best interpretation of how "domain" is used in this book.

Chapters 1–3 heavily emphasized realizing business software strategy through learning and discovery to bring about differentiating innovation. This emphasis on learning and discovery points to the fourth definition for *domain* found in the Merriam-Webster dictionary, and it is the most fitting:

4. A sphere of knowledge, influence, or activity

Every business has a specialized *sphere of knowledge*, which is gained through preexisting expertise and the *activities* of collective and shared learning. Once this knowledge is reflected in software products, it has *influence* on consumers.

Now, dipping into the first three definitions, the results are indeed the intellectual property *owned* within the business *dominion*. It reflects the *distinctive features* of business creativity that are the reward for the investment made in knowledge acquisition and sheer determination to advance the state of the art. This is for certain a *sphere of knowledge, influence, and activity.*

Domain-driven points out that a business drives results through investments in knowledge acquisition within and beyond its current sphere of influence and activity. The business drives its own advancement and growth through steady improvements in its technology-based products. This book continually asserts that it is learning through experimentation-based discovery that will yield the most innovative results.

Innovation within an Agile Methodology

As an example of using a methodology or process execution framework, Scrum identifies four primary reasons to place an item in the product backlog:

1. Features
2. Bugs
3. Technical Work
4. Knowledge Acquisition

It's disappointing that *Knowledge Acquisition* is consigned to last place, because it should always be in first place. How can a team place a new feature in the backlog before they understand it? Even if they do put the feature in the backlog before knowing it well, at a minimum *Knowledge Acquisition* must be given due diligence before attempting to implement it. It's also disappointing that *Knowledge Acquisition* is often described with technical motivations, such as "researching various JavaScript libraries and making a selection." This rationale is also unknown to most developers who consider themselves Scrum practitioners. The fact that such problems exist at all may indicate a larger problem in the methodology or at least the priorities of execution.

If you're using Scrum, promote *Knowledge Acquisition* into first place and label such tasks in terms of domain-driven experimentation, especially those that have a higher potential to lead to breakthroughs that result in differentiating innovations. Pass every new feature-based task under the hammer of traceable business goals through impacts, which might have been first discovered through EventStorming learning sessions.

Using a domain-driven approach requires the prominent and consistent involvement of business experts working with software developers. This aligns precisely with the long-stated tenets of #agile:

- *Agile Manifesto:* "Our highest priority is to satisfy the customer through early and continuous delivery of valuable software. Business people and developers must work together daily throughout the project. The most efficient and effective method of conveying information to and within a development team is face-to-face conversation." [Agile-Manifesto-Principles]

- *Extreme Programming (XP):* "The Customer is Always Available. One of the few requirements of extreme programming (XP) is to have the customer available. [This is] not only to help the development team, but to be a part of it as well. All phases of an XP project require communication with the customer, preferably face to face, on site. . . . You need the expert." [XP]

Admittedly, some aspects of both #agile and XP have shifted over time. Our purpose in noting the importance of "customer" here is not to give a strict definition, but rather to emphasize that those who understand the goals of the domain at hand must be available, and that each must be a member of one or more teams. These individuals might be known as a sponsor, customer, user, product champion, and so forth. There is no need to exhaustively identify every role that a business expert could play in any given subsystem, but you should recognize that there must be one or more who are able to champion the product being developed and drive the software goals to delivery. Everyone involved, including the end users of the product, must be pleased with the results.

Domains and Subdomains

When it comes to equities investments, knowing where to invest and where not to invest is critical to financial success. As the saying goes, "you can't time the market." That reality gives investors all the more reason to invest based on key financial indicators and market conditions, which are sound sources of securities industry knowledge.

When it comes to business software strategy, understanding where to invest the most and where to invest the least is likewise critical to financial success. Although being completely right the first time is rare, it might not matter so much. In the world of business, something that is currently right has a high potential to be wrong later. Constantly monitoring attempted impacts to achieve business goals, as well as studying market conditions that put a spotlight on user satisfaction, are sound ways to gauge the effects of innovation endeavors.

Software reaches across the breadth and depth of an entire business. The entire *domain* or *sphere of knowledge* of all software in a large enterprise is voluminous. It's too complex for any single project or considerably sized business program to include the full domain's vast details in the defined effort's scope. Likely a team will find that most are irrelevant, anyway. Defining constraints for the scope of any given software development effort is essential for successful deliveries.

Because the *sphere* of a *sphere of knowledge* is relative to its specific purpose, it's not surprising that the term *domain* can have a few scopes and nuances. Four are defined for the purposes of this discussion. Figure 4.1 illustrates the four scopes, which are further defined in the list that follows.

1. ***Voluminous enterprise scope.*** All software in a large enterprise is the business's full domain. At this scope, a single source of in-depth knowledge is impossible to create.

2. ***Medium-to-large system scope.*** Commercial licensed enterprise systems, such as ERP, as well as large, custom, legacy systems fall within this scope. In terms of domain knowledge, these are closer to Scope 3, but were likely not well planned and architected. They are often the Big Ball of Mud systems described in Chapters 1 and 2, but that need not be the case.

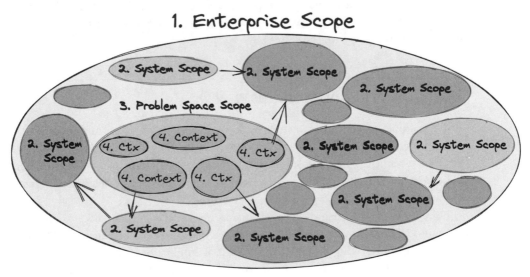

Figure 4.1 *Four scopes of domain knowledge spheres used in this book.*

3. *Medium-to-large problem space scope.* A problem space is a sphere of knowledge that unfolds as a set of solutions are developed, but requires multiple teams whose members have various types of expertise (i.e., Scope 4). Ultimately, the problem space is an effort in system development.

4. *Smallish context scope.* Every single communication context of know-how within a problem space is the sphere of knowledge of a specialized business expertise.

An enterprise architecture framework can assist in managing a large digital enterprise, that of Scope 1. Yet it generally won't provide much deep information about each part of a large enterprise. That's often locked up in the team's tacit knowledge. Such a framework is a schema or ontology, which supports a set of formal and structured viewpoints of an enterprise. Sometimes the framework also assists in the process of defining an enterprise architecture. The power of such a framework is to help in organizing and inventorying a company's digital assets to help with planning and decision making. Two such frameworks are the Zachman Framework [Zachman] and The Open Group Architecture Framework [TOGAF]. Figure 4.1 provides only a limited glimpse into the overall enterprise, and is in no way a reflection of the result of using an enterprise architecture framework.

Scope 2, as seen in Figure 4.1, often reflects a haphazard approach that results in the Big Ball of Mud systems described in Chapters 1 and 2. Still, that need not be the case. A system can be architected and implemented in a manner that doesn't reflect an ad hoc approach. The differences in the two can be seen in Figure 4.1 with the scopes numbered 2 that are brown/dark colored and those that are green/lighter colored, respectively. The Big Ball of Mud systems are generally quite large. Those thoughtfully architected tend to be more medium in size, with new software more focused on a specific solution, and are integrated with the preexisting Big Ball of Mud systems to leverage what works but without getting very dirty hands.

Abstractions Contraptions

This discussion might seem too abstract. If so, think of the Scope 3 problem space as NuCoverage introducing its SaaS-based insurance platform. Consider the Scope 4 contextual divisions within the Scope 3 problems space to be Intake, Underwriting, Risk, Renewals, and Claims. This point is explained in more detail in Chapter 5, "Contextual Expertise." For now, the abstractions are useful for imagining and plugging in the problem space and areas of expertise with a specific sphere of knowledge that exists in any given business.

Figure 4.1 also shows a single Scope 3 strategic initiative that is under way. This area of work is meant to produce some level of breakthrough innovation, which means that the teams lead with experiment-based learning. An overall sphere of knowledge exists here, but a deliberate effort is being made to divide the problem space domain into specialty areas of expertise. This is indicated by the Scope 4 contexts inside Scope 3. This depiction is not meant to create silos, but rather to acknowledge that the different experts view the problem space from different angles. Collectively, the knowledge is gained and used to solve a medium-to-large problem space, while the specialty areas are recognized and strictly honored. As a whole problem space, Scope 3 will have different areas of Scope 4 contextual expertise. Each is managed by a single team. Each team includes at least one expert in that contextual area of expertise. Making one team responsible for a context protects the area of expertise from becoming confused and fractured by the goals and communication-based languages that are developed by other teams.

This leads us to the lowest-level scope. Within the Scope 3 problem space are five Scope 4 *subdomain* contexts of separate specialties. Each of the five contexts represents where specific conversations take place regarding a focused and relatively narrow sphere of knowledge. Every context is where a team of one or more business experts and developers have a shared understanding of what a given term and any number of expressions mean in their conversations. As a goal, no ambiguities should exist inside a given context, although undoubtedly there will be some. When any are detected, conscious exertion is made to clear up the foggy meanings and associated software rules and behaviors.

Scope 4 brings up another term: *subdomain*. A subdomain is a subpart of a domain, and specifically applicable within Scope 3. It's often the case that a subdomain is the same as a business capability. Ideally, a context, such as that seen in Figure 4.1, should align one-to-one with a subdomain. Consider a subdomain as primarily a problem space concept, and recognize that each has a greater or lesser strategic business significance.

In Chapter 5, Figure 5.1 shows the specific contexts represented in Figure 4.1 here. The names assigned to the contexts draw attention to the corresponding subdomains. Problems arise when multiple subdomains exist in a single modular context. Those problems tend to relate to how a single source module becomes overloaded with concepts that are not germane to the central theme of the context, which should be a single, well-defined subdomain. For example, NuCoverage's Policyholder Accounts subdomain becomes problematic as additional insured rewards are defined. Studying the diverging goals makes it clear that a new subdomain has emerged and must be removed from the Policyholder Accounts and located in a new Reward Programs subdomain. When solutions are carefully designed, each subdomain should align one-to-one with a context of the same name.

Does the Scope 3 problem space indicate that all the knowledge for the solution is held inside among the five contexts? That's very unlikely and even more so impractical. At least a few of the five Scope 4 contexts are integrated with preexisting Big Ball of Mud legacy systems. Any amount of effort in a large enterprise will never eliminate all messy and unseemly legacy bits. Leverage what's there because it works. Any given Big Ball of Mud system that is eventually broken apart will still have integrations with the then smaller contexts, each of which represents a single subdomain. Make no mistake—this will be the result of vigorous, concerted effort to overcome the complexity caused by years of neglect.

At least one relevant question remains: Does the Scope 3 problem space represent an architecture where the five contexts are physically contained inside a Monolith? Maybe. Maybe not. As emphasized in Chapter 2, it's a good way to start because it will delay a whole host of problems that the teams shouldn't be required to deal with early on. It's possible that in time the architecture will switch from Monolithic to distributed, but that's a decision to be made at the last responsible moment. For now, Scope 3 is chiefly representative of a strategic problem space where a lot of learning must happen to reach differentiating results.

Summary

This chapter introduced and promoted the concept that every business should be driven to make investments in knowledge acquisition, within and beyond its current sphere of influence and activity. The knowledge reflected in software products is the real business differentiator and has a real influence on the users. Yet, understanding where to invest the most and where to invest the least is likewise critical to financial success, and must also be a recognized component of business software strategy. The domains and subdomains introduced in this chapter help to reinforce the proper application of software as a profit center.

The most essential points of this chapter are:

- Learning through experimentation-based discovery within every core sphere of knowledge of a business will drive the most innovative results.

- Tracing business goals through impacts enables a higher potential for breakthroughs that will result in differentiating innovations.

- The domain-driven approach requires the prominent and consistent involvement of business experts working with software developers.

- Expert is not a title, and business expertise can be gained through roles such as product sponsors, customers, users, product champions, and so on.

- Domains are used to determine the whole business problem space. Subdomains are subparts of the domain with specific contextual scope.

- Each subdomain should align one-to-one with a business capability and a context of expertise, yet business capabilities will be extended over time, and corresponding subdomains will follow suit.

Next, we dive deeper into finding and contextualizing business boundaries of expertise with the help of a technique known as Domain-Driven Design. This technique offers tools for both strategic and tactical software development—those that address the problem space and help transition to the solution space. It fits with the software innovation goals previously discussed and assists with those that remain in this book.

References

[Agile-Manifesto-Principles] https://agilemanifesto.org/principles.html

[TOGAF] https://www.opengroup.org/togaf

[XP] http://www.extremeprogramming.org/rules/customer.html

[Zachman] https://www.zachman.com/about-the-zachman-framework

Chapter 5

Contextual Expertise

Chapter 4, "Reaching Domain-Driven Results," established that contextual divisions with boundaries are necessary to prevent confusion in conversations with experts who use the same terminology but have different definitions of those terms. As explained in the section, "Domains and Subdomains," there are generally multiple perspectives in a single problem space domain. It might be said that different experts view the problem space from different angles. This chapter provides concrete examples of the topics that were discussed more abstractly in Chapter 4. This will clear up any questions that might have been raised in the abstract view.

Bounded Context and Ubiquitous Language

The software development approach known as *Domain-Driven Design* (DDD) [Evans-DDD] addresses the contexts and communications discussed so far in the book. DDD has a name for the specialized set of conversations that take place regarding a relatively narrow sphere of knowledge, such as those depicted in Figure 4.1. In Figure 4.1, they are labeled as Scope 4 with the word *Context* or abbreviated as *Ctx*. In DDD, these conversations form what is known as a *Ubiquitous Language*. This language exists within a context, which is known as a *Bounded Context*.

Yes, Figure 4.1 is abstract because the concepts can be applied to any concrete domain. There are concrete examples of these concepts just ahead in Figure 5.1 and in the section "Business Capabilities and Contexts."

The names Ubiquitous Language and Bounded Context might be unfamiliar and seem mysterious, but there's no need to get hung up on them. They simply identify two of the concepts that have already been discussed extensively. They give software developers applying DDD a means to share a set of names that refer to specific design concepts that everyone involved can use:

- *Ubiquitous Language.* The team-centric common set of terms and expressions spoken in a sphere of knowledge within a specialized business expertise. Often the motivation for creating a common language for the team is the diverse backgrounds of those involved in the project, who might think of some concepts by different names. Even so, the language primarily identifies with accuracy the meanings of various terms used in the team's specific context. That's why outside a given context, the same terms will tend to have at least slightly, if not vastly, different meanings. The word "ubiquitous" might be a bit misleading, as it is not meant to imply that this specialized language (definitions included) is known throughout the business organization. Rather, the language is known within a single team, but is considered ubiquitous in the sense that the terms and expressions from conversations become familiar to that team and permeate the artifacts produced by the team. This is any kind of software modeling, including what's rendered into drawings and the source code model. They all "speak" the same language.

- *Bounded Context.* The context in which a single team speaks and models software using terms, expressions, and defined business rules that reflect a specialized, acquired business knowledge—a Ubiquitous Language. The terms and expressions are not only words, but have clear definitions. The context is bounded in the sense that conversations use clearly understood meanings that occur inside the boundary are not the property of teams on the outside, and the terms and meanings used by other business efforts outside don't penetrate the team's established boundary. In terms of modularization, think of a Bounded Context as a coarse-grained module. How the module is to be deployed is another matter. As described in Chapter 2, "Essential Strategic Learning Tools," modules should be chosen first and deployment options as late as possible.

Figure 4.1 shows five different Bounded Contexts, each with its own specialized Ubiquitous Language. As a rule, a single Bounded Context is owned by a single team. However, one team might own multiple Bounded Contexts. Requiring that a Bounded Context be owned by a single team ensures that conflicting goals and priorities among different teams do not cause confusing conversations and mismatched concepts in a single language.

Finding Boundaries

While participating in EventStorming sessions and using other discovery and learning tools, it might seem overly challenging to identify the correct Bounded Contexts. Finding the "correct" Bounded Contexts is itself a learning process, which means that being wrong so that you can eventually be right is an achievement. It's also true that "correct" today may be not-so-correct in the future.

Recall that the first driver of any kind of modularity is the cohesiveness of concepts, which is learned through the communication and experience. More specifically, the people who are involved in the conversations around solving a very specific problem can be different from the people who are required to participate in other problem-solving conversations. That's because the expertise shifts along with the problem to be solved. If the right people aren't present and must be called on later, their involvement might not take place within the same problem-solving conversation. When multiple experts are together but disagree on the "correctness" of some definitions and operations, they are probably all right. That being so, their multiple perspectives point a spotlight at different contexts. Look for business model boundaries around areas of expertise, indicating the various spheres of knowledge.

The specialized Ubiquitous Language inside a strong boundary allows separate teams to have the same terms for concepts that have slightly or vastly different meanings, including their business rules. Consider, for example, the term *product*. It can have various meanings, including something that you can purchase, such as an insurance product; the result of evaluating a mathematical multiplication expression; and the software that is to be developed by using some project execution techniques. More typically, a single business will use the word *product* with slightly different meanings. In the insurance industry, it could well be that *policy* is a term used across contexts, with each context hosting a different meaning.

Trying to harmonize all the meanings of *policy* into a single software component is fraught with problems. DDD avoids such problems by means of a Bounded Context, which is employed to separate the various uses of the term *policy*. In each Bounded Context, the term *policy* has a well-defined meaning. The idea is to accept and embrace differences across a single business enterprise as normal rather than anomalous.

This strong boundary also allows teams to use different language terms for concepts that are similar. This might be best illustrated by thinking about multiple human languages where the same thing has completely different names. For example, the English *coverage* is three different words in three other languages: French, *couverture*; German, *abdeckung*; and Spanish, *cobertura*. Consider a Bounded Context as a national border behind which a national language is spoken. Although this analogy might seem a bit far-fetched, it is quite true that different areas of a business use completely different terms for overlapping concepts, where those terms have nuanced meanings. The idea of an insurance policy might have the following names across the business:

- Policy
- Coverage
- Contract
- Form

Possibly not readily recognized is that when such differences exist within the same organization, the different languages drive natural coarse-grained decoupling when Bounded Contexts are used to separate these clear language differences. In other words, these different terms will be used within different areas of expertise. It's important to watch for such situations and separate them.

How is it known when the correct term is used? In fact, in the preceding examples, all four names used to refer to a policy are correct. Again, the correctness is determined by the context in which the term is used, because the four different areas of expertise are heralded by the contexts. Figure 5.1 draws attention to this point by referring to each of the five contexts from Figure 4.1 by its context name.

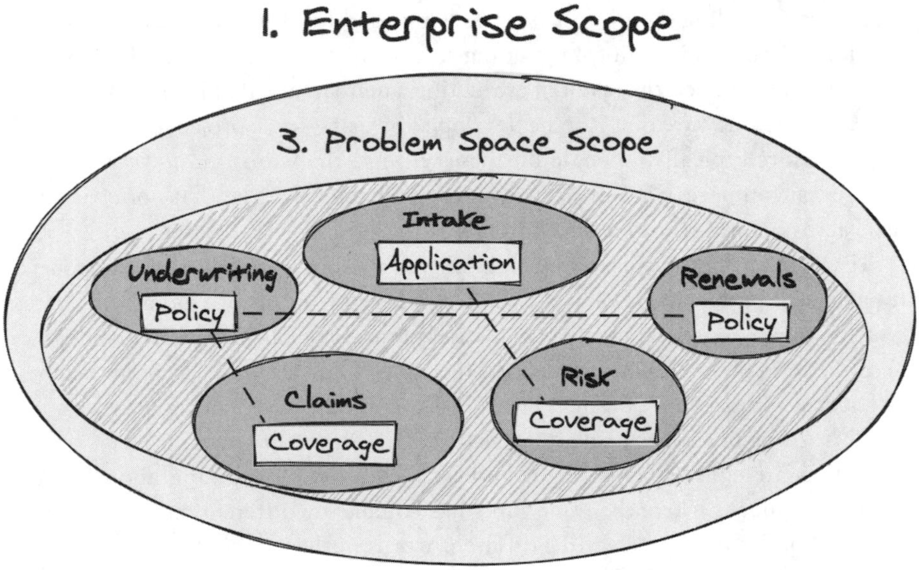

Figure 5.1 *Bounded Contexts are named for their area of expertise and language.*

Each Bounded Context should be named according to its area of expertise. Within that area, the use of every term is relative to the contextual boundary:

- *Intake Context.* The Application for insurance is submitted by an Applicant.

- *Risk Context.* The Coverage contains data from the Application submitted to the Intake Context, which is used to calculate the risks associated with underwriting the policy. The dashed line points out the origin of the data used by Risk—that is, the data comes from Intake. How Risk receives the data is not necessarily indicated by the dashed line. Although the Application data originates with the Intake Context, after it is cleansed and augmented it next flows to the Underwriting Context, and then to the Risk Context.

- *Underwriting Context.* The Policy is the result of receiving the Application details, and then calculating the risk of the coverage and a premium rate. The rate calculation components are not shown here, but the rate may currently be calculated by means of an integration with a Big Ball of Mud legacy system.

- *Claims Context.* The Coverage is based on data from the Policy in the Underwriting Context. The Claims area might or might not hold this data persistently. It could be obtained just in time when a claim is filed. This Coverage is different from the Coverage in the Risk Context.

- *Renewals Context.* This Policy is based on the Underwriting Policy, but is not identical to it. What is needed to renew a Policy is minimal compared to what is needed to underwrite and manage the Policy in Underwriting. The new rate might be determined by reassessing risk (not shown in Figure 5.1), which would be based on any losses filed against the Claim Coverage (or lack thereof), and in turn have an impact on the premium of a renewal.

Each of these contexts aligns one-to-one with the subdomain of the same name. That is, the business capability concept represented by the subdomain is implemented in the same-named Bounded Context.

Core Domain

A *Core Domain* is a subdomain within which a focused core strategic business capability is developed. It is a top-tier differentiator where the investment in radically new and innovative ideas are validated through copious communication and experimentation, and then implemented using a Bounded Context.

A Core Domain is quite literally where a business vision is focused. This is very much where the business *must excel*. In terms of Impact Mapping, the actors, impacts, and deliverables that deliberately drive the business toward a goal will be core. The best of business expertise and software developers compose a core team. Hence, a Core Domain warrants an investment in talent and time.

In Figure 5.1, it's likely that Underwriting starts out as a core initiative because it is responsible for generating business. At first, human underwriters will be responsible for much of the risk evaluation and determining the premiums to match those evaluations. Yet, NuCoverage knows that it must "beat the market" through risk management using machine learning. The website that hosts the Intake and Underwriting interactions with applicants gets the early core focus. All the while, the Risk context is also being developed. At a future point when NuCoverage is confident about taking risk management out of human hands and moving it into smart actuarial mathematical models, the switch gets flipped and Intake and Underwriting become less significant.

This points to the fact that a single business might have multiple core initiatives. Within a large system development effort, there might be only initiatives, such as Underwriting and the back-office effort on Risk. Yet, the actual number of those initiatives will be consistent with the level of innovation required to reach a business goal. It's not as if stating some arbitrary limitation on the practical number of core initiatives is unhelpful. As always, it depends. A key constraint is the talent already onboard and the talent that can be recruited and put into core initiatives.

Our use of the term *talent* here strongly implies that communication with a scientific, experimental mindset is a must. The intelligence, creativity, and drive of these people should be scary, and they will be available only in exchange for compensation equal to their abilities. Innovation has a price tag, kind of like the car driven by a *Fortune* 500 CEO. All the same, talent is no excuse for arrogance and drama. The best people work in teams and know they can't do it all alone, because they understand their own limitations.

Beware of Maintenance Mode

A Core Domain usually receives much attention and investment from the business at the inception of the project until the satisfying delivery is made supporting the defined strategic goal. The team is formed by including experienced senior developers, architects, and business experts who will carry out the work and achieve success.

Most of the time, once the major milestones are achieved and the project deadline is met, the project transitions to maintenance mode. The experienced team is disbanded and a team of juniors are hired to patch bugs and add on any lacking features. Yet, the major breakthroughs in learning occur while the system is running in production for some time. All the while, feedback is gathered from platform monitoring tools, users, customers, and other stake-holders. Adjustments and improvements have to be made. A key problem in this stage is that the original knowledge acquired at the inception of the project has been lost with the disbanding of the experienced team members. The replacements do not have enough perspective, skills, or knowledge to make the right decisions and implementation choices.

This is one reason why a well-architected and thoughtfully structured project becomes a Big Ball of Mud. It would be better to reject maintenance-mode thinking, keep the team together, and continue to invest over the project's entire life cycle.

Early on, a startup business might struggle to focus on one or a few things, but it must learn where its business will earn revenues and how it will succeed. Recalling the germination of an idea and how it was pitched for venture funding can help the organization retain or regain focus. Adopting an Objectives and Key Results (OKRs) process has taken some small startups to valuations of hundreds of billions of dollars [Measure]. If it's not careful, though, a startup might be destined toward entropy—but at least it has the advantage that it doesn't begin in that position. This enables fast innovation.

For a large enterprise, it might be less of a struggle to know what the core focus should be, but the challenges will very likely lie in where and how that focus should be realized. An established enterprise likely starts from a state of entropy and must struggle to deal with not breaking its existing digital assets. The discussion in the section "Context Mapping," in Chapter 6, "Mapping, Failing, and Succeeding—Choose Two," can help the business manage this condition.

Further, a core modeling effort will very likely not remain core over a very long time frame. New investments will continue with necessary new innovations. What is core today might be a supporting part of a newer initiative at some point in the future.

Supporting Subdomains, Generic Subdomains, and Technical Mechanisms

A business can't afford to invest everywhere to the same degree it does in a Core Domain, nor does it need to. Although absolutely necessary to have, many parts of a large system are neither interesting nor worthy of deep investment. These less significant subdomains of a system are there to support the overall function of the core parts.

Such lesser domains tend to fall into two primary areas: supporting and generic subdomains. We can also add to these another typical sideshow that has little to do with the actual business: technical mechanisms.

Supporting Subdomains

A supporting subdomain is one that is necessary to provide support to the functionality of a Core Domain, but does not deserve the steep investment that should go into the core. A supporting subdomain likely does not consist of a commercial software product offering that can be licensed, or for which a subscription is available. If such a supporting subdomain does exist commercially, it is very likely that it is highly configurable and customizable.

Because a supporting subdomain might not be available for purchase, it will almost certainly have to be custom developed. Yet, because it is not core, a team should not run up exorbitant expenses in this supporting area of the system. For one thing, the talent selected to work on this subdomain should not be top-shelf. Although the subdomain talent will undoubtedly need to communicate with the business experts, the necessary discussions might be driven more by a core team because the core team knows what they need to support their efforts.

Another kind of a supporting subdomain is a legacy subsystem with a business capability that can be reused. There will almost certainly be a need to create an interface to the legacy operations that provides a better integration experience than what might (or might not) already exist. Again, the section "Context Mapping" in Chapter 6 addresses the means to deal with this issue in several ways.

As an example, two legacy supporting subdomains for NuCoverage are risk management and premium rate calculations. Integration interfaces must be developed for both because their use is currently internal to the legacy system. In the long run, it will be best to break these assets out of the legacy system and move them into contexts of their own to enable frequent changes to them. This will happen sooner with risk management because it will transition to a Core Domain.

Generic Subdomains

A generic subdomain is complex and requires a great deal of domain expertise to develop, but one that is available through multiple commercial closed source or open source products. Think of two or more products that are compared side-by-side using feature lists with check boxes. For both products, nearly every one of the dozens of check boxes are checked. Which one should be selected? Perhaps the decision should be made based on perceived reputational advantage, greater total number of customers for one of the products, length of time on the market, or other semi-tangible or intangible aspects.

For NuCoverage, examples of generic subdomains might include industry-standard risk models, policy document formatting and generation, photo image scanning for applications and claims, bulk sales and marketing email providers, customer relationship management, enterprise resource planning, identity and access management, and the like.

Technical Mechanisms

Unfortunately, some of the lowest-level areas of software development tend to attract the attention of developers because they are frequently more technical in nature. Management must be careful not to allow the best talent to become pigeon-holed into these areas that might be entertaining in terms of leading-edge technology, but do not yield much bang for the buck when it comes to the business's bottom line. The actual business aspects associated with these tools—if there are any beyond data persistence and movement—are less demanding of thoughtful modeling. The innovation is already present in the mechanism.

Challenge Software Engineers

Good engineers are motivated by challenges. If they are not challenged by the problem they are solving, they will look for challenges in the technology that they employ. The antidote is to supply real challenges so engineers do not have to seek out their own.

In terms of the technology attractions, expect to see some of the latest in cloud infrastructure and application programming interfaces (APIs), deployment containers, databases, web user interface frameworks, network communications, messaging, and anything that promises the potential for large scale and high throughput. Although some doses of these mechanisms that make data move and the enterprise tick are definitely called for, be forewarned that these programmer magnets are not worthy of the undivided attention that they commonly receive. Make business innovation challenges greater than the appeal of leading-edge technology.

Business Capabilities and Contexts

Chapter 2 discussed the importance of organizing teams around business capabilities and capturing critical design communication within the modules separating business capabilities. The Bounded Context, for example, is a top-level, coarse-grained module where a business capability is housed.

Over the long term, the Bounded Context might not remain what it was originally envisioned to be. Boundaries might change. For example, when breaking up a Big Ball of Mud, the teams involved might find a business capability known as Policyholder Accounts. This is where all policyholders of any kind of policies are managed, and it makes sense that this capability includes some knowledge of the kinds of policies they each hold.

Business Capability as a Revenue Generator

A business capability must be directly connected with at least one business goal. There should be no speculation about the need for a company to define a business capability. A business capability answers the "What?" question regarding the means by which the company will generate revenues. A substantive question with regard to a business capability is "How?" Impact Mapping, discussed in Chapter 2 in the section "Strategic Delivery on Purpose," explains driving software deliverables starting with the question "Why?" By the time a team starts work on a business capability in a specific context of expertise, there should be no question "Why?" The "Why?" must be stated as a clear business goal, yet the deliverables are determined by asking "How?" Some impacts will change the behavior of "Who?" actors (e.g., customers and competition) to reach the "Why?" goal. This leaves no room for the *contractor model* to push for features and functionality that are not already identified by one or more Impact Mapping exercises. The impacts might change over time based on the success or failure of each, but the goal won't change until the business decides that it's no longer a necessary goal.

One of the concepts held inside this module is digital policy documents acknowledging rewards given to exemplary policyholders. Because car insurance was the first business in which NuCoverage engaged, the one supported reward is the Safe Driver Reward. It seemed logical to maintain the Safe Driver Reward with mainstream policy information. Yet, over time NuCoverage began to introduce new insurance products, including new kinds of rewards. For example, health insurance products are associated with Good Health Rewards, and similar rewards are offered with life insurance. These rewards are meant not only to improve the driving and health of individual policyholders, but also to lower the risk of auto accidents, healthcare costs, and premature death as financial impacts on NuCoverage.

As these rewards began to grow in number, clearly a new business capability and a new area of expertise began to form. Now it makes sense to break out the rewards from Policyholder Accounts into their own specific coarse-grained module.

The Reward Programs Context is the chosen name of the new Bounded Context. Rewards-related conversations and learning opportunities are addressed inside this context. At some point in the future, it might be best to break specific rewards into their own Bounded Contexts.

A well-designed microservice should encompass the business capability, which means that a first good step is to consider a microservice as a Bounded Context. This determines what you put inside the service—namely, a modeled business capability that is reflected in a Ubiquitous Language. The service should be autonomous, supporting a model as data and operations with business rules. This approach should be used as extensively as possible over a whole system solution, leaving no questions about where the business capabilities are within the whole. Of course, this doesn't mean that every Big Ball of Mud can be replaced in the short term, but using Context Mapping (described in more detail in Chapter 6) is a way to fabricate an explicit surfacing of a subdomain.

A Bounded Context containing a single business capability transcends technology boundaries. If the architectural layers include a web user interface, then some form of client code running as JavaScript will be involved in expressing the Ubiquitous Language. Further, the primary services will be implemented using a foundational runtime platform, such as Java or .NET. Unsurprisingly, the model-based business capabilities might use a polyglot of programming languages as well as runtime platforms to capitalize on the specific technical advantages afforded by these supports.

The enterprise business divisions, departments, or lines are not always a good indication of where the business capabilities are found. Computing has gradually had an increasing impact on business operations, where workflows were previously driven by file cabinets and memos moving from desk to desk. Now there's much greater use of electronic folders, files, email, and workflow routing. Yet, none of the previous or current business operations and data access practices defined the capabilities of a business. Thus, business capabilities should not be confused with business processes (operational details ending in "ing," such as pricing), which might encompass multiple business capabilities to fully address a business operation.

To fully understand how to implement a business capability using #agile requires an examination of the user working in their natural environment. Otherwise, the team risks missing out on collecting important steps and gestures within the daily workflow of users. Such an investigation will almost certainly uncover pain points and workarounds that should be addressed by improving the system. For example, suppose you observe a user who has one or many sticky notes on their display, or a spreadsheet containing usage instructions, to help them remember how to navigate to and use important software features in the application. That points to a problem that must be recognized and remedied. This is part of fully developing a sphere of knowledge within each business capability.

Not Too Big, Not Too Small

The section "Are Microservices Good?" in Chapter 1, "Business Goals and Digital Transformation," established that Microservices are not about size but rather about the purpose. The word "micro" is misleading in the way that it implies some kind of size constraints. Yet, it should not convey those connotations. Refer back to the discussion in Chapter 1 for more details.

As far as Microservices or modularized Monoliths are concerned, the same kinds of modularizations and design practices apply because these are all focused on Bounded Contexts. Thus, you might instead ask: How large is a Bounded Context? Although this is sort of the wrong question, the answer is another question: How large is the Ubiquitous Language within the context? In other words, size cannot be accurately measured as a standard goal because it is highly contextual.

A Bounded Context is the encapsulation of a business capability, and each business capability must have a complete implementation. There shouldn't be any part of a given business capability left over or implemented outside of its Bounded Context. The only design driving force for Bounded Contexts should be the *scope* of the business capability and its Ubiquitous Language, and not the *size*.

Nested Bounded Contexts?

It's not uncommon for this question to be raised. It's uncertain if those asking this question actually understand what a Bounded Context is and how it is designed. Think about the implications provided in these three examples:

1. If there were a context within a context, it would stand to reason that either the outer context or the inner context would "speak" a superset of both languages, and the other would "speak" a subset of them. It seems most likely that the outer context would "speak" the superset. The question is, to what end? This seems unwieldy, but might be viable to some. See the section "Shared Kernel" in Chapter 6, which describes what some might have in mind. Yet, a Shared Kernel is not generally meant to be used in this way.

2. Another possibility is that the "inner" context is not nested at all, but separate (e.g., Microservice) and reachable only through the "outer" context. Encapsulation and detail hiding are well-known principles. For example, the Law of Demeter is known as the "law of least knowledge." This seems more appropriate than the first example, but isn't an earth-shaking idea. It's (a) one subsystem integrating with (b) another, that in turn integrates with (c) another, where (c) is unknown to (a). This is a common service composition.

3. Perhaps the question is less about nested contexts than it is about a single context having inner components that "nest." If this is the case, then the components in the context are simply multiple elements of the bounded language that have some visibility scoping. This is also a common pattern.

There are likely other ideas about how nested contexts could work, which could be considered more or less useful.

With these considerations in mind, a Bounded Context is typically not tiny-tiny, as in 100 lines of code. And although it's unlikely that a full business capability could be implemented in 100 lines of any programming language code, it could be, if that's what it takes to implement it. Further, a single Bounded Context on its own would be very unlikely to be a Monolith.

It's fair to conclude that a Bounded Context will tend to be smallish. When that's true, thinking of a Bounded Context as a Microservice is a good enough place to start. If other drivers cause the corresponding business capability to change in some way, such as being divided into multiple business capabilities, then transform it into multiple Bounded Contexts according to the drivers. A reason for this was demonstrated previously with the growing number of policyholder rewards. Conversely, if there is a rate of change, or technical scale and/or performance drivers, then respond to those drivers. In these three cases, the deployments might change, but the logical Bounded Context remains intact. Assuming that these drivers exist from the start, but with no empirical evidence, will harm the system under design. Making any necessary changes at the last responsible moment is #agile thinking, and a better choice.

Summary

This chapter introduced Domain-Driven Design with a focus on two strategic modeling artifacts, the Ubiquitous Language and the Bounded Context. The specialized Bounded Context known as a Core Domain is where a strategic business capability is developed. The chapter also offered views on different kinds of business subdomains and how they connect to the business capabilities and their Bounded Contexts.

The most salient points are:

- A Ubiquitous Language represents the conversations that take place in a relatively narrow sphere of knowledge that is contextualized by a Bounded Context.

- Each business concept, the meanings of various terms, and the constraining business rules used in the specific language of a context are both accurate and unambiguous.

- Bounded Context delimits the applicability of its Ubiquitous Language.

- Each Bounded Context should be owned by a single team, but a team can own several Bounded Contexts.

- The Core Domain is where the business vision is focused and an investment in talent and time is made.

- The size of the Bounded Context should be delimited by the scope of the business capability and its Ubiquitous Language.

Chapter 6 introduces tools to help map team relationships, collaboration, and integrations between multiple contexts of expertise. The mapping types address a broad range of inter-team situations, communication channels, and ways to exchange information and request behavior from integration sources.

References

[**Evans-DDD**] Eric Evans. *Domain-Driven Design: Tackling Complexity in the Heart of Software*. Boston, MA: Addison-Wesley, 2004.

[**Measure**] John Doerr. *Measure What Matters: How Google, Bono, and the Gates Foundation Rock the World with OKRs*. New York: Portfolio, 2018.

Chapter 6

Mapping, Failing, and Succeeding—Choose Two

In any project involving a Core Domain, it's almost inconceivable that this context of innovation would not need to integrate with any other systems or subsystems, including Big Ball of Mud legacy systems. It's even likely that some other new supporting and generic subdomains will be implemented as Bounded Contexts that a Core Domain must lean on for "remote" functionality. Here, "remote" might refer to contextual modules in the same Monolith that are segregated from the others but without a network between them, or it might actually mean physically remote.

This chapter starts with mapping team relationships and integrations between multiple contexts of expertise. Later, we see a number of warnings about poor modeling practices that cause failures. These are not the quick failures that eventually result in good outcomes, so they must be avoided. Next, we explore practices that tend to lead to success. Finally, we demonstrate how to apply the experimentation and discovery tools within a problem space and its solutions.

Context Mapping

The mappings between any two Bounded Contexts are known as *Context Maps*. This section provides diagrams and explanations that effectively describe the various kinds of mappings. Diagrams are great, but Context Maps go beyond drawings. They help teams recognize the situations they face and provide tools to spot and address specific modeling situations. The primary roles of Context Maps are as follows:

- Cross-team communications
- Project thinking, learning, and planning
- Integration situation discovery and desired solutions

Context Maps are recognized as real inter-team relationships and implemented as source code integrations patterns. This section discusses how any two Bounded Contexts can integrate with each other using Context Maps.

A Context Mapping between any two Bounded Contexts is represented in a diagram as a line between the two contexts, as illustrated in Figure 6.1. The line can have multiple meanings, including the kind of team communication that exists or that must be established to succeed and the way integration will be achieved.

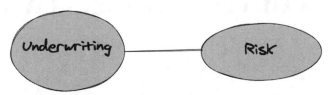

Figure 6.1 *A Context Mapping of two Bounded Contexts is represented by the line between the contexts.*

In mapping the reality of which conditions currently exist, an effort is made to assess the actual relationships and communications between teams as the result of the organizational structure and politics. This realistic view makes it clear that it might not be possible to change most of the dynamics, but highlights where concerted efforts to improve could pay off.

Before venturing into the individual Context Mapping types, consider a few salient points about the various patterns. First, Context Maps are initially useful for mapping what exists. There will almost always be some preexisting systems, which will comprise subsystems with which the new context must integrate. Show what those existing subsystems are, and indicate the current relationship that the new context's team has with each of the teams in the external subsystems and their integration offerings. The Context Mapping patterns are not mutually exclusive—they will tend to overlap. For example, a Partnership could include the use of a Shared Kernel and/or a Published Language. A team might seek some goals to improve its mapping of situations from what exists to what would be most useful. Sometimes that works.

Now consider an overview of the different Context Mapping types:

- *Partnership.* Two teams work together as an interdependent unit to achieve closely aligned goals, which generally must be delivered in unison.

- *Shared Kernel.* Two or more teams share a small model of domain concepts that the teams agree upon. The agreement includes sharing the language of the small model. Each of the individual teams is free to design additional model elements that are specific to its language.

- *Customer–Supplier Development.* A team is in a customer position as an integrator with a supplier team. The customer is said to be downstream from the supplier because the supplier holds sway over what the customer's integration mechanisms will have.

- *Conformist.* A downstream team must integrate with an upstream model, such as with Customer–Supplier Development. For any number of reasons, the downstream cannot translate the upstream model into its downstream language, but instead must conform to the upstream's model and language.

- *Anticorruption Layer.* A downstream team must integrate with an upstream model, such as with Customer–Supplier Development. The downstream team translates the upstream model so that it fits into its own model and language.

- *Open-Host Service.* An open API is offered by a context's team that provides a flexible means to exchange information between its context and others.

- *Published Language.* A standardized format with language-based type names and attributes is developed for exchanging information between two or more contexts. This language is published, meaning that it offers well-defined schemas including documents for query results, commands for operations, and events of outcomes.

- *Separate Ways.* A downstream team could integrate with an upstream model, such as with Customer–Supplier Development; however, to avoid that in exchange for limited benefits, it chooses to create its own one-off solution.

Now let's consider the details of each Context Mapping pattern.

Partnership

As is common with partnerships, there are two parties involved in this one. Some partnerships involve more individuals or organizations, but generally we think of a partnership as being only two-sided. In the discussion of this Context Mapping type, let's limit a Partnership mapping to being one that occurs between two teams.

Each team owns its own Bounded Context, but of course these must work together in some constructive and mutually beneficial way. In Figure 6.2, the tight inter-team dependencies are depicted by the thick line between the two Bounded Contexts. Thus, the point of the Partnership is largely centered on the relationship between the teams, but there is also the possibility that they understand each other's languages more than would normally be the case.

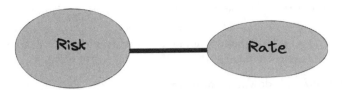

Figure 6.2 *Two teams responsible for different Bounded Contexts may require a Partnership.*

It's often true that two teams have aligned goals and neither one can succeed without the other. They must align their efforts and communication closely with those shared goals, which means they must coordinate a lot in terms of supporting features, integrations, testing, and timelines. For instance, if the teams depend on each other, then they likely share some sort of model and the two ultimate deployments cannot go live separately. At least one must be deployed shortly before the other, or both together.

Now, in terms of autonomy, this isn't the best idea; actually, it's not a good idea at all. But sometimes it's necessary. For the sake of building team autonomy into the organizational culture and structure, a Partnership might be only a short-term measure to accomplish a strategic initiative. Indeed, maintaining this relationship over the long term might be stressful for the operations of both teams and autonomy won't be possible. In some of the upcoming concrete examples we present in this chapter, it's clear that maintaining a high-contact Partnership over the long haul is unnecessary.

It's less of a burden when the two teams are actually just subteams creating subdomains within the same single team's responsibilities. In other words, a team of seven might have all seven team members working on a Core Domain, but then split off two or three members to create a Supporting Subdomain because it seems best to cleanly separate a model that isn't really a core part of the strategy. Or perhaps it is core, but the experts involved and the pace of change between the two efforts are far different because they are driven by different strategic priorities.

As an example, consider the Risk subdomain team. The Risk team is to become more focused on actuarial tasks through machine learning. This team gradually realizes that they have also, by default, inherited the job of calculating policy premium rates. After all, the rates are very closely tied to the outcomes of the risk determinations. The team understands that although this is a necessary part of the business, and possibly even core in its own right, the actuarial risk-based algorithms are driven by different business experts and change at a different pace than the rate calculations do.

Undoubtedly, the actuarial outcomes will produce disparate data types over time, but the Risk team doesn't want to take on the added burden of designing a standard information exchange specification for the rate calculations to consume. The Risk team would prefer that this standard be developed by a team that is focusing more intently on the premium rate needs. It might be that a separated Rate team would even implement the standard.

Creating a separation between the two contexts (Risk and Rate) means that there must be two teams. Even so, the two teams must work closely together for two reasons:

- The information exchange standard must be specified by the Rate team but approved by the Risk team, so it requires ongoing coordination.

- Both the Risk and Rate products must be ready for release at the same time.

It won't be a good idea to maintain this Partnership over the long haul, so the two teams will address breaking their close ties in the future when less coordination is necessary. They'll rely on other Context Mapping patterns for that.

Shared Kernel

A Shared Kernel is a mapping in which it is possible to share a small model among two or more Bounded Contexts—a sharing that is actually embraced as part of each consuming context's Ubiquitous Language. A Shared Kernel is both an inter-team relationship and a technical, code-centric relationship.

Inter-team communication is key here; otherwise, it's less likely that any teams involved would know one team already possesses a model that could be shared, or even be aware of the need and potential to share. Alternatively, two or more teams might need to recognize that there will be shared concepts between contexts in a large system, and understand that they should form a bit of a standard around it. The complexity and precision of the model in this scenario are high enough that not sharing it would be worse for all potential beneficiaries.

As an example, perhaps a given system or even several subsystems within an entire organization require a standard money type. Programmers who do not understand how monetary calculations and exchanges between currencies should be handled can cause some really big problems with money—even legal problems. Because most monetary schemes employ a decimal point to indicate a fraction of the whole denomination, it's common for programmers to think that floating-point numbers are the best type to use. Actually doing so would cause monetary losses and/or gains that would eventually cause large financial discrepancies. Floating-point values are the *worst* way to model money within a given business. First, the practice of rounding is fraught with peril for both single- and double-precision floating-point numbers. If decimal precision is needed for financial calculations, then using a "big decimal" type offers precision to a few billion decimal places. Second, a monetary value is often best treated as a whole integer without a decimal point, scaling, or rounding. In this case, there is an implied and visual formatting decimal point placed so many digits from the right in the whole string of digits. Currency conversions and support for multiple currencies also come into play here.

If a system doesn't provide a shared money type with the versatility and correctness required to meet financial standards, as seen in the Monetary Shared Kernel in Figure 6.3, everyone involved should go home and rethink their life.

Note that Figure 6.3 does not indicate that Monetary is a separate Bounded Context. It is not—but it is also not just a library. Monetary is a portion of a model that at least two teams agree to share. To make this point clearer, a Money object or record *is not persisted* by the Monetary model. Rather, the Bounded Contexts that share and consume the Monetary model are responsible for persisting Money values in their own separate storages. That is, Underwriting persists any Money values in its owned data storage, and Risk persists any Money instances in its separately owned data storage.

Such shared models are important in other domains as well. For example, consider equities trading that supports fixed bid prices for buy trades by collecting share prices across several sell orders, which together average out to the fixed price of the buy. This model concept is sometimes referred to as a "quote bar." It could be part of a Shared Kernel that provides common trading components in a model that is consumed by various specialty trading subdomains.

Another potential problem arises with the use of national or international coding standards. For instance, the medical and healthcare domains use ICD-10 codes, which are recognized in nearly 30 nations for billing and reimbursement collection purposes. More than 100 nations use ICD-10 codes for reporting statistics on causes of death. These kinds of standards form natural Shared Kernel models.

One common mistake is to consider some kinds of information (such as events) exchanged between Bounded Contexts to be a Shared Kernel. This is not typically the case because often an event, when received by a consuming Bounded Context, is translated into a command or a query at the outer boundary. When this kind of translation occurs, the specific external event type is never known at the heart of the consuming Bounded Context—that is, in its domain model. Performing a translation

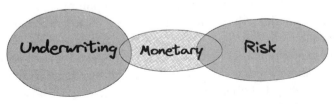

Figure 6.3 *A Shared Kernel named Monetary includes Money and other monetary types.*

from an external language to the local language means that the external language is not consumed as an acceptable language for the local context. Because it is not part of the local context's Ubiquitous Language, it is not shared between two contexts.

The local domain model treats a truly shared type, such as money, as if it were part of its Ubiquitous Language. If an external event were permitted to have meaning in the local domain model, then it might be considered part of a Shared Kernel. That's actually not a good practice because it creates a strong coupling between the producer and the consumer of such events. Translating from the external event to an internal command is a better choice.

Customer–Supplier Development

Consider the dynamics involved when there is a high degree of autonomy between teams:

- There are two teams.
- One team is considered upstream.
- The other team is considered downstream.
- The downstream team needs integration support from the upstream.
- The upstream team holds sway over what the downstream team gets.

This relationship provides autonomy for the upstream team. The downstream team can also achieve a high degree of autonomy, but they still have a dependency on the upstream. The downstream remains in a favorable situation only as long as the upstream provides the necessary integration features for this team. The downstream might need only what the upstream already provides, which would leave each team in a good position to remain on their own pace. Yet, the opposite could be true if the upstream doesn't have and can't/won't provide what the downstream needs. It might also be that the downstream team's voice is big enough and their demands sufficiently impactful on the upstream that it sets the upstream team back on their heels with respect to their own planned feature releases. The relationship might even have negative enough consequences that the downstream pressure causes the upstream team to cut corners, which results in making their own model brittle. Given a significant measure of these consequences applied to both sides, the efforts of the two teams could be derailed unless care is taken to help them work together. In fact, this kind of political clout could actually serve to flip the upstream and downstream relationships altogether.

For example, suppose that in an effort to remain autonomous, the upstream team intends to make rapid progress on their own model. However, these achievements might come at the expense of the downstream. That would happen if the upstream changed in a way that no longer supported the downstream, such as breaking previously established information exchange protocols and schemas. A typical case is when other pressures on the upstream force incompatible changes for one or more previously dependent downstream contexts. The regression first hurts the downstream team, but without a doubt the upstream team will soon suffer as they must fix their broken exchange contracts.

Creating a formal Customer–Supplier Development relationship puts both the upstream and downstream teams on more solid footing. The following is necessary:

> Establish a formal relationship between the two teams that keeps each side honest in their communication and commitment toward support, and in being a customer that understands they are not the solitary pressure that their supplier, and possibly a former partner, faces.

Although it is possible for the upstream to succeed independently of the downstream, establishing a formal, named relationship tends to reinforce an understanding that there must be agreement between the two teams, but not to the extent of Partnership. Agreement is essential for overall success.

This pattern might be more difficult to effect outside the same organization. Yet even if the upstream team is entirely external as a separate organization, they must still embrace the understanding that their customers count and have a say. Although customers are not really always right, it helps to acknowledge that they do pay the supplier real money, and that's what makes them "right." Otherwise, customer retention will be impossible—and so will job retention. The larger, more powerful, and more influential the supplier, the less likely it is to exercise altruistic behavior—that is, unless the customer is similarly larger, more powerful, more influential, and paying a lot for the service.

Having the upstream team establish API and information schema standards for their offerings will help. Even so, the upstream supplier must be willing to accept some responsibility to deliver on the requests of the downstream customers, which further necessitates some negotiations on what is to be delivered and when. Once these parameters are in place, measures must be taken to ensure that the downstream customers will receive some reliable stream of necessary support.

The previous discussion of the Partnership relationship between Risk and Rate determined that maintaining this interdependency over the long haul would be stressful on the operations of both teams and autonomy would not be possible. In time, as their synchronized releases lead to reliable stability, it will be possible to transition out of the Partnership. It's likely that the teams can then establish a Customer–Supplier Development relationship moving forward. Figure 6.4 depicts the Context Map for this relationship.

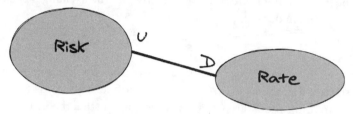

Figure 6.4 *A Customer–Supplier Development relationship between two teams.*

It might at first seem that the Rate Context would be upstream, because under the Partnership it is responsible for specifying the information exchange protocol and schema. Yet, even in that relationship Risk has the power to accept or reject the specification. In actuality, there is already a bit of Customer–Supplier Development relationship built into the Partnership, albeit a small one because coordinating release priorities tends to overrule taking a hard line on schema quality. The teams would like to establish a more versatile specification that might better support future risk determinations. At the same time, they know that attempting to achieve this outcome will be less than fruitful, especially very early on. Thus, they decide to push this effort off to the last responsible moment. The teams agree that a second or third version of the contract will need to be developed later, at which point they will have learned enough to better determine how a more flexible schema might be established.

Conformist

A Conformist relationship is in force when at least two of a few conditions exist. An upstream model is large and complex, and . . .

- A downstream team cannot afford to translate an upstream model, generally related to time, ability, and/or team bandwidth. Thus, they conform out of necessity.

- The downstream team will not realize any strategic advantage from translating the upstream model. This might be a matter of determining that the downstream model can be sufficiently close to the upstream model; or the downstream solution might be temporary, so it would be wasteful to make the solution more elaborate.

- The downstream team can't come up with a better model for their context.
- The design of the upstream integration information exchange schema is a one-to-one mapping of the upstream internal model structure, and changes to the internal model are reflected directly into the exchange schema (this is a poor upstream design).

In such cases, the downstream team decides to (or is forced to) conform entirely to the upstream model. In other words, the downstream uses the Ubiquitous Language of the upstream, and the structure or shape will be one-to-one.

One way to think about this pattern is by recognizing that the API of the upstream is used to exchange information and perform operations, with no attempt to more optimally adapt it to the local downstream model. If data from the upstream must be manipulated in any way, or even persisted, and later sent back to the upstream, it exists in the downstream much as it would be in the upstream.

As shown in Figure 6.5, the downstream Rate Context is a Conformist to the upstream Risk Context's Assessment Results model. This is because premium rate calculations are based on risk assessments, and there is no need to change that for rate calculations. The Rate Context team has a major influence on the upstream Assessment Results model specification, which makes consuming the exchange schema and conforming to the model language and structure more than palatable.

There is no reason to translate the upstream, as doing so would be unnecessary, time-consuming, and pretentious work that would also increase risk. If translation was chosen as the preferred approach, every time that the upstream Assessment Results model changed, the downstream model's translation layer would have to change as well. Of course, the Rate team will have to react to the upstream changes to the Assessment Results model, but because they have a strong influence on the specification, they can actually plan ahead for the necessary consumer code modification(s).

Ideally, each team's context will be as cohesive as possible and as decoupled as possible from the other contexts. Coupling and cohesion are defined in terms of the amount of work it takes to change something [StrucDesign]. If either of the two

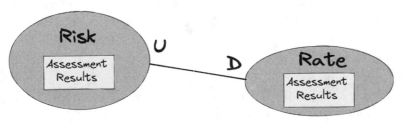

Figure 6.5 *A downstream Conformist consumes an upstream model as is.*

contexts don't change that often, the coupling is not really an issue. It is a good rule of thumb to consider the frequency of changes and to prevent coupling if it will impact teams in a negative way.

It really makes no sense to translate in this particular case, but it is not possible to make a blanket rule. Instead, those decisions should be made on a case-by-case basis. Due consideration should be given to the compatibility of the upstream Ubiquitous Language to the downstream consumer's Ubiquitous Language, but the other factors listed previously must also be weighed. In addition, the following Context Mappings identify other consequences of adopting a translation approach.

Anticorruption Layer

An Anticorruption Layer is the exact opposite of a Conformist. This pattern takes a defensive integration perspective by making every effort to prevent the upstream model from corrupting the downstream model. The downstream is the implementer of the Anticorruption Layer because this team must take responsibility for translating whatever is available in the upstream into the language and structure of their consuming model. It is also possible that the downstream will have to send data changes back upstream. When that takes place, the downstream model must be translated back to what the upstream understands.

In many cases, the upstream system is a legacy Big Ball of Mud. If that's true, don't expect the upstream to have a rich client-facing API and well-defined information exchange schema. Integration with the upstream might require being granted a user account for the upstream database and performing ad hoc queries. Although this book is not meant to make technology recommendations, it does seem appropriate to acknowledge that the introduction of GraphQL represents a game-changer for such jobs. Yet, we shouldn't consider the existence of GraphQL an excuse to design integrations in a substandard way that requires its use.

Even if the upstream model does have a rich client-facing API and a well-defined information exchange schema, the downstream team might still decide to translate the upstream model to its own Ubiquitous Language. Imposing one or many loanwords[1] from the upstream context might not fit well with the downstream Ubiquitous Language. The team might decide that forming a calque[2] is natural for some local terms, and/or that defining an entirely different term might be even better. All of these options could be mixed together as deemed appropriate. The translation decisions belong to the downstream team.

---

1. A loanword is one or more words taken into a target language exactly as is from another language. For example, all languages other than French that use "déjà vu" are using a loanword.
2. A calque is composed of one or more words from one language that are transliterated into a target language. For example, the English "beer garden" calques the German "biergarten."

The point is not necessarily that the upstream model is a mess, which is difficult to readily exchange information with, and that heroic feats must be performed to translate it for downstream consumption. Rather, the salient point is that if the downstream does not think and speak in terms of the upstream, then a translation would be helpful and could even be appropriate from the standpoint of downstream team time and abilities.

Figure 6.6 depicts an Anticorruption Layer accessing a Big Ball of Mud legacy system that has the current NuCoverage premium calculation rules. This is done as a Risk Context team interim step, which will suffice until an improved model can be fully implemented locally.

The model shown in Figure 6.6 will be more versatile in terms of adding, editing, removing, enabling, and disabling rules. These rules can, in turn, be used for experimental A/B testing in production. Until that time, the Rate Context team has put in place what they consider to be a fairly good representation of their fully designed future model. Thus, they will translate the upstream rules into their local model as a means of testing their assumptions regarding the new local model. At the present time, it is less important to have a versatile model when a working model is a necessity.

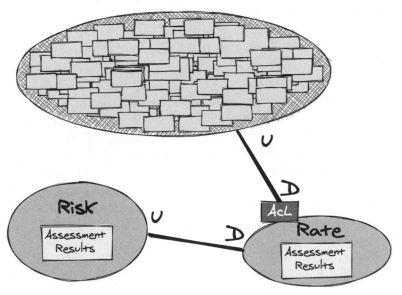

Figure 6.6 *The Rate Context queries a legacy system for premium calculation rules.*

Open-Host Service

Sometimes teams have foreknowledge of the needs of current and future integration clients and enough time to plan for them. At other times a team might not know of any integration needs and then later get caught trying to play catch-up. Creating an Open-Host Service can be the answer to both of these situations.

Think of an Open-Host Service as an API for exchanging information, where some exchanges might require the API provider to support data mutations from downstream onto their upstream model.

Now, consider the following potential integration situations in which the upstream team may find themselves. Let's look at the Rate team as an example.

Team Knows Early

During a lunch conversation, the team implementing a Rate Context learns that at least one other downstream team will require access to their model. The downstream team is interested in analytics around the calculated premium rates. During the same lunch, the newly downstream analytics team declaring their dependency suggests that another team, and possibly more, will also be in need of the same kinds of integrations. The now (suddenly) upstream team hasn't interviewed the other teams, and is only aware of the one. Should they go to the effort of providing an API for the single dependent downstream team of which they currently are aware? Or should they just provide a database user account for this team?

Assertion: Sharing Access to a Database with Even One Downstream Client Is Never a Good Idea

This approach gives deep access to the persistent data, and potentially creation and update rights. Imagine the damage that could be done with "willy-nilly" data mutations happening while the owning team remains blissfully unaware of them. The deep dependency also makes changing the database schema later very difficult for the upstream, or very impactful to the downstream, or both. In time, it might become difficult to know who is and who isn't dependent on the database, and often that's a lesson learned the hard way. Once the system is running in production, performance can decrease and, even worse, deadlocks on different tables can bring the whole system to a grinding halt. As a rule of thumb, using shared resources tends to hide coupling where instead it should be explicitly modeled. For these and other reasons, sharing direct access to a persistence mechanism is a really bad idea.

The upstream Rate team could design an API that takes care of the single downstream client, but without many bells and whistles. This might require the downstream analytics team to take on a bit of overhead to translate the consumed model on their own from less than optimal exchanges with the upstream API. At least for now it seems to be a read-only API, meaning it's simply query-based.

If the upstream Rate team were to interview the other potential downstream clients, they could make a better determination of the broader needs. If they get an affirmative answer from one or more clients, it could be worth putting more effort into the development of the API, especially if the other teams need to exchange information beyond queries. The Rate team conducts some interviews and learns that now at least three teams, including analytics, will need API access, and the other two teams will need to push new and changed information back to the Rate Context.

The Team Is Surprised

One of the worst situations faced by teams expected to provide open integrations occurs when they are surprised by requirements that show up late. This problem might be caused by the organization's poor communication structure. Recall Conway's Law: The systems produced by an organization will reflect its communication structures. Now think of what happens when communication happens latently and the teams that declare their dependencies need the support in short order. The reality is exactly the sad scene anyone would expect. The outcome of the API will reflect the condensed timeline available to implement it. If properly handled, the debt will be recorded and paid. More realistically, if additional teams pile on with similar "oh, BTW" requests for support, the situation will only get worse before it gets better.

Although visible efforts are sometimes made to improve the organizational communication channels, some organizations are too large and complicated to entirely prevent this unhappy situation, at least in the short run. No organization should accept this status quo, because there are ways to break through the silence and walls between teams. Address these barriers early for the good of the teams, projects, and company. Consider implementing weekly lightning (10- to 15-minute) talks across teams working on the same system. Between four and six teams can present their progress in one hour. These meetings must be attended by all parties involved, and the presentations must not consist of fluff or focus on bragging rights. Instead, the teams must share what they have of value, where they are struggling, and what they need.

Another approach is to incorporate an engineering discipline into the system by identifying *responsible engineers* on each team who must collaborate with a *chief engineer* to ensure integrations are planned and correctly synchronized. The chief engineer will employ what are known as *integrating events* or *sync and stabilize events*—the result of forming purposeful organizational communication structures. These events are planned at intervals and tracked to confirm that all integrating teams deliver subsets of new functionality with working integrations across subsystems. Good integrating events will bring out hidden problems and interactions, as well as places where suboptimization is killing the organization's overall ability to succeed with this new product. If there are problems in meeting team schedules, the responsible engineer must communicate with the chief engineer as early as these issues become known, but at the latest they should surface at integrating events. This kind of engineering-focused approach is not project management, but rather a matter of engineers working together to meet technical milestones that align with and deliver on business goals.

Suppose the surprise happened to the Rate team because the lunch date got canceled due to a production problem—this situation, even in a relatively small organization, could easily occur. In the previous scenario, it was only serendipity that allowed the Rate team to learn about the Analytics team requiring information exchange. Likewise, it was only by happenstance that the Rate team got a hint that other teams would eventually require dependencies. If the lunch is rescheduled for the following week, the work topic could be preempted by the goings on at the French Open, the Champions League, the WNBA, or that awesome Oceansize album. And, then, surprise!

The major problem in not making time to handle these unplanned bad situations is that the other teams might be forced to go their separate ways, or even integrate with a legacy Big Ball of Mud that might be falling behind the curve as it is replaced, for example, by the new Rate Context. It will also take a lot of effort to integrate with the legacy system and maintain the wishful thinking that what is exchanged will still be relevant after weeks and months, and possibly even years. There's no way that the Rate team can force integration by delaying the schedule of the other team, even if communication was foiled.

The best that the Rate team can do in the short term is offer to provide some not-so-good access to the downstream. Perhaps opening a set of REpresentational State Transfer (REST) resources would make this solution more acceptable to both teams and enable the time crunch to be met. It might be possible to enlist the help of the downstream team, and that team might indeed have to incur some pain for their latent communication. In fact, probably even a limited API on the modernized Rate Context will be much better to work with than the crufty legacy system.

Still, all of these troublesome situations can be largely avoided by introducing an engineering discipline such as the ones noted here.

Service API

In both of the preceding scenarios, the Rate team and their dependents end up in the same place—all parties face pressure from the outside. With more time to think, plan, and implement, the Rate team would stand on more solid ground. Even so, delivery is the only practical choice, so the team plows forward.

After discovering that three teams will depend on Rate, the challenges seem to lie less with the complexity of the API itself than with the information exchange schemas involved. Because the premium rate rules and calculations will ultimately be altered, perhaps even multiple times per day, and the constant flux in the number of new rules might be substantial, the information exchange schemas will be a moving target. The next section, "Published Language," describes dealing with this challenge in more detail.

One consideration is that some information might best be made available as a stream of events that have occurred in the upstream Rate Context. Because all three dependents are interested in some subset of the changes that occur in the upstream, the Rate team can make part of the query API a way for the downstream to "subscribe" to the total number of happenings in the Rate Context that they are willing to share. This query API would likely be offered as REST resources. The Risk team might instead place the events on a pub-sub topic.

There are advantages to both strategies. As outlined in Chapter 2, "Essential Strategic Learning Tools," the organization can use Architecture Decision Records (ADRs) to outline the possible decisions; in this case, there are two. Integration tests can be used to demonstrate the options. The familiarity of downstream teams with either approach might be the deciding factor, but not necessarily. When the decision is made, include it in the ADR.

The Rate team must keep in mind that their event stream might not carry the full payloads that consumers need. If so, the API must support queries that provide deeper information views than the events carry, or perhaps the events themselves should carry richer payloads. One problem with query-backs is the challenges associated with making available the data versions that the events reference. The data now considered current in the upstream could have transitioned one or more times since the event that causes the eventual query-back could be processed by the downstream. Mitigating this scenario might require the upstream to maintain snapshot versions of the potentially queried data. Alternatively, as previously indicated, the events could be designed to carry a large enough payload about the state at the time of the event to negate the query-back. As another possibility, the downstream might have to understand how to deal with query-back results that no longer contain what happened before the current state. The Rate Context provides the Rate Calculated event to consuming downstream contexts, as Figure 6.7 illustrates.

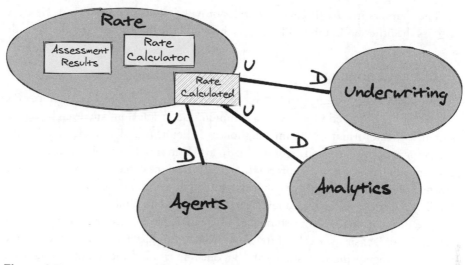

Figure 6.7 *An Open-Host Service with multiple downstream consumers.*

It might not have been expected that Underwriting is downstream, because it is upstream from Risk, and Rate calculates the premium based on the Risk's Assessment Results. Yet, it's understandable that Underwriting must consume the calculated premium somehow. If Underwriting doesn't subscribe from a downstream position, it would have to perform some pretty strange gyrations to obtain the premium. Importantly, the Rate Calculated event must carry an identity that correlates to the original Underwriting Application or some other type of entity that caused the risk to be assessed and the rate to be calculated. Expectedly, the Analytics Context also consumes the event. Likewise, the Agents Context consumes the event, giving WellBank and other agents the opportunity to see the processing activity shortly after each step happens.

The remainder of the API should be designed with a minimalist mindset, providing only what is absolutely necessary. This API can be offered as REST resources or via asynchronous messaging. It seems almost silly to consider Simple Object Access Protocol (SOAP)–based remote procedure calls (RPC) in contemporary system design, but they are still available for use, and will likely exist in some legacy systems. If RPCs are desired today, normally gRPC would be used rather than SOAP. More to the point, the API should be built up over time as downstream clients drive the functionality and information exchange schemas. This can be achieved by means of *Consumer-Driven Contracts* [Consumer-Driven-Contracts], which are drawn up as consumers express their needs. When this approach is used, the contracts can be tailored for each consumer. It's also possible that all consumers might be given the superset of all information determined by the merger of all consumer needs.

The chapters in Part III cover the styles of API designs in more detail. Next, we discuss the other half of the API—that is, how will the information be exchanged?

Published Language

A Bounded Context is often the source of information needed by one or more other collaborating Bounded Contexts in a common system solution, and even by outside systems. If the format of the information is difficult to understand, then its consumption will be tricky and error prone. To avoid this predicament and enhance the exchangeability of pertinent information, organizations can employ a standardized strong schema. In domain-driven terms, this is known as a Published Language. A Published Language can take a few forms, as outlined in Table 6.1.

The international schema standards listed in Table 6.1 are only a small representation of those available throughout various industries. There are obvious trade-offs when using such standards, but one important thing to note is that using the beefy canonical models has a definite disadvantage for internal enterprise use. These models are not only more difficult to adhere to, but also carry a lot higher transport overhead. If the enterprise is on the cloud, this will have an impact on cost.

Figure 6.8 shows three Published Language examples within NuCoverage. The Risk Context has its own Published Language, with one element being the event

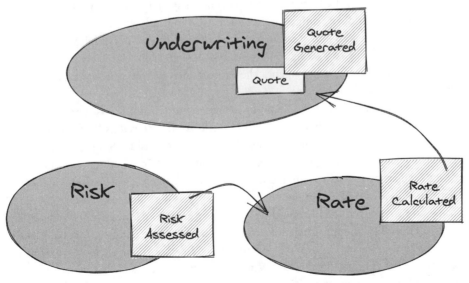

Figure 6.8 *The Risk, Rate, and Underwriting provide their own Published Languages.*

Table 6.1 *Published Language Schemas from International to Single Enterprise Services*

Type	Example	Consequences
Industry-wide strong schema defined by an international or national working group supported by a governing organization	Health Level 7 (HL7) digital healthcare exchange standard: It may be a requirement for all subdomains in a whole-system solution, and for those across systems, and between organizations, to exchange healthcare clinical and administrative information using HL7.	HL7 is a strong schema in terms of supporting definite record types, but it is weak in the definition of fields within each record type. This can result in the schema being misused and potentially requiring interpretation by a business entity using it, which might be different from the use by other organizations. Even with HL7, inter-organization digital healthcare exchanges may require translation or retooling of data generation and parsing.
	GS1 global data identification standards. This is the origin of the barcode and other standards around B2B information exchange, including ecommerce.	There is a well-defined standard, ever within each record type, but it can require a large number of records to define a very small dataset. In one ecommerce usage example, between 300 and 350 record types were required to correctly define a dataset of fewer than 20 total lines of product order information. Creating the source code implementation of the standard, the producer output writers, and the consumer input readers was a time-consuming experience. This emphasizes the downsides to the "canonical data model" pattern in which an attempt is to make a one-size-fits-all standard. This approach causes bloat because it attempts to define the superset of all possible needs across a broad number of industries.
	ICD-10 is the 10th revision of the *International Statistical Classification of Diseases and Related Health Problems*, a medical classification list developed by the World Health Organization.	This is a large, but clear and straightforward, set of medical codings.

Continues

Table 6.1 *Published Language Schemas from International to Single Enterprise Services (Continued)*

Type	Example	Consequences
Organizational internal standard governed by principals within a specific business entity	These standards are defined by each organization on a case-by-case basis. External businesses integrating with the standard-defining organization might be (or are) required to use the standard. Possibly even internal systems must exchange information using the same standards.	Provides flexibility in the definition, and clear direction for outside integrations. However, this approach can add unnecessary overhead to exchanges inside the organization's enterprise of systems because inter-system and inter-context exchanges might be required to provide more information than is practical or even possible.
Contextual/subdomain standard	Each Bounded Context can define its own digital exchange standard. Every other Bounded Context, subdomain, and whole-system solution must use the strong schemas defined by each given Bounded Context.	Provides optimal information exchange schema definitions for each subdomain á la the Bounded Context. It might be difficult for a single Bounded Context that requires integrations with several other Bounded Contexts to deal with all the different schemas. Yet, having many integrations might point to other problems. Further, the context/subdomain standard might be insufficient for integrations external to the organization's enterprise. Even so, the individual schema standards can be used more globally by entering them into the superset of those defined for inter-organization exchanges.

named Risk Assessed. The Rate Context has a different Published Language, with one element being Rate Calculated. The Risk Assessed event has an impact on Rate, and the Rate Calculated event is consumed by the Underwriting Context. In turn, the Underwriting Context builds a Quote from one or more Rate Calculated events and emits a Quote Generated event for each completed Quote.

One way to maintain an international, national, and organization-defined Published Language and make it available to consumers is by means of a schema registry. A worthy schema registry supports business contextual schemas of any number, each with multiple versions, and provides for appropriate compatibility checks between versions. One such schema registry is available as part of the open source, reactive VLINGO XOOM in its Schemata tool [VLINGO-XOOM].

Separate Ways

When a team might integrate with another Bounded Context but the cost is likely to be higher than the potential benefits gained, that team might decide to go their Separate Ways. Teams that go their Separate Ways create their own one-off solutions, or make simpler modeling decisions that help them make short work of the problem they face.

It's possible that a given Bounded Context might have no integrations at all with other contexts. However, this pattern can be applied on a case-by-case basis. In other words, the team under discussion might integrate with one or more Bounded Contexts, but not with others.

The downside to taking this route appears when the solution chosen creates *significant* silos of data and/or domain expertise expressed in software that are roughly duplicates of other areas of a system. Some amount of duplication is not always bad, but too much is too much. Don't Repeat Yourself (DRY) is an adage that applies to knowledge, not code. Creating *large* silos of duplicate data and repeating knowledge by way of expertise codified in multiple contexts is not the desired effect of the Separate Ways pattern.

Topography Modeling

While participating in an EventStorming session, it might seem difficult to find boundaries. As previously advised, participants should think in terms of business capabilities and recognize communication drivers among experts. These are the best ways to organize boundaries and the best places to start. More refinement will happen as the business grows and changes, and new business capabilities become essential.

Another tool that can help define boundaries and clarify how the boundaries will work together is the *topographic* approach. *Topography* can mean a few things. According to the Merriam-Webster dictionary, its definitions include these:

1. **a:** The art or practice of graphic delineation in detail usually on maps or charts of natural and man-made features of a place or region especially in a way to show their relative positions and elevations.

   b: Topographical surveying.

2. **a:** The configuration of a surface including its relief and the position of its natural and man-made features.

   b: The physical or natural features of an object or entity and their structural relationships.

All of these definitions are applicable using this approach.

Yes, the communication within a Bounded Context helps teams understand what belongs inside, but the communication and mapping between Bounded Contexts further inform the contexts themselves. These elements include Context Maps, but grasping the actual flow of detailed information exchange schemas by means of enhanced visual mapping models helps even more. Modeling with topography is a way to better understand the shape and character of your system. Figure 6.9 provides a template for Topography Modeling.

Several areas of the template in Figure 6.9 can be filled in with information (see Table 6.2). The resulting models can be placed on a table top or on a wall in the order of processing flow, similar to an EventStorming timeline. The template provides teams with a number of placeholders that can be used to show more context than is given at a single point in an EventStorming timeline. Additional placeholder areas can be added to any part of the modeling map as needed. This template purposely omits architectural details that, although necessary for runtime operations, serve only to obfuscate the more important parts of the model.

Using paper and pen to simulate the processing flow of the system being designed promotes continued additional conversation drivers that can lead to deep insights into the software's inner workings. Are there missing business capabilities that are needed for complete functionality through collaboration and integration? Do there seem to be areas warranting refinement or areas needing further clarification? Making changes with pen and paper is a lot faster and cheaper means to fail fast, learn, and reboot.

Every team involved in the integrations can carry away copies of their context(s) and the surrounding contextual topographies that collaborate. Each opportunity to discover and learn leads to confidence and a chance to innovate.

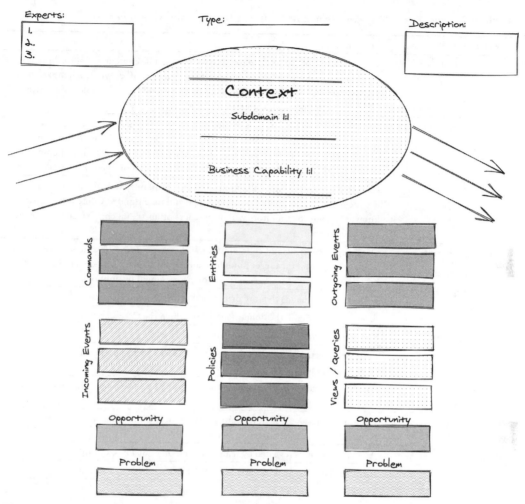

Figure 6.9 *Topography Modeling template diagram.*

Table 6.2 *Topography Modeling Template Areas and Descriptions*

Area Type	Description
Experts	Write the names of the business experts who contribute to the sphere of knowledge of the communication context.
Type	The subdomain type: Core, Supporting, or Generic.
Description	A brief summary of the context's purpose.
Context	Write the name of the communication context (i.e., the Bounded Context's name) on the line above.

Continues

Table 6.2 *Topography Modeling Template Areas and Descriptions (Continued)*

Area Type	Description
Subdomain 1:1	Write the name of the subdomain of this context. The context and the subdomain should have a one-to-one relationship. If the names conflict with each other, there is a problem with subdomain alignment. If there tend to be multiple subdomains, there might be a problem with model focus.
Business Capability 1:1	Write the name of the business capability provided by this context. The context and the business capability should have a one-to-one relationship. If the names conflict with one another, there is a problem with business capability alignment. If there tend to be multiple business capabilities, there is a problem with model focus.
Arrows, left side	Incoming integration and collaboration points available, and which contexts use them. Name the Context Mapping type and the Bounded Context using it, if known. Known collaborators will be partners or upstream contexts; downstream will be unknown.
Arrows, right side	Outgoing integration and collaboration with other contexts. Name the Context Mapping type and the target Bounded Context, if known. A known target might be a partner or an upstream context; downstream will be unknown.
Commands	Prominent commands that are dispatched to the domain model.
Entities	Prominent entities in the domain model to which the Commands are directed.
Outgoing Events	Prominent events emitted by the Entities.
Incoming Events	Prominent events received by the Bounded Context through the left-side arrows representing integration points.
Policies	Any business rules to be applied to the Incoming Events or the Commands being dispatched to the domain model.
Views/Queries	Prominent query model views onto which model changes must be projected to ensure the related queries will provide viewable data.
Opportunities	Any opportunities revealed by team learning that must be exploited.
Problems	Any problems revealed by team learning that must be addressed.

Ways to Fail and Succeed

Failure can lead to good because of the learning opportunities it produces. That kind of controlled failure is based on a scientific approach using experimentation and ultimately leads to success. Although learning can come from the failures discussed in this section, these are not the kind of failures that can help the organization in the short term. Instead, these kinds of failures can and should be avoided. They relate to misusing the domain-driven tools, and often lead to overall failure to meet the business goals.

Failure when applying a domain-driven approach is generally related to several different mistakes, all of which might be at play, or possibly just a few of the most insidious ones. Consider the following common pitfalls:

1. *No strategic focus.* Disregarding the strategic discovery and learning opportunities is missing the point of the domain-driven approach. It will also lead to software development as usual, with all the problems already discussed, because business experts will not be involved and developers will create a divide of tangled components as before. The developers imagine that following some technical ideas from the domain-driven approach is all that is needed, but not applying strategic learning is a big mistake.

2. *Doing too much too soon.* Using strategic discovery, but only at a cursory level as an excuse to start coding, is fraught with problems. It's roughly the same as not using strategic design at all, although some boundaries might be discovered that are appropriate in the short term. Even so, problems will occur when trying to apply Bounded Contexts with distributed computing before the teams have a good reason to, or when trying to understand the strategic goals and solve business problems using single-process modularity first. Such a bias will likely lead to over-engineered technical approaches, putting too much emphasis on the solution rather than on the strategy. A domain-driven approach is about discovery, learning, and innovation.

3. *Tight coupling and temporal dependencies everywhere.* Especially when things move too quickly, too little attention is given to upstream and downstream dependencies between Bounded Contexts. Often this is also due to the style of integration used. For example, REST and RPCs can lead to very tight coupling, both in API dependencies and temporally.[3] Making an effort to disentangle data type dependencies is rarely even considered. Frequently, this neglect leads to nearly every integration becoming a Conformist to upstream contexts. Generally, when using REST and RPCs, there is a sense that the network doesn't exist between two services, even though it does. When the network is unstable, even for a short period of time, that can wreak havoc on integrations, causing cascading failures across a whole system. Even when using messaging and events, the coupling can still be a liability rather than an asset when there is no effort to decouple the data types between contexts.

4. *Replicating data broadly.* Every single piece of data has a system of record—that is, an original source and an authority over the data. When any

---

3. Temporal coupling is harmful because one distributed service will fail when another completes more slowly than expected or tolerable.

single piece of data is replicated and stored in another location other than its source, there is a risk of losing the source and authority over it. Over time, those employees who understand that the data copy should not be used for conclusive decision making might leave the project, or new employees working on their own might make a wrong assumption about ownership, use the data inappropriately, and possibly even provide a copy of it to others. This can lead to serious problems.

5. *Technical failures.* There are a few different varieties of these failures:

   a. Producing quick fixes to bugs or model disparity can lead to progressive distortion of the Ubiquitous Language.

   b. Developers may pursue highly abstract type hierarchies upfront in an effort to open the door to unknown future needs, which rarely prove correct in the long run. In general, abstractions adopted in the name of code reuse or even emphasis on concrete reused goals will lead to unwanted baggage at best, and potentially extensive rework.

   c. Assigning insufficiently skilled developers to the project will lead to near certain failure.

   d. Not recognizing or recording debt due to business modeling knowledge gaps, or lack of follow-through to pay the recognized and recorded debt, is another technical failure.

Most of these major project failures—from which it might be impossible to recover—have already been addressed in one way or another in this book. The saddest part is that they are all avoidable. With the assistance of one or two domain-driven experts to get a project or program effort under way, and with some guidance over each month of the projects, teams can be both brought up to speed and helped to grow and mature. The following are ways to succeed:

1. *Understand the business goals.* All stakeholders must keep clearly in mind the business goals to be achieved through a domain-driven effort. Understand that current knowledge is all that is available, and new knowledge can change the project direction.

2. *Use strategic learning tools.* Once business goals are firmly established in everyone's mind, dig into the problem space domain by building teams with good organizational communication structures that stand up to Conway's Law, by using Impact Mapping, EventStorming, Context Mapping, and Topography Modeling. Everything is an experiment until it isn't. Don't be

discouraged if that time never arrives. Failing in small ways, and doing so rapidly and inexpensively, is discovering and learning at its best.

3. *Take time to digest learnings.* Don't be in too big a hurry to start developing concrete solutions. Code should be written very early, but with the intent to experiment, leading to discovery and learning. Sometimes it can take a few days for the context boundaries to settle, and even when these seem correct, at least minor adjustments will likely be necessary. Sometimes the boundaries are correct but some concepts and data are misappropriated. Be willing to move some concepts around to different Bounded Contexts, and recognize when concepts have become more clearly identified with their rightful ownership. This can happen even a few days or more into the project. These kinds of concept and data migrations seem to require more time to settle on when working on legacy modernization and large enterprise digital transformations.

4. *Adopt loose coupling and temporal decoupling techniques.* The less one Bounded Context knows about another Bounded Context, the better. The less one Bounded Context accepts another Bounded Context's API, information, and internal structure into its own, the better. The less one Bounded Context depends on another Bounded Context's ability to complete a task within a given time frame, the better. The less one Bounded Context depends on another Bounded Context to provide information in any order relative to any others, the better. Loose coupling and temporal decoupling are our friends.

5. *Respect data origins and authorities.* Stakeholders must learn to avoid replicating data outside its authority and access it for single-use operations. Chapter 5, "Contextual Expertise," provides ways to access data from disparate services while respecting the original sources.

6. *Use appropriate tactical tools.* This book is light on detailed implementation techniques, but the authors provide a follow-on technical book, *Implementing Strategic Monoliths and Microservices* (Vernon & Jaskuła, Addison-Wesley, forthcoming), on deep implementation patterns and practices. In brief, avoid technical tools that are unnecessary for the context and that tend to lead to more expensive designs without justification for them.

Champion simplicity in the strategic and tactical tools and approaches used to wrangle with the already complex business domain at hand. Winning strategies guide teams toward delivering on business goals that lead to the ultimate business aspiration: richly rewarding innovations.

Applying the Tools

The section "Applying the Tools" in Chapter 3, "Events-First Experimentation and Discovery," depicts a recording of an EventStorming session in which NuCoverage discovers a problematic issue: Applicants are dropping out of the application process before it is completed. One opportunity that the team has identified to address this problem is to use machine learning algorithms to assess the risk and calculate the rate; however, it was not clear to the NuCoverage team how machine learning would fit into the overall application processing. They decided to hold another EventStorming session closer to the design level to help them with this specific challenge. After some intensive discussions between team members and business experts, the design of the new application process started to take form.

Recall from Chapter 3 that the current application process is constantly exchanging messages between the Risk Context's assessment and the Rate Context's premium calculations so that it can obtain the most accurate projected premium quote to present to the applicant in real time as they progress through the application form. This feeds into the ongoing application information gathering effort by evaluating whether the applicant must answer additional questions. All this dynamicity is used in an effort to simultaneously keep the current projected premium quote before the applicant and allow NuCoverage to assess risk more precisely and (re)calculate an up-to-date premium. Unfortunately, it has produced a long and cumbersome application process that the team will attempt to simplify by introducing machine learning algorithms.

The new application process requires a bare minimum of data from the application form, with nearly zero complexity demanded of the applicant. The complexity will instead be encapsulated in the machine learning risk assessment and premium price calculation models. What stands out as a result of this discovery and learning iteration is that to achieve the team's goal, a specific business process is needed to handle interactions between the application forms, risk assessment, and premium rate calculation. The team decided to name it the *Application Premium Process*. In Figure 6.10, this process is shown on a purple (or lilac or mulberry) sticky note. Once the application form is complete, the *Application Submitted* event occurs. It is handled by the *Application Premium Process*, which guides the subsequent next

Figure 6.10 *The team identified the Application Premium Process.*

steps. The team continues iterating on the EventStorming session in an effort to discover what the individual processing steps will be.

The risk assessment based on machine learning algorithms is quite complex. This process will need to access several external data sources and handle complex algorithm calibration steps. As illustrated in Figure 6.11, the NuCoverage team thought it would be best to model the assessment as a *Risk Assessor* stateless domain service, as described in Chapter 7, "Modeling Domain Concepts." It starts the risk assessment step upon receiving the *Assess Risk* command from *Application Premium Process*. The outcome of the risk assessment is captured in an *Assessment Result* aggregate, and the *Risk Assessed* event is emitted. This event is handled by the *Application Premium Process*, which will cause the next processing step.

The next step started by the *Application Premium Process* triggers the premium rate calculations by issuing *Calculate Rate* command. The rate calculation processing is likewise a complex step because any number of different calculation rules could apply based on the assessment results, risk weights, and other criteria defined by the specific agent's business experts. Yet, the calculation step itself is stateless. When these considerations were taken into account, designing the *Rate Calculator* as a domain service seemed the best option (Figure 6.12). It can change in the future,

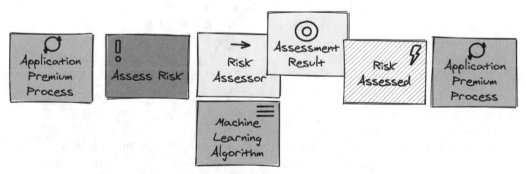

Figure 6.11 *Design of the risk assessment step with machine learning.*

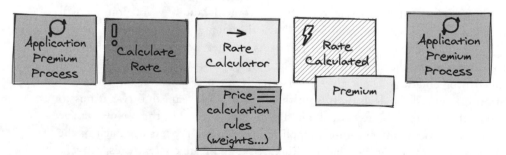

Figure 6.12 *Design of the premium rate calculation step.*

but given the current knowledge, a domain service is the right choice. After the rate has been calculated, a *Rate Calculated* event is emitted that contains the calculated *Premium* as its payload. This event is handled by the *Application Premium Process*, which will again cause the next step.

Following the previous steps, a quote can be provided to the applicant. The *Application Premium Process* further drives the application process by issuing the *Record Premium* command. This command results in a *Policy Quote* being generated for the applicant, and presented in the UI. Figure 6.13 illustrates this process.

Figure 6.13 *Final step of storing a premium for and issuing a policy quote.*

The team decided to review the entire process design once again, with the intention of identifying the different contexts in play for the application-to-quote processing. As indicated by Figure 6.14, the team employed pink stickies placed over the various steps to identify the contexts involved across the timeline. This timeline is the entire result of the EventStorming session. Currently, everybody is happy with the outcome, but they all realize that there is even more to learn.

The identified Bounded Contexts playing a role in the application process are *Underwriting*, *Risk*, and *Rate*. The *Underwriting Context* is responsible for gathering application form data at the beginning of the process and issuing a policy quote at the end. It makes sense that the *Application Premium Process* driving all the steps of the application lives in the *Underwriting Context*. The *Risk Context* assesses risks with the help of its associated machine learning algorithms. The *Rate Context* calculates the premium rates using the appropriate standard rules and those applicable to the specific agent.

As the final step of the design session, the team decided to use Context Mapping to indicate relationships between the different contexts and how integrations will work, making these explicit. Figure 6.15 shows this mapping.

In the "Partnership" section earlier in this chapter, we noted that when the Risk team realized they had by default inherited rate calculations, that assignment seemed problematic to them given their already intense tasks ahead. This realization influenced the decision to split the original Risk team into two teams to manage the separate contexts, Risk and Rate. Thus, a total of three NuCoverage teams will work on the end-to-end application-to-quote processing. Each of the three teams will work on the Underwriting, Risk, and Rate contexts, respectively. Initially, a pragmatic decision determined that Risk and Rate should work within

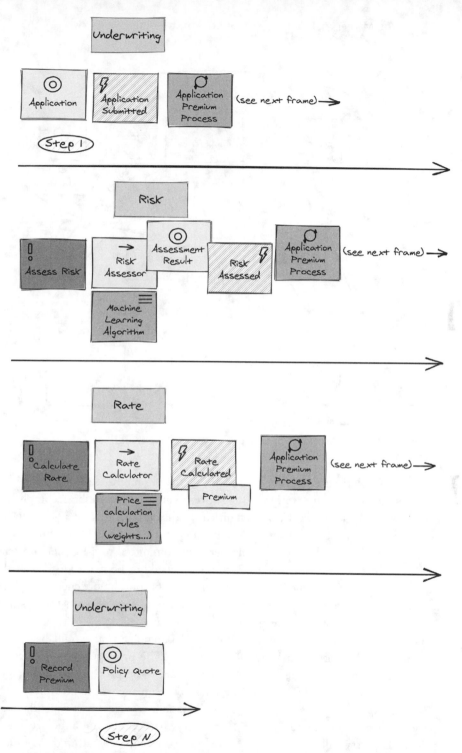

Figure 6.14 *The new application process as a result of the EventStorming session.*

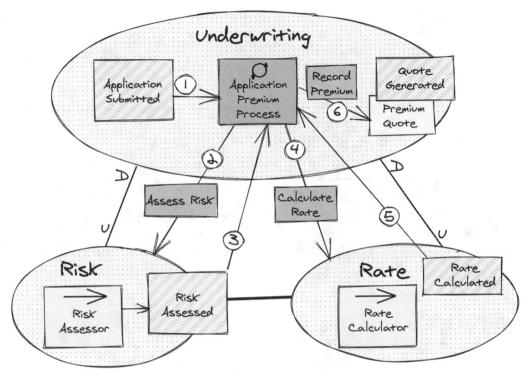

Figure 6.15 *Context Mappings between Underwriting, Risk, and Rate.*

a Partnership relationship. These two teams' goals are interdependent, at least in the early stages of implementation, and the overall quoting cannot be accomplished without the success of both. In fact, significant calibration is required between the assessed risk and rate calculation models. It would be unnecessarily difficult to synchronize their designs if the two teams were not committed to a Partnership relationship. As previously explained, a Partnership need not be maintained over the long term. At some point, the Partnership is likely to become a bottleneck, blocking one or both teams from making progress independent of each other as the business moves forward with unrelated priorities.

The teams considered designing a Published Language that would be shared between the Underwriting, Risk, and Rate contexts. This proposed language would include the commands and events necessary to drive the processing. Ultimately, though, it was determined that a single Published Language would be unnecessary because the *Application Premium Process* will manage cross-context dependencies, whether upstream–downstream, peer-to-peer, or whatever else might be necessary. A Schema Registry will be used to maintain loose coupling even within the *Application Premium Process* that is implemented inside the Underwriting Context.

The Underwriting Context is downstream to Risk and Rate because they depend on the assessed risk and calculated premium rate. These are decidedly Customer–Supplier relationships. The Underwriting team must synchronize with the Risk and Rate team to implement the application-to-quote process as a whole. Both the Risk and Rate contexts will define their own limited, but independent Published Languages, which the *Application Premium Process* will use. The Underwriting Context must communicate the application data to Risk Context, but the application data must be formatted according to the Risk Published Language. In contrast, the Rate Context communicates its Rate Calculated and Premium model elements to the Underwriting as its own Published Language. These considerations help normalize those exchanges and provide for the highly desired loose coupling between the contexts.

Summary

This chapter promoted the use of Context Maps to identify relationships between any two teams and their respective Bounded Contexts. Context Mapping helps teams recognize the situations they face and provides tools to recognize and address specific modeling challenges that result in whole-system solutions. Using a topographic approach to Context Mapping assists in defining boundaries and specifying how various Bounded Contexts work together. Warnings were offered about the common pitfalls of misusing the domain-driven tools, which can lead to costly, overall failure. These warnings transitioned to useful guidance for succeeding with proper use of the same tools.

Follow these guiding principles:

- Discover the actual existing inter-team relationships by applying Context Maps to each integration point, and (possibly) attempt to work out better circumstances by improving a given relationship and means of integration.

- Correctly apply the appropriate Context Mapping options, such as Partnership, Customer–Supplier Development, Conformist, Anticorruption Layer, Open-Host Service, and Published Language, to current and future modeling situations.

- Topography modeling is a means of understanding the shape and character of your system and grasping the flow of detailed information exchange between Bounded Contexts.

- Carefully avoid misusing the domain-driven tools. Doing so can lead to failure of entire projects and, in turn, to failure to meet business goals.

- Most domain-driven pitfalls can be avoided. Engage and retain a domain-driven expert to help launch and keep the system architecture and development on track.

Chapter 7, "Modeling Domain Concepts," introduces the tactical domain-driven modeling tools, which are used to express a sphere of knowledge in source code free of confusion that results from ambiguity.

References

[Consumer-Driven-Contracts] https://martinfowler.com/articles/consumerDrivenContracts.html

[StrucDesign] W. P. Stevens, G. J. Myers, and L. L. Constantine. "Structured Design." *IBM Systems Journal* 13, no. 2 (1974): 115–139.

[VLINGO-XOOM] https://github.com/vlingo and https://vlingo.io

Chapter 7

Modeling Domain Concepts

Many projects could benefit from carefully crafted domain models, but don't. Oftentimes the lack of thoughtful modeling is due to the concepts of a business being perceived as data. After all, we are constantly reminded that "data is the most important asset of the business." Given the strong affinity for big and fast-moving data, it might seem difficult to argue against this reasoning. But even if you assign the highest importance to data, that data means nothing without smart people who learn how to process it to the point of extracting the greatest possible value from it.

This is where tactical modeling comes in. Once you have a fairly good understanding of the strategic direction to be taken, more focus can be given to the implementation. When the implementation of the business model is primarily based on data, the outcome is mostly composed of the following elements:

- *Big nouns* are the modules. When there's a data-centric focus, the modules generally take on characteristics of data manipulation tools rather than business drivers: factories, entities, data access objects or "repositories," data transfer objects, data services, and data mappers.

- *Medium-sized nouns* are entities, business-centric services, and data manipulation tools. These were all listed in the previous point.

- *Small nouns* are the fields, attributes, or properties of the entities or other data-centric tools. Think of the detailed parts of any data object—those are small nouns.

During their training and consulting engagements, the authors enjoy asking others to describe their day from the time they awoke until the present time of that same day, but only with the use of nouns. Although perhaps expecting to hear several in the group speak up and rattle off "alarm, bathroom, closet, clothes, kitchen," and the like, it might be surprising that most have difficulty even getting started. That's because people don't think in nouns.

Instead, people think in concepts that, when communicated to other people, must be described by means of expressiveness. To do so, they need word forms and figures of speech that include nouns, but go far beyond them. When software is implemented without people making these efforts, it leaves software in a state of confusion. Each reader of source code must interpret the meaning from hundreds or thousands of big, medium-sized, and small nouns. This approach is so complex and fraught with peril that projects regularly fail as a result. It is simply impossible to keep in mind every single noun, or even a small number of them, and their impacts on all the many others. Clarity, narrow meaning, and clear behavioral intentions are vital.

This chapter highlights the importance of modeling business concepts using rich expressions, and augmenting the data and business rules with language that conveys the best ways for the business work that is done with the software to be carried out. Doing so will convey explicit meaning. Other guidance is available on these topics, such as the books *Implementing Domain-Driven Design* [IDDD] and the quick-start guide *Domain-Driven Design Distilled* [DDD-Distilled]. Here we consider the tools in less detail, but with enough information provided to understand the concepts.

Entities

An entity is used when modeling a conceptual whole that is an individual thing. Giving an entity individuality is done through generating and assigning it a unique identity. Its uniqueness must be achieved within the scope of the entity's life cycle. If the entity is considered a top-level concept within a modeling context, it must be assigned a globally unique identity. If an entity is held inside a parent entity, the child must be uniquely identified only within its parent. Note that it's the combination of the entity's module name, concept name, and generated identity that collectively make a given entity instance unique.

In the following, two entities are both assigned identity value 1, but they are globally unique because of their different module names and concept names:

```
com.nucoverage.underwriting.model.application.Application : 1
com.nucoverage.rate.model.rate.PremiumRate : 1
```

An entity can also be mutable (modifiable), and an object-based entity is very likely to be mutable, but that alone does not qualify it as an entity. That's because an entity can be immutable instead. Its uniqueness is the key to an entity being an entity, an individual thing in the model. In Figure 7.1, the `Application` is an entity and `applicationId` holds its unique identity.

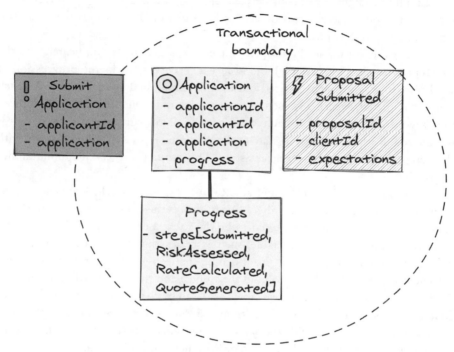

Figure 7.1 *An Entity and Value Object that compose an Aggregate as a transactional boundary.*

Value Objects

A Value Object is a modeled concept with one or more data attributes or properties that together compose a whole value; thus, it is a constant, an immutable state. Unlike an Entity, which has a unique identity, a Value Object's identity is not meant to be unique. It can be said that a value has no identity, but it does have a concept of identity. A value's identity is determined by its type name and all of its composed attributes/properties together; that is, its full state identifies each value. In the case of values, uniqueness of identity is not expected. Two values with the same identity are equal. Whether or not value identity makes sense to you, what's most important to understand is that equality between two or more values is quite common.

An example of a value is the integer 1. Two integer values of 1 are equal, and there can be many, many values of 1 in a single software process. Another example value is the text string "one". In some modern programming languages, the integer value 1 is a scalar, one of the basic single-value types. Other scalars include `long`, `boolean`, and `char`/`character`. Depending on the source of its definition, a string might or might not be considered a scalar. Yet, that's not important: A string is generally modeled as an array of `char` and its functional behavior provides useful, side-effect-free operations.

Other value types in Figure 7.1 include `ApplicationId` (indicated by the `applicationId` instance variable) and `Progress`. `Progress` tracks the progression of workflow processing steps carried out on the parent `Application` entity. As each step is completed, `Progress` is used to capture each individual step along with those that have already occurred. To achieve this tracking, the current state of `Progress` is not altered. Rather, the current state of the previous steps, if any, is combined with the new step to form a new `Progress` state. This maintains the value immutability constraint.

The logic of a value being immutable can be reasoned on when considering the value 1. The value 1 cannot be altered; it is always the value 1. It would make no sense if the value 1 could be altered to be the value 3 or 10 instead. This is not a discussion about an integer variable, such as `total`, that can hold the value 1. Of course, a mutable variable `total` itself can be changed—for example, by assigning it to hold the value 1 and later to hold the value 3 and then, later still, the value 10. The difference is that while the variable `total` can be changed, the immutable value that it holds, such as 1, is constant. Although a `Progress` state is more complex than an integer, it is designed with the same immutability constraint. A `Progress` state cannot be altered, but it can be used to derive a new value of type `Progress`.

Aggregates

Generally, some business rules will require certain data within a single parent object to remain consistent throughout the parent object's lifetime. Given that there is the parent object A, this is accomplished by placing behavior on A that simultaneously changes the data items that are managed within its consistency boundary. This kind of behavioral operation is known as atomicity; that is, the operation changes an entire subset of A's consistency-constrained data atomically. To maintain the consistency in a database, we can use an atomic translation. An atomic database translation is meant to create isolation around the data being persisted, similar to A's atomic behavioral operation, such that the data will always be written to disk without any interruption or change outside of the isolation area.

In a domain modeling context, an Aggregate is used to maintain a parent object's transactional boundary around its data. An Aggregate is modeled with at least one Entity, and that Entity holds zero or more other entities and at least one Value Object. It composes a whole domain concept. The outer Entity, referred to as the *root*, must have a global unique identity. That's why an Aggregate must hold at least one value, its unique identity. All other rules of an Entity hold for an Aggregate.

In Figure 7.2, `PolicyQuote` is the root entity that manages the concept's transactional boundary. The transactional boundary is needed because when an Aggregate is persisted to the database, all business state consistency rules must be met when the atomic database transaction commits. Whether we're using a relational database or a key–value store, the full state of a single Aggregate is atomically persisted. The same might not be possible for two or more such entity states, which emphasizes the need to think in terms of Aggregate transactional boundaries.

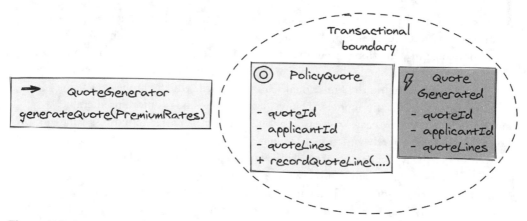

Figure 7.2 *A Domain Service is responsible for guiding a small business process.*

Domain Services

Sometimes a modeling situation calls for an operation to apply business rules that are not practical to implement as a member of the type on which it operates. This will be the case when the operation must supply more behavior than a typical instance method should, when the operation cuts across two or more instances or the same type, and when the operation must use instances of two or more different types. In such a modeling situation, use a Domain Service. A Domain Service provides one or more operations that don't obviously belong on an Entity or a Value Object as would normally be expected, and the service itself owns no operational state as does an Entity or Value Object.

Figure 7.2 shows the Domain Service named `QuoteGenerator`. It is responsible for accepting one parameter value named `PremiumRates`, translating it to one or more `QuoteLine` instances (which comprise a specific coverage and premium), and recording each on the `PolicyQuote` Aggregate. Note that when the final `QuoteLine` is recorded, the `QuoteGenerated` event is emitted.

An important difference between an Application Service and a Domain Service is that an Application Service must not contain business logic, while a Domain Service always does. If an Application Service is used to coordinate this use case, it would manage the transaction. Either way, the Domain Service would never do that.

Functional Behavior

Many approaches to domain modeling exist, but to date the object-oriented paradigm has completely dominated. There are ways,[1] however, of expressing domain behavior using pure functions rather than mutable objects. The section "Functional Core with Imperative Shell," in Chapter 8, "Foundation Architecture," discusses the benefits of leveraging the Functional Core approach, which emphasizes using pure functions for domain models. The result is that the code is more predictable, more easily tested, and easier to reason about. While it is easier to express functional behaviors in purely functional language, the good news is that there is no need to switch away from an object-oriented language to a functional one, because functional fundamentals can be used with practically any programming language. Contemporary object-oriented languages, such as Java and C#, incorporate functional constructs that enable functional programming even beyond the fundamentals. Although they don't have all the features of a full functional language,[2] implementing a domain model with functional behavior is readily achievable with such languages.

Domain modeling using the Domain-Driven Design approach works well with models expressed as functional behavior. Eric Evans, in his book *Domain-Driven*

---

1. Some people would say "better ways" to highlight the fact that the recent hype around the functional programming paradigm might make object-oriented programming appear to be outdated. However, the authors stress that each programming paradigm has its strengths and weaknesses, and that no single paradigm excels in every use case.

2. Functional programming features have been added to several object-oriented languages as new versions have streamed out to the market. This has resulted in multiparadigm languages, which make it easier to switch from object-oriented programming to functional programming, and back. Questions remain about how effective mixing paradigms in a language is, and whether it in some way hinders the expression of the business software model under development.

Design [DDD-Evans], stresses the importance of using "side-effect-free functions" to avoid unwanted and unintended consequences of calling an arbitrarily deep nesting of side-effect-generating operations. In fact, Value Objects, as described above, are an example of one way to implement functional behavior. When side effects are not avoided, the results cannot be predicted without a deep understanding of the implementation of each operation. When the complexity of side effects is unbounded, the solution becomes brittle because its quality cannot be ensured. The only way to avoid such pitfalls is by simplifying the code, which might include employing at least some functional behavior. Functional behavior tends to be useful with less effort. (There are plenty of examples of poorly written code in both paradigms, so don't expect any silver bullets delivered with a functional programming language.)

Consider an example of quoting a policy based on the risk and rate. The NuCoverage team working on the Underwriting Context has decided to use a functional behavior approach when modeling `PolicyQuote`:

```
public record PolicyQuote
{
    int QuoteId;
    int ApplicantId;
    List<QuoteLine> QuoteLines;
}
```

In this example, the `PolicyQuote` is modeled as an *immutable* record. Immutability describes the means of creating the record such that its state cannot be changed. This has at least two benefits:

- `PolicyQuote` instances can be passed to different functions without any fear that a function will modify their state. The unpredictability associated with mutable objects is eliminated.

- Instances can be shared in concurrent environments across threads because their immutable nature negates locking and the potential for deadlocks.

Even though these points might not be the main decision drivers for the NuCoverage team, it is helpful to understand that these benefits are available for free when immutability is designed in.

Defining immutable structures for domain concepts is the first step when employing functional behavior. Following this, NuCoverage must define the concrete behaviors with pure functions. One of those operations is recording `QuoteLine` instances to be composed by `PolicyQuote`. With the traditional OOP approach, a `RecordQuoteLine` operation would be invoked on a `PolicyQuote` instance, with its internal state being mutated to record the new QuoteLine. With the functional behavior approach, this kind of behavior is not permitted because PolicyQuote is immutable and once instantiated cannot be changed. But there is another approach, which does not require any mutation at all. The RecordQuoteLine operation can be implemented as a pure function:

```
public Tuple<PolicyQuote, List<DomainEvent>> RecordQuoteLine(
  PolicyQuote policyQuote,
  QuoteLine quoteLine)
{
  var newPolicyQuote =
        PolicyQuote.WithNewQuoteLine(policyQuote, quoteLine);

  var quoteLineRecorded =
        QuoteLineRecorded.Using(quoteId, applicantId, quoteLine);

  return Tuple.From(newPolicyQuote, quoteLineRecorded);
}
```

In this example, RecordQuoteLine is defined as a pure function: Every time the function is called with the same values, it yields the same result. This is meant to work similarly to the pure mathematical function, where the function power = x * x will always yield 4, if 2 is passed as an input parameter. The RecordQuoteLine function simply returns a tuple[3] composed of the new instance of PolicyQuote with a new QuoteLine appended to the new instance of the current collection of quote lines, along with a QuoteLineRecorded domain event.

Note that the input parameter policyQuote is never mutated. The primary advantage of this approach is that the RecordQuoteLine function has improved the predictability and testability of its behavior. There is no need to look into the implementation of this function, as there cannot be any observable side effect or unintended mutation of the current application state.

Another important benefit of the functional paradigm is that pure functions can be readily composed if the output type of the function to be composed matches the input type of the function composing it. The mechanics are beyond the scope of this book, but are provided in a follow-on implementation book, *Implementing Strategic Monoliths and Microservices* (Vernon & Jaskuła, Addison-Wesley, forthcoming).

The main takeaway of functional behavior is that it simplifies the surface of the abstractions used in the model, improving their predictability and testability. Given

---

3. A tuple represents a composition of two or more arbitrary types as a whole. Here, PolicyQuote and List<DomainEvent> are addressed as a single whole. Tuples are frequently used in functional programming because a function may return only one type of result. A tuple is a single value that holds multiple values.

the capabilities of modern object-oriented languages and the benefits they offer, there is a strong incentive to use them. At least initially, attempt functional programming using the "Functional Core with Imperative Shell" approach.

Applying the Tools

Domain modeling is one of the best places to experiment, and is exemplified by the rapid event-based learning described in Chapter 3, "Events-First Experimentation and Discovery." Experiments should be quickly performed, using names and behavioral expressions that best describe the business concepts being modeled. This can be done with sticky notes, with virtual whiteboards and other collaborative drawing tools, and—of course—in source code. These tools are applied in the remaining chapters of this book.

Many examples of these modeling techniques can be found in the books *Implementing Domain-Driven Design* [IDDD] and the quick-start guide *Domain-Driven Design Distilled* [DDD-Distilled].

Summary

This chapter introduced Domain-Driven Design tactical modeling tools, such as Entities, Value Objects, and Aggregates. The appropriate use of these tools depends on the modeling situations that they are intended to handle. Another modeling tool, functional behavior, is used to express domain model behavior using pure functions rather than mutable objects.

The primary messages within the chapter are as follows:

- Use an Entity when modeling a conceptual whole that is a uniquely identified individual thing and has a stateful life cycle.

- A Value Object encapsulates data attributes/properties that together compose a whole value, and provides side-effect-free behavior. Value Objects are immutable and make no attempt to identify themselves uniquely, but only by the whole value of their type and all combined attributes/properties.

- Aggregates model a whole concept that can be composed of one or more Entities and/or Value Objects, where a parent Entity represents a transactional consistency boundary.

- Use a Domain Service to model a business operation that is itself stateless and that would be misplaced if included as behavior on an Entity or Value Object.

- Functional behavior houses business rules in pure function, but doesn't require the use of a pure functional programming language. In other words, a contemporary object-oriented language, such as Java or C#, can be used to implement pure functions.

This concludes Part II. We now transition to Part III, "Events-First Architecture," which discusses software architectural styles and patterns that offer pragmatic purpose rather than technical intrigue.

References

[**DDD-Distilled**] Vaughn Vernon. *Domain-Driven Design Distilled*. Boston, MA: Addison-Wesley, 2016.

[**DDD-Evans**] Eric Evans. *Domain-Driven Design: Tackling Complexity in the Heart of Software*. Boston, MA: Addison-Wesley, 2004.

[**IDDD**] Vaughn Vernon. *Implementing Domain-Driven Design*. Boston, MA: Addison-Wesley, 2013.

Part III

Events-First Architecture

Executive Summary

This part of the book introduces the software architecture styles and mechanics that lead to highly versatile and adaptable applications and services. It does take on a more technical slant, but the illustrative diagrams and explanations should be palatable for many who do not regularly practice software development. At a minimum, it is recommended that executives and other senior management have a fundamental understanding of making good software architecture decisions, which help practitioners avoid the bad ones. Armed with this knowledge, feel free to converse with software architects and developers, and inquire about the choices they've made. Challenge them about these decisions, which must stand up to the test of time and relentless change.

Chapter 8: Foundation Architecture

Every software architecture must start somewhere, and this chapter provides the building blocks to begin such an effort. As expected, some foundational principles must be set and followed to make a software architecture flexible enough to host any number of decisions made early, mid-term, and late in the software development life cycle.

- You must understand which software architecture styles and decisions are commonly used, and which ones fit more narrowly defined system-building situations.

- Using the Ports and Adapters style can establish the most flexible architecture possible, and leave openings for early and late decisions as needed. Further, consider four options that can be used inside the Ports and Adapters style, depending on the specific context being constructed.

- Consider using modularization to address contextual divisions for both Monoliths and Microservices, and for hybrids of both.

- Gain a primary understanding of REST, a widely used Web style of browser-to-server communication, while discovering that REST is much more versatile than most developers think.

- Grasp the critical nature of supporting architectural requirements that are not driven by user feature–based functionality: security, privacy, performance, scalability, resilience, and complexity.

Chapter 9: Message- and Event-Driven Architectures

There are numerous reasons to use message-based and event-driven architectures. Depending on familiar request–response introduces multiple points of failure, including ones that are notorious for causing cascading outages. The nature of distributed systems that operate over networks, as well as in cloud and multi-cloud environments, calls for tolerating latency, whose scale is unpredictable at any given time. It would be better for systems and subsystems to embrace latency, by designing architectures that deal gracefully with it. That is exactly what messaging infrastructure supports, and messaging is the way the events are generally offered for consumption. This approach all but erases concerns over network latency, and makes it possible to deliver more responsive systems because the message-based foundation underpins and supports elastic and resilient subsystems and their internal runtime components.

- A common use case in a large system is for multiple business capabilities to share in a step-by-step workflow, taking it from start to finish. For example, when an applicant requests an insurance policy, (1) their application must be validated for correct and full data. Next, (2) a risk assessment must be performed on the application. If the risks are acceptable, (3) a premium rate must be calculated. At that point, (4) a quote is generated, and (5) the applicant is given the opportunity to accept it. If the offer is accepted, then (6) the policy is underwritten.

- All of the steps must be managed by the system, and this chapter explains two options that can be used to do so: choreography and orchestration.

- Choreography is a process in which the decision to fulfill a given workflow step is left up to the individual subsystems. Each contextual subsystem must understand the stimulus, such as an event notification, that signals that a given step must happen next. Choreography is best reserved for simpler process workflows with few required steps.

- Orchestration is a process in which a central control mechanism guides the workflows steps by commanding each one to take place when and as directed. Orchestration is most useful when a process includes several or many complex steps, such as the policy underwriting workflow.

- Doing the simplest thing that could possibly work is generally the best choice. One such thing is to feed events to interested subsystems through a Web-based request–response procedure. This technique uses event logs stored in disk files similar to Web server static content (e.g., HTML pages and images), which are served to clients one log at a time upon request. It's based on the scale and performance of the Web. The fact that the server might not be available from time to time is generally not problematic. Clients already assume latency exists between things that have happened on the server subsystem and one or more steps required in reaction on the client subsystem to bring them into harmony.

- An architectural technique is introduced as a means to track all data changes in a subsystem, such that audit trails of the changes are maintained over the subsystem's life cycle. This approach is generally most useful when government or industry regulations demand proof of which data changed and when that change happened.

- Sometimes it's helpful to treat the data that changes on user command differently than the data that the same user views to make decisions about which data changes should be commanded. This is the case when the shape and content of the data that users view is a richer aggregation of information than the more limited data that changes on command. This architecture technique creates a division between the two kinds of data, so that each side can be custom optimized for how it is used.

There is no need to be a software architect to appreciate the simple power packed into the architecture guidance offered in the chapters in Part III. Every executive and other senior managers who invest in software innovation as a competitive differentiator must be conversant with the architectural decisions being made on their behalf. Part III provides a highly approachable treatment of this topic for executives and software professionals alike.

Chapter 8

Foundation Architecture

It seems that every book that discusses software architecture in any way attempts to define software architecture. Some examples from other sources follow.

> The software architecture of a program or computing system is the structure or structures of the system, which comprise software elements, the externally visible properties of those elements, and the relations among them. [Software Architecture in Practice]
>
> The fundamental organization of a system embodied in its components, their relationships to each other, and to the environment, and the principles guiding its design and evolution. [ISO 47010]
>
> All architecture is design, but not all design is architecture. Architecture represents the significant design decisions that shape the form and function of a system, where significant is measured by the cost of change. Every software-intensive system has an architecture: some are intentional; a few are accidental; most are emergent. All meaningful architecture springs from a living, vibrant process of deliberation, design, and decision.
>
> —Grady Booch

Okay, these are good. There are probably some ideas that are implied, but not explicitly stated. Maybe another attempt is worthwhile. The following is the authors' attempt to freshen the older definitions. This one reflects what this book discusses, and has been used for several years.

> There are at least three major sets of statements that help define software architecture. (1) Architecture is the result of team communication that leads to a shared understanding of business goals, how to balance the goals of various stakeholders, and how to understand and address the quality attributes–related impactful

features; that is, there cannot be effective architecture without a purpose, and purpose cannot be well understood without socializing intent through communication. (2) The architectural intent is captured and articulated as a set of current and future decisions for the whole system and individual services by specifying purposeful flexibility and constraints that support the software's initial and ongoing development. (3) The architectural intent and decisions are spoken, rendered into visual form—graphical and/or textual—and expressed in software artifacts that have modular structure and well-defined component-to-component protocols.

Note that there's a lot of communication going on within all three parts of this definition, and it seems to be communication that is lacking in the more traditional definitions. Sound architecture cannot be developed in a vacuum. No part of the definition suggests specific tooling or formats, which should be chosen by the teams involved. That's all part of socializing the software's intent through communication, and the best way to capture and articulate that intent should be determined by those who create it. Accepting feedback is an invaluable skill to be developed.

The authors also recommend reading another book in the Vaughn Vernon Signature Series—namely, *Continuous Architecture in Practice* by Murat Erder, Pierre Pureur, and Eoin Woods. It provides in-depth advice on how to apply a continuous approach to software architecture and contains in-depth guidance for addressing key quality attributes and cross-cutting concerns, such as security, performance, scalability, resilience, data, and emerging technologies, all illustrated using a start-to-finish case study [Continuous-Architecture].

It's not uncommon for software architecture to be thrown under the bus, dismissed as some sort of formal and useless rite of common programmers seeking a higher pay grade. There are indeed overengineered architectures, but those come from the immature. Here's the point:

> If you think that good architecture is expensive, try bad architecture.
> —Brian Foote [BBoM]

You can pay for architecture now, or you can pay for it later. The authors suggest now would be best. All the same, there is no need for good architecture to be expensive. This chapter backs up that claim and throws overengineered architectures under the bus.

We'll consider a number of architectural styles and architecture patterns that specifically support events-first systems. This is where the understanding gained from previous chapters that feature business drivers now point toward making wise decisions based on how the overall software architecture will support the business goals. There is clearly a danger of selecting among a broad collection of arbitrary architectural choices just because they seem useful, or even cool, as if a potpourri of architecture decisions will automatically produce benefits. Again, the purpose of architecture decisions is to achieve the quality attribute requirements, such as flexibility, security, performance, and scalability. Without those requirements, architecture decisions are meaningless and often harmful. Deep details are out of scope for the book, but are provided in our follow-on implementation book, *Implementing Strategic Monoliths and Microservices* (Vernon & Jaskuła, Addison-Wesley, forthcoming).

Next up on our agenda are a selection of modern architecture options, each of which is described in terms of its overall definition, but also qualified according to its strengths and weaknesses. As with everything involved in software development, the architectural decisions made by teams will tend to have both positive and negative consequences.

Architectural Styles, Patterns, and Decision Drivers

To reiterate, not every architecture style and pattern will suit any set of arbitrary business, technical, scale, performance, or throughput constraints. The specific set of constraints will drive a purposeful architecture. Likewise, not every Bounded Context is equally important in terms of business strategic goals, which has an important influence on architectural decisions.

The architectures discussed here include those at both the system level and the service/application level. A system-level architecture defines how various subsystems work together to address the quality attributes related to shared impactful features, including software collaboration and integration. A service/application architecture defines how a single subsystem (service/application) addresses the quality attributes related to its own impactful features.

Chapter 2, "Essential Strategic Learning Tools," discussed Architecture Decision Records (ADRs) as a means to determine the business and technical drivers around each decision made regarding software architecture. ADRs are used by teams to help explain why various styles and patterns are helpful, but they also highlight the potential negative consequences of applying those choices in a given solution.

Ports and Adapters (Hexagonal)

One of the most versatile architecture styles is Ports and Adapters, also known as Hexagonal. This style inherits concepts from the traditional Layers architecture [POSA1], but it emphasizes different strengths and has much less overhead. Some of the highlighted strengths are based on contemporary software drivers, such as tests and loose coupling.

> Allow an application to equally be driven by users, programs, automated tests, or batch scripts, and to be developed and tested in isolation from its eventual run-time devices and databases. [PortsAdapters]

Sometimes problems are encountered due to the fundamental differences between the external devices and other mechanisms used to interact with a software service or application. These mechanisms might be a browser, a mobile phone or tablet, another service or application, a streaming or messaging mechanism, batch processing, tests, or other computing resources. The service or application should not be exposed directly to the interactions with the outside world because that will interfere with the technology-independent business logic and processing.

To sidestep the potential problems of coupling the service or application to various kinds of input–output devices and mechanisms, create a layer of adapters between the two sets of concerns. As Figure 8.1 illustrates, the Ports and Adapters architecture style defines such a separation by considering one part of the architecture as the *outside* and the other as the *inside*. On the outside left are a number of driver types, also called *primary actors*: HTTP, externally called procedures or functions, and flowing streams or messages. On the outside right are a number of driven types, also called *secondary actors*: payment gateways, databases, procedure or function outward calls, and flowing streams of messages. The locations of the ports are shown by the bold border around the inside circular Application area.

> **Note**
> The outside-left driver actors send input requests or notifications. The outside-right driven actors are driven by the application inside to fulfill use cases: Some are bidirectional, providing both requests and responses; others receive one-way notifications. The outside-left adapters are needed to adapt incoming requests or notifications to data types that the Application can consume to carry out its supported use cases. The Application uses adapters on the outside right to persist and query, as well as to deliver notifications. Only the outside left is aware of the existence of use cases on the inside. The outside-right driven actors are oblivious to use cases.

Figure 8.1 does not contain an exhaustive set of incoming and outgoing adapter types. Any given adapter type is not limited to creating a single instance. The adapters shown are those typically used by services and applications. There need not be a single database type or instance, for example, or a single stream source and sink, or one messaging topic. The elements in Figure 8.1 are only representative of the large number of possibilities.

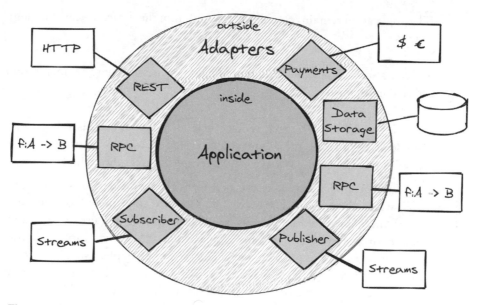

Figure 8.1 *Ports and Adapters architecture, also known as Hexagonal, Clean, and Onion.*[1]

Some of the distinct advantages of Ports and Adapters are as follows:

- Each of the two main layers can be tested in isolation; that is, any adapter can be tested without the need for a specific application implementation, and the application may be tested without any given adapter implementation.

- All device adapters can be backed by both mocks/fakes and with actual mechanisms. (This does not mean that the concrete adapters aren't tested, because they always are. Rather, mocks/fakes are used to test units that are dependent on the adapters.)

- Each actual mechanism might have multiple types (e.g., Postgres, MariaDB, HSQLDB, AWS DynamoDB, Google Cloud Bigtable, or Azure Cosmos DB).

- New adapter types can be introduced as needed without big upfront architecture/design; that is, the team can employ an #agile and emergent architectural design.

- Multiple outside adapters can use the same inside Application layer facilities.

---

1. Some consider Onion architecture to be closer to Layers, which does not distinguish the outside and inside in terms of adapters. Some consider Onion to be synonymous with Layers. Rather than have several thousand people complain about the omission of Onion, it is mentioned here, along with a potential caveat (or at least a specific nuance).

- The application remains completely isolated from the device-level technology details.

There can also be disadvantages, depending on decisions regarding integration with external mechanisms:

- The use of data mappers, such as object-relational mapping tools, might cause complexity. However, this disadvantage is due to the choice of persistence integration, not because Ports and Adapters itself forces these choices.

- The domain model can make use of integrations with remote services and applications through an interface. The interface implementation can leak underlying implementation details, such as exceptions and errors caused by network and service failures. This can be avoided by a few means, including those discussed in this chapter and Chapter 9. For example, using Functional Core with Imperative Shell keeps the domain model entirely isolated from external remote integrations. The Imperative Shell must do all integration work separately and not involve the Functional Core. The Functional Core provides only pure, side-effect-free functions.

- Other disadvantages may include additional complexity by requiring more layers; creation and maintenance cost; and lack of guidance on organizing code (directories and layers). The authors have not experienced these claims in the least, and wonder if those who cite these so-called problems have read the literature and understand Ports and Adapters at all. Experience has shown us that a basic, well-structured architecture can be constructed in a matter of minutes, with far fewer layers than a typical N-tier application requires. The chosen mechanisms and related adapters can increase the system's complexity, but those have nothing to do with the architecture style. Such a system would have at least the same complexity without the use of a Ports and Adapters architecture.

The Ports and Adapters architecture isolates the inside Application layer from the details of device input–output. The Application is focused solely on business-driven use cases. Multiple outside-left adapter types may effectively reuse Application ports to perform operations rather than a separate port type being required for every adapter type.

This architectural design can employ the Dependency Inversion Principle [SOLID], in which the infrastructure becomes dependent on the Application, rather than the Application being dependent on the infrastructure. The Application can steer clear of concrete device dependencies because any such dependencies on the outside-right secondary actor types are managed through adapter interfaces. The adapter interfaces are provided to the Application by means of its service constructors/initializers or possibly container-based dependency injection.

Adapters should adhere to the Single Responsibility Principle [SOLID], meaning that a single adapter should focus on adapting input–output that it is designated to support and no more. No adapter should depend on another adapter.

Some have claimed that Ports and Adapters is an unnecessarily heavyweight style of architecture, but frankly this criticism is both unfounded and unsubstantiated when one considers the facts. As Figure 8.1 illustrates, a Ports and Adapters software architecture includes exactly the number and kinds of adapters needed for a given input and output port—no more, no less. There are also only two primary layers.

Certainly any architecture style and pattern can suffer from overengineering. Don't expect Ports and Adapters to, on its own, prevent such poorly executed implementations. As Figure 8.2 shows, the nature of the Application inside is quite versatile; that is, the pattern doesn't define how the Application inside should work. What is more, not even one of the four natures shown is at all complex, although each has its advantages (as described in the sections that follow).

Service Layer with Transaction Scripts

A Service Layer is described as follows:

> Defines an application's boundary and its set of available operations from the perspective of interfacing client layers [i.e., port adapters]. It encapsulates the application's business logic, controlling transactions and coordinating responses in the implementation of its operations. [Fowler-PEAA]

A Service Layer supplies application-specific services, typically known as Application Services, as depicted in the first two variants, from left to right, in Figure 8.2. At the top left of this figure is a Service Layer composed of only Application Services. This example uses some form of Transaction Scripts, Active Record, or Data Access Objects [Fowler-PEAA]. These three patterns are used for Create-Read-Update-Delete (CRUD) operations without incurring the overhead of a domain model. They are all useful when the Bounded Context is mainly focused on data collection and performs simple creates and updates, and occasional deletes. There is no business-driven complexity. In terms of Cynefin—as explained in Chapter 2, in the section "Using Cynefin to Make Decisions"—this is clear/obvious/simple. The primary work lies in using the Application Services for writing and reading, with possible encapsulation of data accesses to and from a database, but any such access encapsulation is purposely kept trivial.

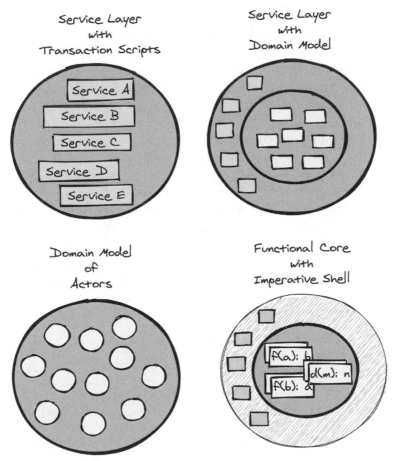

Figure 8.2 *Ports and Adapters architecture with varying Application types.*

Service Layer with Domain Model

In the top-right Service Layer in Figure 8.2, the Application Services are accompanied by a domain model at the heart of the software below the Application Layer. A domain model is used when (as described in Chapter 7) domain[2] complexity needs to be solved in an innovative, core, differentiating business software initiative. In the system depicted in Figure 8.2, the Application Services are used to manage the use case coordination and database usage, including transactions.[3]

---

2. Here again, *domain* means a sphere of knowledge.

3. Use cases and transactions may be managed by other means, such as in the adapters, negating the Service Layer. Even so, you should be careful not to place too many responsibilities on adapters.

Domain Model of Actors

The Actor Model is a form of message-driven object model that provides specialized and well-insulated capabilities in a highly concurrent and scalable compute environment, as further described in Chapter 9, "Message- and Event-Driven Architectures."[4] The incoming adapters dispatch directly into the domain model objects. Although there are no Application Services, the domain model might provide actor-based Domain Services.

This implementation of Ports and Adapters provides the simplest and most concise rendering of this architecture style, packing tremendous power into a small form factor.[5] An actor, by design, is physically isolated from other actors—which emphasizes even more strongly the sound distinction between business logic and infrastructure concerns.

Functional Core with Imperative Shell

Functional Core with Imperative Shell bridges the gap between Ports and Adapters and Functional Programming. Although inspired by functional programming principles, Functional Core is readily applicable even with programming paradigms that are not purely functional. For example, the fundamental strengths of functional programming can be achieved with object-oriented programming languages such as Java and C#. The idea behind this approach is to write pure functional code for the domain model, while moving the side effects[6] of imperative code to the surrounding environment, known as the Imperative Shell. The Functional Core is thus predictable, more easily testable, and used where it counts most.

The predictability comes from the fact that a pure function always returns the same result for the same input and never causes observable side effects. Likewise, pure functions are easier to test, because the focus is on meaningful inputs and outputs. There is no need to create mocks or stubs, so no knowledge of unit test internals is needed. Actually, avoiding mocks altogether is one of the goals of Functional Core with Imperative Shell.

Another advantage is that this approach decreases the risk of leaking technical concerns when domain code calls a side-effectful domain service through

---

4. This is different from the Service Layer with Domain Model because the underlying actor platform is designed to take this burden off of application developers, rather than to move it elsewhere in the team's code.

5. Although typically a hardware term, *form factor* seems appropriate here because individual actors in an Actor Model have been referred to as tiny computers.

6. A side effect is the modification of some state variable value(s) outside its local environment; in other words, the operation has an observable effect besides returning a value (the main effect) to the invoker of the operation. For example, execution of an I/O operation such as a network call or database call is a side effect.

an interface. For example, error handling can be problematic. Using a REST-over-HTTP endpoint can result in not just expected kinds of errors, such as `404 Resource Not Found`, but also unexpected errors, such as network failures. Error-handling logic can be challenging to test and, unless extreme caution is used, can propagate throughout the whole of the domain model. Deep details of this issue are beyond the scope of this book but are provided in the follow-on implementation book.

Ports and Adapters Architecture Nature Comparison

Table 8.1 compares the four natures described here and outlines how they differ in usefulness, complexity, model isolation, evolvability, quality attributes, and testability.

Modularization

The importance of modularity has already been established, and we've even provided a few examples of it. This section applies an architectural focus to modularization. Figure 8.3 provides an example of a modular Monolith.

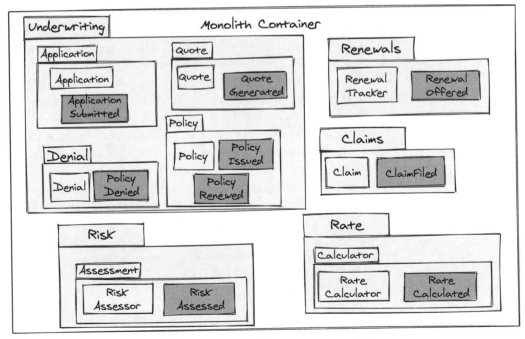

Figure 8.3 *Monolith container with five Bounded Contexts as modules.*

Table 8.1 *Comparison of Different Architectural Approaches to Domain Model Implementation and Their Impacts*

	Service Layer with Transaction Scripts	Service Layer with Domain Model	Domain Model of Actors	Functional Core with Imperative Shell
Isolated domain model	No; focused on data updates	Yes	Yes	Yes
Business complexity	Low; not many or no business rules, mainly data focused	High	High	High
Domain model isolation from infrastructure	Low technical overhead, but the domain model is not present, so it involves mainly data access encapsulation. Very close to infrastructure concerns, which pose a risk for long-term maintenance.	Domain model is well isolated from infrastructure but requires constant effort to keep the isolation free of infrastructure concerns. It may require application services for coordination.	Domain model is very well isolated from infrastructure concerns. Isolation is embedded in the underlying Actor Model implementation, which helps to maintain domain models while keeping them free of any infrastructure concerns.	Domain model is very well isolated from infrastructure concerns because it is based on pure functions. This design prevents pure functions from interacting with infrastructure and directly causing side effects, which is guaranteed to keep the domain model isolated.
Evolvability	Low. The lack of a domain model makes it difficult to evolve toward more complex business scenarios.	Medium to high. Depends on how the domain model is kept isolated from other infrastructural concerns.	Very high. It is very simple to add business behavior.	Very high. It is very simple to add new business behavior.
Scalability, performance, and concurrency	Very low.	Low to high. It may require implementation of technical code around the domain model to keep up with scalability and concurrency requirements. The domain model itself is not geared toward concurrency so the surrounding code has to take care of it.	Very high. The Actor Model implementation guarantees the scalability, performance, and concurrency out of the box.	High. The domain model is based on pure functions, which means it is concurrency enabled. However, the Imperative Shell code may require some tenacity to make it more scalable and performant.
Testability	Low. May be difficult based on how infrastructure concerns are managed.	High. Domain model is well isolated, so it is simple to test.	High. Every aspect is testable.	High. The domain model is very simple to test. However, the Imperative Shell is not easily tested except through integration tests.

The container itself is not necessarily special in its own right. It's just a way to deploy a body of executable software. It might be a Docker container, and might even have a Kubernetes Pod around it for a co-located, co-scheduled, and shared runtime context. Yet, the focus in the Monolith container is on the five major modules inside. Each of these modules represents a Bounded Context. As previously noted, a Monolith is a great place to start early in software architecture development, and possibly even a long-term solution.

The fact that the five modules are deployed together in a single container is not an excuse for the Bounded Context modules to be tightly coupled or to have any strong, infiltrating dependencies between them. That is absolutely not acceptable, in the same way that it is unacceptable to have such dependencies between Microservices. The loose coupling between Bounded Contexts can be achieved using Context Maps, like those described in Chapter 6, "Mapping, Failing, and Succeeding—Choose Two." Figure 8.3 indicates the formation of Published Languages among the contexts. Moreover, the related events might be communicated across contexts using an asynchronous messaging mechanism, which is practical even in a Monolithic solution, but a lightweight choice rather than heavyweight component.

Inside each of the five Bounded Context modules are internal modules specific to the respective Ubiquitous Language. Each internal module shown encompasses cohesive model components, with no dependencies on other modules, or perhaps acyclic ones.

Over time, it is observed that two of the major modules, Risk and Rate, have a tendency to change at a pace that is significantly faster than the rate of change for the other three modules; the Risk and Rate modules also changes in ways that are different from each other. As a result of this observation, the teams determine that it would be best to split the Risk and Rate modules off into two independent Microservices. Figure 8.4 shows the outcome. The solution has now become three outer containers, which have a similar or identical nature as the original Monolith container. Possibly each is a Docker container, and each of those might have a respective Kubernetes Pod containing it.

The three separate containers have a network in between them, which introduces the challenges associated with distributed systems. Even so, if care was taken early on in the process of creating the original Monolithic architecture, having a messaging mechanism between modularized contexts should have forced each message publisher and subscriber to design around concerns related to nondeterministic latency, unsequenced order, and multiplicity of deliveries. As previously stated, the original introduction of a messaging mechanism for the Monolith could be lightweight, but now this would be replaced with a more robust mechanism. There will likely be some challenges beyond these when a cloud network and other infrastructure are involved, but they should not be major surprises—unlike when networks are perceived as a "free lunch."

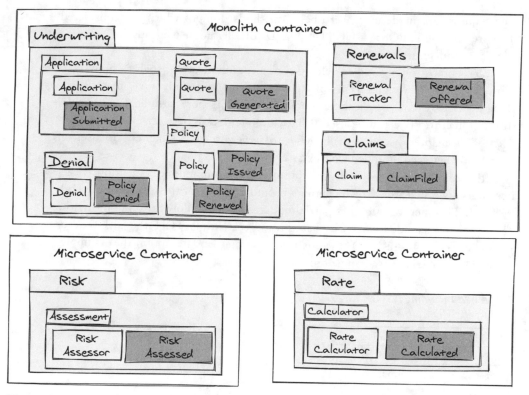

Figure 8.4 *A Monolith container and two Microservice containers with five total Bounded Contexts.*

All of the aforementioned rate-of-change and nondeterministic messaging drivers demonstrate that the system architecture serves a purpose, rather than the system becoming the host of an architecture that meets the desires and curiosities of its architects.

REST Request–Response

The REST architecture style and pattern supports requests and responses generated during the exchange of application resources. The exchanges of application state generally use non-native representations (e.g., digital data is rendered in a text-based format). The industry-standard implementation of REST is HTTP, which is not only a network transport protocol but also a protocol for exchanging and modifying information. HTTP even supports application workflows by means of hypermedia, meaning that links to related data are embedded in the resource exchanges.

The requests are made using verb-based methods, four of which are considered the bare minimum: POST, GET, PUT, and DELETE. These methods are meant to operate on full entity-based resources.

REST is most often used for client–server communication, such as between a browser and a server. REST is often considered useful only for Create-Read-Update-Delete (CRUD) applications, but it is actually far more versatile. For example, this architecture style can be used to provide integration between Bounded Contexts. This chapter discusses the browser-to-server use case. Chapter 9 focuses on integration between Bounded Contexts.

Although only four methods are considered the minimum, as mentioned earlier and shown in Table 8.2, the authors promote the use of the fifth verb method, PATCH. This method supports partial updates—which allow for pinpointing the specific changes made to an entity-based resource. With PATCH, the CRUD acronym is extended to CRUUD; there is now a second Update option that is implemented for partial entity changes only.

Table 8.2 *Including PATCH for Partial Updates Forms CRUUD Rather Than CRUD*

POST	Create
GET	Read
PUT	Update
PATCH	Update, Partial
DELETE	Delete

In a PUT-based update, the intention is to replace the entire entity state. When doing so, if only a small portion of the entity is actually modified, it is difficult for the server-side application to determine what specific update occurred. If the use case implementation is to produce an event-based outcome, it's overly complicated to identify what the fine-grained event should be. This results in events being very coarse-grained. When the entire state of the entity is packed into a single event, and that event is named, for example, *Application Updated*, both everything and nothing are communicated at the same time. The consumer of the event must perform some sort of difference comparison based on an older state; otherwise, it might apply the full state in a destructive or error-inducing way.

As indicated by Figure 8.5, cumbersome state modification determination is not the case when using PATCH. With a partial update, it is straightforward to determine what the fine-grained event-based outcome is for the use case, because it is clear exactly what changed. A key advantage of the architecture shown in Figure 8.5

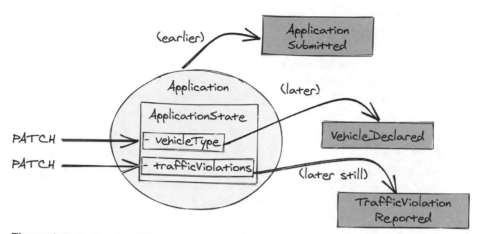

Figure 8.5 *Performing CRUUD partial updates makes pinpointing event types and their content simple.*

is that subsequent risk reassessment and rate recalculation can be performed more quickly because only the limited amount of data changed is precisely communicated by a specific event.

> **Note**
>
> Something similar to PATCH can be accomplished using PUT, but the submitted entity must indicate what in the full payload has changed. Using PUT reduces the number of exposed URIs that are required by PATCH,[7] and it may be considered a way to reduce the client's awareness of additional URIs. Yet, if the team is employing the ideas of HATEOAS,[8] there is no need for the client to hard-code access to resources.

Chapter 9 discusses how REST supports message- and event-driven architectures.

---

7. PUT creates overhead: The full entity payload must cross the network twice; the client must understand how to indicate a partially changed entity; and the server must know how to dispatch by means of the indicator.

8. Hypertext As The Engine Of Application State (HATEOAS): This acronym, which many don't know how to pronounce, represents the idea that once a client uses GET on a top-level, "minted" URI, all other resources are available through links provided in the response payload. This continually guides the client through everything the service/application makes available to that client.

Quality Attributes

The foundation architecture includes quality attributes. Among the many possible quality attributes, we have chosen to discuss here a subset that we consider to be the most salient: Security, Privacy, Performance, Scalability, Resilience, and Complexity. The sections that follow discuss the trade-offs involved in each of these.

> **Note**
> Readers interested in learning more about addressing quality attributes can refer to *Continuous Architecture in Practice* [Continuous-Architecture], a book in the Vaughn Vernon Signature Series.

Security

Nowadays, it is difficult to imagine a company not handling at least a part of its business activities using online technologies. Exposing the business enterprise to even partially open access can be dangerous, though. Whether it relies on a publicly accessible website, HTTP APIs, or diverse integration endpoints with partners reaching in through private networks or VPNs, open access poses multiple threats to business security.

For example, data might be stolen or corrupted. General computing resources running day-to-day operations might be infected with viruses and compromised. There is also the possibility that various attacks and infiltrations might require considerable time to detect, and might even go unnoticed until severe damage is done. In the worst of cases, the damage might bring the whole business down. Such potential threats can cause security team members to "sleep with one eye open."

Consider one of the most devastating cyber-attacks ever [CyberAttack]. Within hours of its first appearance, the malware known as NotPetya wormed its way beyond a small Ukrainian software business to countless devices around the world. It paralyzed global shipping corporations, including FedEx, TNT Express, and Maersk, for several weeks, causing more than $10 billion in damages. Not every cyber-attack has such extensive penetration or such dramatic consequences, but according to data collected by Juniper Research [Juniper] and *Forbes*, cyber-crimes accounted for $2 trillion in losses in 2019 alone. Further, it is estimated that total losses could reach three times that number sometime in 2021. The University of Maryland found recently that a cyber-attack takes place every 39 seconds, while security firm McAfee reported 480 new high-tech threats are introduced every minute. According to one research reference, a large percentage of data breaches are caused by application security problems, rather than by infrastructure [Verizon-SEC].

That it is essential to develop systems with thoroughly designed security features might be the understatement of a decade. Security must be a design goal [Secure-By-Design] and it must be complete [Agile-SEC]. Otherwise, a breach of business assets might lead to extreme financial losses and damage to a firm's reputation via headline news. Far too often, security is implemented or strengthened only as an afterthought, leading to exposure of the system to would-be attackers through unknown gaps.

Note that Microservices have different attack surfaces that can make threats more serious due to the myriad opportunities for exploiting them. These opportunities are generally due to the services' distributed state, network access, and distributed security mechanisms. A Monolithic architecture can use an in-process security context that is naturally available to the whole application. In contrast, because Microservices are composed of multiple distributed services, the security context has to be passed from one service to another.

The most prominent example of inter-service security dependencies is seen with establishing and verifying user identity. In a Monolithic system, user identity can be established once when a user signs in, and remains available to every module until the user finally signs out. When architecting a Microservice-based system, it is inconceivable that users be required to sign in to every service that is required to fulfill the business system's operations.

When working within the constraints of a Microservices architecture, it can be quite challenging to correctly implement viable security. This leads to legitimate fears of getting it wrong amidst the challenges and unknowns related to which aspects might be vulnerable. Yet, companies have a wealth of industry standards and tools on which they can rely. Modern application developers must implement at least two aspects of security:

- *Authentication:* The process of verifying the identity of a human or another software component attempting to access a Monolith or Microservice. The main goal is to verify the user's credentials, such as a user identity and password, or a secret key that provides access to an API. Many different kinds of authentication protocols exist, but the most commonly used is OpenID Connect, which employs Access Tokens (JWT) as proof of authentication.

- *Authorization:* The process of verifying that the authenticated user is allowed to perform a requested operation in a specific business context and on specific data. Most of the time, this involves a combination of role-based security along with associated access control lists (ACLs) or permissions, which support fine-grained authorization. The former grants broad permission for legitimate users to access certain high-level business functionality.

The latter grants authentic users authorized access to specific operations on specialized components by ensuring each plays the necessary user role and has the required permissions to do so.

Modern authentication and authorization protocols rely heavily on the use of security access and bearer tokens, and system security architectures should require tokens to be included in specific HTTP, RPC, and messaging requests. Access/bearer tokens are highly secure and are retrieved through authentication. A token carries enough information to prove user authenticity and authority to use a given service offering. Tokens might expire after a standard time frame but can be renewed through regeneration. The regeneration ensures that appropriate access is still available to the user while preventing attackers from breaking the token's secret encoding by limiting its lifetime. That's accomplished by making the security mechanisms' cryptography a moving target.

The following practices can be incorporated very early on in the development process to design systems with security as a central concern:

- **Design for security:** Security must not be an afterthought, as that lackadaisical approach results in designs that are brittle, are fragile, and lack optimal security.

- **Use HTTPS by default:** Transport Layer Security (TLS) is designed to ensure privacy and data integrity between computer applications. HTTPS requires a certificate. Certificates can be generated through a cloud provider. A certificate grants permissions to use encrypted communication via the Public Key Infrastructure (PKI), and also authenticates the identity of the certificate's holder.

- **Encrypt and protect secrets:** Applications will likely have secrets that they use for communication. These secrets might be an API key, or a client secret, or credentials for basic authentication. All of these secrets should be encrypted and should be stored and managed by third-party cloud services. The Azure Key Vault is one example of a key manager.

- **Security checks as part of the deployment pipeline[9]:** Static Application Security Testing (SAST) tools are designed to analyze source code or compiled versions of code to help find security flaws. Proactively use these SAST

---

9. These techniques are helpful and good to use, but tools are lacking, which can make it challenging to accomplish the intended aims fully. SAST reveals only limited types of security flaws. Thus, it is necessary to perform a number of other security tests, both automated and manual.

tools to uncover flaws through invaluable, immediate feedback; don't rely on late discovery of vulnerabilities.

- **Don't create your own security mechanisms or crypto code:** Not everyone is a security expert. Rely on external tools and libraries that are battle tested through use by many thousands of developers, systems, and individual services.

There are many other points to consider when implementing systems and individual services, whether using Monoliths, Microservices, or both together. Taking into account the points outlined here will certainly contribute to improved security. The follow-on book provides detailed information on architecting and implementing security.

Privacy

Disk storage has become very inexpensive. That being so, many businesses desire to capture and store as much information as possible, even when that information has undetermined value and may potentially be discarded later. Data has become known as the most valuable business asset, so incurring the limited expense of storing data, even though it potentially has no value seems, worthwhile. Useful knowledge about customers, competitors, and markets can be gained through crunching huge amounts of data by means of machine learning (ML) algorithms that yield opportunities to transform data into business intelligence. In this effort, businesses always collect some data that could be used to derive information about individual humans. Although potentially valuable, care must be taken when storing and processing such personal information.

Storing copious amounts of data about individuals can be a double-edged sword. One downside is that snatching vast amounts of personal information, or even small amounts of high-value personal information, is often the aim of those who launch security attacks. Indeed, theft of sensitive data is one of the greatest motivations of malicious individuals. One can cite many examples of credit card numbers being stolen, even from tech giants such as Apple. Storing the bare minimum of data required for a business to operate eliminates this security threat, since it reduces the business's value as a target.

In some countries, governmental policies define how personal data can be collected, stored, and used. The most well-known policy is the "General Data Protection Regulation" [GDPR]. Its primary aim is to give individuals control over their personal data. GDPR guarantees individuals the right to erase any of their personal data, such as their email address, government-issued identity, IP address, name, street address, date of birth, age, and gender. This law is aimed at all businesses operating within the territories of countries that belong to the European Union (EU), but other personal data protection policies have been established in other countries outside the EU. In all such cases, businesses functioning within the jurisdiction of the policies must comply if they want to operate within those markets.

Figure 8.6 illustrates how events that must reference privacy data can do so from a distance, so that the events remain unchanged and the privacy data exists only until it must be deleted.

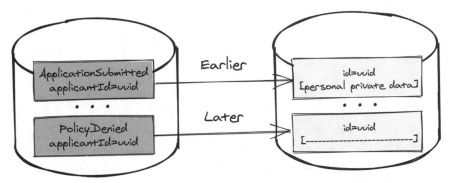

Figure 8.6 *Store the bare minimum of anonymized and separated private data that can be deleted.*

In addition to the elements illustrated in Figure 8.6, additional procedures can be considered that will save a lot of work when taking into account data related to personal privacy. Consider the following as the minimum steps needed:

- *Store the bare minimum of private data.* The less data that is stored that could be personally identifiable, the less work the business must undertake to comply with privacy protection policies, such as GDPR. Individuals within the EU territory can at any time request that their personal data be deleted, and businesses are required to comply. This reduces the threat that those individuals' sensitive data will be stolen.

- *Involve the legal team.* Work with the legal team on privacy requirements and understand the privacy policy under which users will be signing up.

- *Understand the purpose.* Make sure the purpose of storing every piece of data is well understood.

- *Have a retention plan.* Ensure there is a well-defined data retention policy and implement it.

- *Know which data is identifiable and destroyable.* There must be an established way to find and delete all privacy data relating to a specific individual on demand, per GDPR requirements.

- *Anonymize and separate private data.* Some data cannot be easily deleted, or it might be necessary to retain for legal, auditing, or historical reasons. When using Event Sourcing, for example, some Domain Events might tend to contain user information that is protected by a private data protection policy. In such cases, it is advisable to design data privacy as an application feature rather than considering it to be a patch. All personal data that is obligatory to store for a long time must be anonymized, and no personal information can be derived from what is anonymized. To correlate anonymized data with streaming data, such as Domain Events, replace the actual user personal data with a global unique identity, such as a universally unique identifier (UUID) token. The unique identity points to a highly secure storage record. All records holding private data can then be scrubbed upon request. It might be that the unique identity will continue to exist, but will point to data devoid of sensitive information. All that remains is data without any meaningful user information.

People everywhere are demanding freedom from uninvited intrusion and surveillance. Systems should be designed for privacy, even in countries, such as the United States, where privacy laws are a tough sell [WP-Privacy]. This is even more so the case when US and other non-EU businesses expect to succeed in markets beyond their national borders.

Transparency in how businesses collect, manage, and protect private data is vital to building trust and accountability with customers and partners who expect privacy. Unfortunately, many companies have learned the importance of privacy the hard way. Ensuring their data privacy demonstrates that the company is operating in the best interests of its customers. To be successful in that endeavor, data protection processes and procedures must be considered fundamental to the design of systems architectures.

Performance

The most salient aspect of performance is *latency*. With Microservices, the fact that the physical network is involved in the communication between services increases latency. Marshalling and unmarshalling data as well as sending bytes over the network takes time. The speed of light is very fast. No matter how quickly data is transmitted, relatively short distances require time for light to travel over a fiber network. Light travels at top speed in a vacuum, and fiber-optic networks aren't vacuums. Consider the example round-trip times in Table 8.3 [Fiber-Latency].

Table 8.3 *Routes on Optical Fiber with Round-Trip Times in Milliseconds*

Route	Optical Fiber Round-Trip
New York to San Francisco	42 ms
New York to London	56 ms
New York to Sydney	160 ms

Further, a few or several milliseconds (i.e., less than one second) at observable human scale are indivisible and thus seemingly nonexistent. Computers operate on a much tighter time scale, one characterized by extremely small fractions of a second. It's common to measure computer operations in nanoseconds, where one nanosecond is one billionth of a second. To better visualize how latency affects processing, we can express computing time at the human scale. Brendan Gregg, in the book *Systems Performance: Enterprise and the Cloud* [SysPerformance], scaled the relative time of various computer operations by making a single CPU cycle equivalent to one second. As Table 8.4 illustrates, the results were stunning.

Table 8.4 *Computing Time with Nanoseconds Scaled Up to Seconds*

Event	Actual Latency	Human-Scale Latency
One CPU cycle	0.4 ns	1 s
Level 1 cache access	0.9 ns	2 s
Level 2 cache access	2.8 ns	7 s
Level 3 cache access	28 ns	1 min
Main memory access (DDR DIMM)	~100 ns	4 min
Intel Optane memory access	<10 µs	7 hr
NVMe SSD I/O	~25 µs	17 hr
SSD I/O	50–150 µs	1.5–4 days
Rotational disk I/O	1–10 ms	1–9 months
Internet operation: San Francisco to New York City	65 ms	5 years
Internet operation: San Francisco to Hong Kong	141 ms	11 years

Network operations, shown at the bottom of Table 8.4, when expressed as human-scale latencies, require years to complete. That's because there are many billions of nanoseconds in 65 milliseconds and 141 milliseconds.

It is inaccurate to say that the latency of every network operation between Microservices accumulates linearly. Assuming asynchronous messaging is used for at least some inter-service communications, all of those asynchronous message requests run in parallel. With the publish–subscribe (i.e., fanout) pattern, one message sent by a producer can be delivered to a virtually unlimited number of consumers.

Latency can also be mitigated by services keeping copies of data from other services locally, thereby eliminating the network operations needed to constantly retrieve that specific data. Yet, when non-owners cache data, other problems can occur, such as when the data becomes stale. What happens when the service that caches non-owned data acts upon that data after it becomes stale? It depends on the data in use and whether the service contracts are based on accuracy, assuming someone realizes the need to think of that point during contract negotiations. Some service contracts can be fuzzy, whereas others must be precise. Problems can be avoided by evicting stale data, refreshing it on a just-in-time basis, or not caching data that has a high sensitivity to time and service demands for the sake of accuracy.

Total latency is reduced as more operations execute simultaneously. Executing in parallel all operations that are required to solve a given problem yields the completed result in the amount of time required for the slowest of all those parallel operations. The Monolith has no network latency, other than what's required for database access and a possible messaging mechanism, because all normal operations are in-process. Even in a perfectly parallelizable world, Monoliths will still be faster and have higher throughput, especially for workloads that cannot be easily scaled to multiple machines.

Additionally, performance is closely related to scalability. One affects the other in an opposite way; that is, they have an inverse relationship.

Scalability

Before delving into the scalability property of Monolithic and Microservices architectures, it's helpful to consider the potential demand on computing resources. Given:

- Both a Monolith and a set of Microservices are assigned the same work
- Each Microservice is:
  - Run in a Docker container
  - Orchestrated by cluster management tools such as Kubernetes
  - Uses log aggregation and monitoring

Even without digging through and surfacing exact figures, it is safe to assume that the way Microservices are run will require some processing overhead not required by a Monolith. Despite that, Microservices are capable of providing smarter resource usage. Because the cluster manager can allocate specific computing resources based on demand for use of specific components, the overall resource utilization can be much lower for the Microservices that are less heavily used. With

Monoliths, the opposite is true. Because a small portion of the overall Monolith code requires the greatest number of resources, demand-based scaling carries a disproportionate cost. Thus, Microservices can independently scale the resource-intensive parts of the code, while every instance of a Monolith must have access to the peak number of resources demanded by its most resource-intensive part.

Although Monoliths are not easily scaled, there are ways around that limitation. As explained in the section "Serverless and Function as a Service," in Chapter 9, it's possible to deploy a cloud-native modular Monolith as serverless[10] and reap all the benefits of infinite scale for the least possible financial cost on the cloud. Although that approach isn't free, it is attainable. The system must be well designed and meet a few cloud-native design requirements. In fact, running both modular Monoliths and Microservices in a serverless fashion yields equal benefits.

Resilience: Reliability and Fault Tolerance

Resilience is a software quality that is resistant to cascading failure when small components inevitably fail. There is a big difference between a modularized Monolith and a Big Ball of Mud Monolith. The modularized Monolith can be designed with reliability and fault tolerance in mind, similarly to Microservices, but with less technical overhead. Running in the same process doesn't require complex mechanisms to guarantee reliability. In contrast, the Big Ball of Mud Monolith is unreliable because testing the application thoroughly is very difficult, and quality tests rarely exist. The lack of extensive tests means that bugs can easily make their way into production. It is generally quite difficult to augment a Big Ball of Mud Monolith with effective reliability measures as an afterthought. These points have been well established, and obviously this book's concern and focus is on architecting, designing, and developing modularized Monoliths.

Microservices are also difficult to test extensively because each individual service might interact with and/or depend on functionality provided by other Microservices. Making these work well together by testing their collaboration and integration is a challenging undertaking. It's not unusual for defects to be found in production rather than during testing.

As previously established, operations that occur inside modular Monoliths are in-process and direct. Any network failure cannot impede such operations

---

10. We don't mean to suggest that a legacy Big Ball of Mud would be deployed as a serverless entity. The Monolith spoken of here would be designed to be serverless, with a cloud-native nature. The key benefit of deploying a well-designed Monolith as serverless is the decreased operational complexity, which would be incurred if the system were instead designed as hundreds of small Function as a Service (FaaS) components. There will be some size limitations to serverless solutions, however. At the time of this book's writing, an AWS Lambda must run in 10 GB of memory. This is a lesser limitation than the previous 3 GB.

because the network is not involved. Even if network operations are guaranteed to be 99.9%[11] reliable, 0.1% of the time there will be issues. An uptime Service Level Agreement (SLA) of 99.9% means that the system will be down 8.77 hours per year, 43.83 minutes per month, 10.08 minutes per week, and 1.44 minutes every single day. It should be abundantly obvious that the more nines in the availability criterion, the better. Nonetheless, a full-day outage that falls outside the SLA, as an unexpected anomaly, will certainly have the greatest impact of all. Using the network less rather than more has a very big advantage.

Even if a modularized Monolith has much to offer, unlike Microservices, it cannot easily guarantee fault isolation. If an unhandled exception occurs in one module—or worse yet, an unrecoverable exception such as an out-of-memory condition due to a memory leak—it can potentially crash the whole process that is running all services. With Microservices, just one service is lost when it crashes, but only if attention is given to the measures noted in the section "Mental Preparation with Resolve," in Chapter 11, "Monolith to Microservices Like a Boss." As stated there, failure supervision can prevent widespread system crashes.

Microservices should be designed with network and other kinds of failure in mind. When a service experiences a network outage or a full crash, the resource manager (e.g., Kubernetes or a cloud-provider–specific program) can rapidly bring the service down and spin up another service instance.

Another way to ensure fault tolerance is through the purposeful creation of chaos as a test. Netflix developed a test tool, ChaosMonkey, which randomly terminates a service so as to ensure that fault tolerance is properly achieved [ChaosMonkey]. The assertions for proper recovery include (1) a new service instance replaces the downed service; (2) network calls are rerouted; and (3) the overall architecture is reliable and continues to run as expected.

Complexity

Whole-system complexity embodies a number of challenging aspects. It stems from the complexity of deployments, the complexity of code under development, the complexity of running the whole system in production, and the ongoing challenge of monitoring and observing the system. From the perspective of the codebase, the Monolith application code is often kept in a single repository, known as a mono-repo. The inter-module communication between services is easier to trace with this setup, and with the help of an integrated development environment (IDE) static analysis, the processing flow can be quickly discovered.

---

11. Availability is usually expressed as a percentage of uptime in a given year within the SLA. It is usually expressed as "N nines," such as 99.9%, or "three nines" (https://en.wikipedia.org/wiki/High_availability).

We don't mean to imply that Microservices cannot make use of the mono-repo[12] feature. On a practical level, though, Microservices may be built by mixing languages and technologies, which increases the overall system complexity. Additionally, dealing with different libraries and frameworks, and different versions of each across services, is quite complex.

Deployments and auto-scalability of the system can be very complex as well. Monoliths are simple to deploy because they are self-contained and the company likely has decades of accumulated experience in deploying business software to a single machine. Scaling Monoliths is a matter of spinning up a new instance of one deployment unit. By comparison, deployments and scalability are much more complex with Microservices. Deployments to different computer nodes can be quite complex to coordinate, and tools used for scaling, such as Kubernetes, require real expertise.

And then there's the challenge of running the system in production. Logging and monitoring may be less or more complex depending on the use of Monoliths or Microservices, respectively. When running a Monolith in production, there is generally only one or a few log files to search and inspect, making debugging issues much less complex. It's a different story with Microservices: Tracking an issue might involve checking multiple, even many, log files. Not only is it necessary to find all the relevant log output, but it's also critical to aggregate and merge all of the logs in the correct order of operational occurrence. Often, tools such as Elasticsearch are used to aggregate and find all the relevant log output across services.

Applying the Tools

Architecture decisions should not be pushed abruptly into concrete. It might be too early, and the team might not know enough, for a sound decision to be made on any given architectural concern. It's never wrong to wait until the decision is actually required, rather than making decisions based on speculation. Making a decision without a confirmation of need is irresponsible and potentially harmful. Recall that all decisions should be made at the last responsible moment.

Part IV of this book demonstrates the application of the specific architectures and patterns discussed in Part III.

---

12. A mono-repo is a single source code revision tracking repository that holds all the source code for potentially many projects in a large system. For more information, see https://en.wikipedia.org/wiki/Monorepo.

> **Modules First**
>
> A fair question is, would it make sense to promote the internal modules (Intake, Processing, Policy, Renewals) to top-level modules of their own? That's a possibility to consider in time, and there might be advantages to doing so. But let's fall back on the earlier advice that in essence asserts, "The team doesn't yet have enough information to accept that decision." It would be irresponsible to go there now. Future conversations might lead in that direction, but jumping to a conclusion now doesn't make sense.

Summary

This chapter began by reviewing some of the many definitions of software architecture, then proposed a fresh definition with new insights. A number of architectural styles and architecture patterns were considered that specifically support events-first systems. In particular, the Ports and Adapters (Hexagonal) architectural style can be adapted to high-level architecture decisions, supporting variety at lower levels. A significant benefit of Ports and Adapters is its support for just-in-time decisions. It is a sound and versatile architecture on which to base additional architecture decisions and their respective implementations. In summary, the chapter made the following key points:

- Ports and Adapters can be expressed in several ways, including Service Layer with Transaction Scripts; Service Layer with a Domain Model; compressed layers with a Domain Model of Actors; and Functional Core with Imperative Shell.

- Modularization is key to adaptive architectures, where Monoliths lead to a blend of both Monolith and Microservices, or to entirely Microservices, depending on the purpose served.

- The REST architecture is often used for limited CRUD applications, but can be extended to domain-driven and event-driven architectures by using CRUUD-based partial updates.

- The purpose of architecture decisions is to achieve quality attribute requirements, such as flexibility, security, privacy, performance, scalability, and resilience, while reducing complexity.

- Not every architecture style and pattern is suitable for all system and subsystem constraints.

- Some architecture decisions meant to address certain quality attributes can work against others, requiring trade-offs to be made.

References

[Agile-SEC] Laura Bell, Rich Smith, Michael Brunton-Spall, and Jim Bird. *Agile Application Security: Enabling Security in a Continuous Delivery Pipeline.* Sebastopol, CA: O'Reilly Media, 2017.

[BBoM] http://laputan.org/mud/

[ChaosMonkey] https://github.com/netflix/chaosmonkey

[Continuous-Architecture] Murat Erder, Pierre Pureur, and Eoin Woods. *Continuous Architecture in Practice.* Boston, MA: Addison-Wesley, 2021.

[CyberAttack] https://www.wired.com/story/notpetya-cyberattack-ukraine-russia-code-crashed-the-world/

[Fiber-Latency] https://hpbn.co/primer-on-latency-and-bandwidth/

[GDPR] https://en.wikipedia.org/wiki/General_Data_Protection_Regulation

[ISO 47010] ISO 47010; was IEEE Standard 1471; https://en.wikipedia.org/wiki/IEEE_1471

[PortsAdapters] https://alistair.cockburn.us/hexagonal-architecture/

[POSA1] Frank Buschmann, Regine Meunier, Hans Rohnert, Peter Sommerlad, and Michael Stal. *Pattern-Oriented Software Architecture Volume 1: A System of Patterns.* Hoboken, NJ: Wiley, 1996.

[Secure-By-Design] https://www.manning.com/books/secure-by-design

[Software Architecture in Practice] Len Bass, Paul Clements, and Rick Kazman. *Software Architecture in Practice*, 3rd ed. Boston, MA: Addison-Wesley, 2013.

[SOLID] https://en.wikipedia.org/wiki/SOLID

[SysPerformance] Brendan Gregg. *Systems Performance: Enterprise and the Cloud*, 2nd ed. Boston, MA: Addison-Wesley, 2021.

[Verizon-SEC] https://enterprise.verizon.com/resources/reports/dbir/

[VLINGO-XOOM] https://vlingo.io

[WP-Privacy] *Washington Post*. https://www.washingtonpost.com/news/powerpost/paloma/the-cybersecurity-202/2018/05/25/the-cybersecurity-202-why-a-privacy-law-like-gdpr-would-be-a-tough-sell-in-the-u-s/5b07038b1b326b492dd07e83/

Chapter 9

Message- and Event-Driven Architectures

A message-driven architecture is one that emphasizes sending and receiving messages as playing a prominent role throughout the system. In general, message-driven architectures have been chosen less often compared to REpresentational State Transfer (REST) and remote procedure calls (RPC). This is because REST and RPC seem more similar to general-purpose programming language paradigms than does messaging; the former approaches provide abstractions that give the impression of procedure calls and method invocations, with which many programmers are already familiar.

Yet, REST and RPC are brittle mechanisms in comparison to general-purpose programming languages. It's highly unlikely that a procedure call or method invocation will fail due to brittle mechanisms within a programming language. With the REST-over-HTTP and RPC approaches, it is very likely that failures will occur due to network and remote service failures. When failure does occur, the temporal coupling between one remote service and another will tend to cause a complete failure of the client service. The more remote services or subsystems that are involved in the given use case, the worse the problem can become. As Leslie Lamport, a distributed systems expert, described it:

> A distributed system is one that prevents you from working because of the failure of a machine that you had never heard of.

That sort of cascading failure tends to be avoided when systems use asynchronous messaging, because the requests and responses are all temporally decoupled. Figure 9.1 highlights the relaxed temporal dependencies across subsystems involved in a choreographed event-driven process. To be clear, events capturing and communicating business interests are (generally) a form of message, and message-driven processes are a superset of event-driven processes.[1]

Choreographed and Orchestrated Processes

These are two primary styles of process management: choreography and orchestration. Choreography comprises a decentralized style of process where, for example, events are published using messaging, and each subsystem context must determine whether the event is relevant to it, and if so, apply the event to its state. One or more events emitted in response by the subsystem in context will be relevant to one or more other subsystems. Choreography is relatively simple to understand and is most practical when processes have only a few steps. One disadvantage of this process management style is that when the process stalls somewhere, it can be difficult to determine where it went wrong and why. Another disadvantage is that event dependencies become coupled to subsystems that don't own the events, and must be subjectively interpreted and applied to their own purpose. And, of course, dependencies on events can become quite tangled as system and process complexities increase.

Orchestration, in contrast, features a centralized style of process manager (i.e., Saga) that receives events emitted by any number of subsystems involved in the process, and then creates command messages that drive subsequent steps of the process to relevant subsystems. The advantages of using orchestrated processes include reduced dependencies across subsystems involved in a given process because the orchestrator takes on the entire responsibility of translating from event to command. The orchestrator can be a central point of failure, but that's generally not a significant concern given the scalability and failover strategies common to well-designed distributed systems. Typically, an orchestrator is designed and implemented by the team most interested in its ultimate outcome. They might become a blocker when changes are made across subsystems involved in the process that must be applied inside the orchestrator. An orchestrator might be too complex for controlling processes with less complexity. The orchestrator must not become a dungeon for business logic; it must be used only to drive steps of the process.

---

1. Some use a strict definition of a message, specifying that it must be directly sent peer-to-peer from sender to receiver. They may also constrain events to only those sent via pub-sub. The authors hold the opinion that this is an overly limiting perspective. The next section discusses using poll-based REST as a means to read event logs. Although many consumers might read such a feed of events, it is not the same as the push model of pub-sub. Of course, anyone can hold an opinion, so neither view is necessarily wrong.

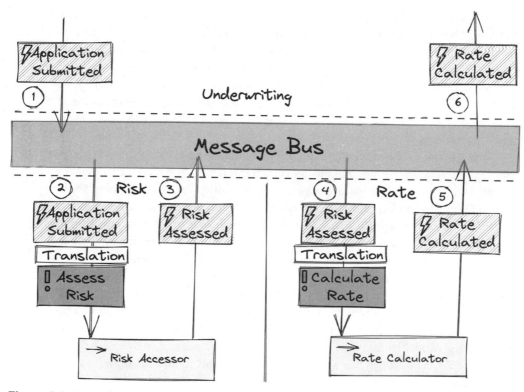

Figure 9.1 *Event-driven choreography: events over a message bus translated to commands.*

The overall system works by means of the events that occur in a given subsystem being made available to other subsystems via a message bus. Message-driven architecture is also a Reactive architecture because the components, as seen in Figure 9.1, are passive until message stimuli occur, and then the appropriate components react to those stimuli. In contrast, imperative code drives responses by means of REST and RPC procedure calls or method invocations. Reactive is defined as having four primary characteristics: responsive, resilient, elastic, and message-driven [Reactive].

In Figure 9.1, the six steps executed across three subsystem contexts (Underwriting, Risk, and Rate) collectively provide the calculated rate needed to quote a policy premium for an applicant over the Web. The Underwriting subsystem context is blissfully unaware of the details involved in reaching the result. At some time in the future after the *Application Submitted* event occurs, Underwriting will be informed that a quotable premium rate is available.

The desired Underwriting outcome could require 2 seconds or 12 seconds to achieve. There is no failure in Underwriting because of the infrastructure being pre-configured to time out after 5 seconds, which would hold sway over the response to a REST request. It's not that 12 seconds is an acceptable long-term Service Level Agreement (SLA)—but it is perfectly acceptable in the face of full failure of the Risk or Rate subsystem, followed by full recovery on a different cloud infrastructure, and possibly even in another region. Neither ordinary REST nor RPC would survive that pathway.

Note a detail of the process in Figure 9.1 that's due to the nature of choreography: Events sent on the message bus must be translated by the receiver so that the internal stimulus is cast in the language of the consuming context. The event *Application Submitted* means nothing to Risk—but it does after it's translated to *Assess Risk*. The same goes for *Risk Assessed* in the context of Rate: When translated to *Calculate Rate*, it makes perfect sense because a rate can be determined from an *Assessment Result* that's available as part of the *Risk Assessed* event.

While message bus communication is typically used for collaborative computing across subsystem contexts, it's not a practical fit for message-driven communication within a single subsystem context. As Figure 9.2 illustrates, the individual components within a subsystem context might be implemented as actors that function in an Actor Model runtime. Every actor component is message-driven, such that actors are Reactive. When one actor wants another actor to do something, it sends a message to the other actor that will be delivered asynchronously. Although each message delivery executes asynchronously, the flow shown in Figure 9.2 functions in sequence according to the step numbers.

In Figure 9.2, every individual actor is represented by a circular element (as opposed to rectangular ones that represent plain objects). The message sending between actors can be different from that based on the message bus. For example, steps 1 and 2 indicate that the Message Bridge actor, a driver adapter, receives an *Application Submitted* event message from the message bus and adapts it to a message sent on to the Risk Assessor actor. What appears to be a normal method invocation is not one typically used in object-to-object communication. This method invocation packs the intent of the invocation into an object-based message that is enqueued in the Risk Assessor actor's mailbox. The assessRisk(facts) message will be delivered as an actual method invocation on the Risk Assessor actor implementation as soon as possible.

The nature of the Actor Model ensures that all computer processors are used all the time, making for highly efficient compute solutions that *drive down the monetary cost of operations* on both on-premises and cloud infrastructures. This is accomplished by the Actor Model runtime using the compute node's limited number of threads, along with scheduling and dispatching that are performed cooperatively

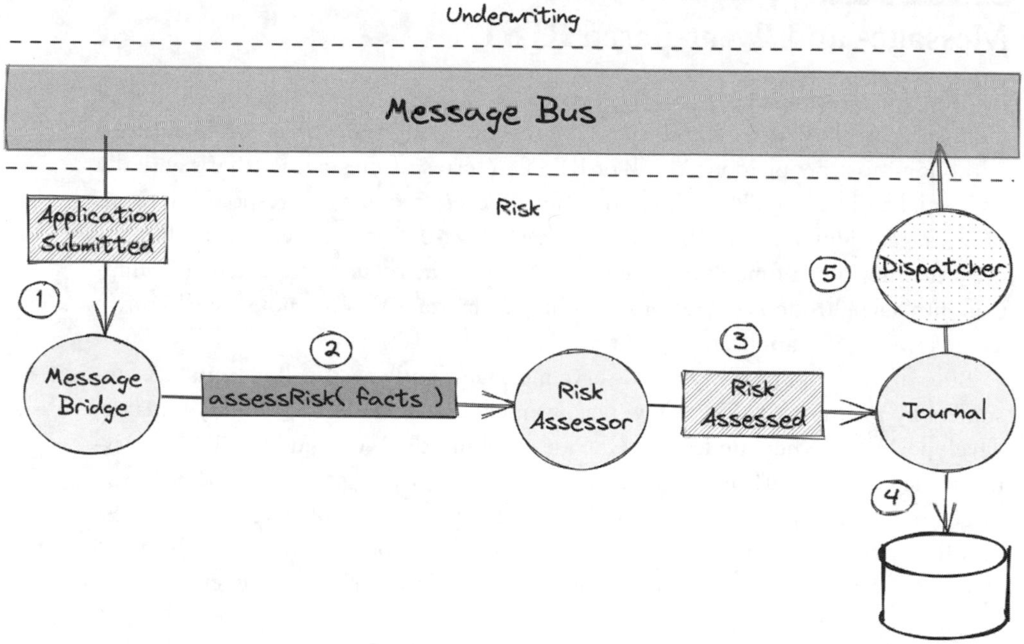

Figure 9.2 *Reactive architecture inside a subsystem context is achieved by using the Actor Model.*

by all actors. The limited number of threads must be distributed across any number of actors. Each actor that has an available message in its mailbox is scheduled to run when a thread becomes available for it, and will (typically) handle only a single pending message while using that thread. Any remaining messages available to the actor are scheduled to be delivered after the current one completes.

This highlights another benefit of the Actor Model. Every actor will handle only one message at a time, meaning that actors are individually single-threaded, although many actors handling messages simultaneously over a short period of time mean that the overall runtime model is massively concurrent. The fact that each actor is single-threaded means that it need not protect its internal state data from use by two or more threads entering simultaneously. State protection is further strengthened by the rule that actors must not ever share the mutable internal state.

The types of use cases highlighted in Figure 9.2 and throughout this book are specifically supported by VLINGO XOOM, a free and open source (FOSS) Reactive toolset based on the Actor Model for Monolith and Microservices architectures [VLINGO-XOOM].

Message- and Event-Based REST

As discussed in Chapter 8, REST can be used for integration across Bounded Contexts, but how does REST support message- and event-driven architectures? Although most people don't think of REST in terms of messaging, that's actually its specialty. The HTTP specification refers to every request and response in terms of messages. Thus, REST is by definition a message-driven architecture, and events are a distinct type of message. The trick is to turn the requests for event consumption into asynchronous operations. It's these techniques that are not as well known as are typical Web application patterns.

But why would anyone want to serve messages, and specifically events, to consumers by means of REST? A few reasons include that the Web is highly scalable, developers everywhere understand the ideas behind the Web and HTTP, and serving static content is quite fast (and cacheable on the server and client). Developers in general tend to be unfamiliar with message buses and brokers, or at least less familiar with them than with HTTP. Being uncomfortable with message buses and brokers should not prevent the use of message- and event-driven architectures.

Event Logs

As a basic rule of thumb, every event persistently stored must be immutable; that is, it must never be changed. A second and related rule is that if an event is in error, rather than patching its persistent state, there must be a compensating event that is persisted later and eventually "fixes" the data in error when consumers apply the event over top of the data that they produced before the error was known. In other words, if consumers have already consumed an event in error, changing it later will not help those consumers. They should never start over and apply all events again from the beginning—that would likely lead to disaster. Carry these rules forward when considering the following points.

As events occur in a subsystem context, they should be collected persistently in the order in which they occurred. From the sequence of events, a series of event logs might be created, either virtually or physically. Figure 9.3 provides a depiction of these logs.

This can be done by using a formal database (as opposed to a flat file or directories of flat files) that supports a reliable sequence number that is assigned to each event and then incremented. Relational databases support this process through a feature known as *sequences* or with another feature called *auto-increment columns*. The event logs are created logically by determining a maximum number of entries in the individual logs and then creating a virtual moving window to serve each log dynamically.

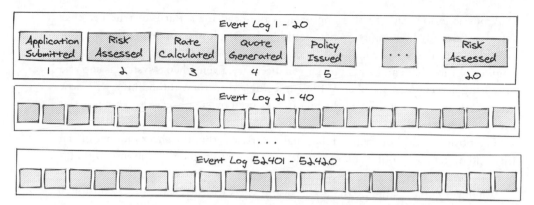

Figure 9.3 *Event logs starting with 1–20 and continuing to nearly 1 million total events.*

Some negative trade-offs with a relational database include somewhat slow event log serving compared to purpose-built log databases. If a vast number of events is stored, the disk space used to maintain them over the long term could be problematic; however, if the system uses cloud-enabled relational databases, that concern will likely never become an actual problem. Even so, it might make sense to create a virtual array of tables, where each table will hold only a maximum number of events and excess events will then spill over into the next logical table. There is also the risk that users might be tempted to modify an existing event in the database, which must never be done. Because the logs are records of past occurrences, it would be incorrect to patch an event.

A good relational database and a developer with advanced skills in its use can not only support many millions of database rows in a single table, but also enable fast retrieval by means of correct key indexing. Although this statement is true, the viewpoint it expresses assumes that many millions of rows in a single database table are enough. In reality, some systems produce many millions or even billions of events every single day. If a relational database still makes sense under these conditions, a virtual array of tables can help. It might also seem obvious that such a system could use a highly scalable NoSQL database instead. That would also solve a set of problems, but it wouldn't work well to insert new events using a monotonically increasing integer key. Doing so generally greatly hampers the sharding/hashing algorithms employed by such databases.

There are other ways to handle this situation. As pictured in Figure 9.3, maintaining event logs can be accomplished by writing a series of flat files to a normal disk that are servable REST resources. After each log file is written, the content would be available as static content. The static flat files can be replicated to a few or many servers, just as would be done when scaling typical website content.

A possible downside to this approach is the need for a flat-file structure that specifies not only how many events should be written into a single log flat file, but also how the files will be laid out on disk. Operating systems place limits on the number of files that can be held in a given directory. Even when a system is capable of storing a very great number of files in a single directory, these limits will slow access. An approach similar to the hierarchies used by email servers can make flat file access very fast.

The positive trade-off with a relational database is that the sheer number of flat files and directory layouts will offer little temptation to patch the contents. If that is not a deterrent, then secure access to the filesystem can be.

Whatever choice is made, there are several ways for the events to be consumed using REST, as described in the sections that follow.

Subscriber Polling

Subscribers can use simple polling of the log resources:

```
GET /streams/{name}/1-20
GET /streams/{name}/21-40
GET /streams/{name}/41-60
GET /streams/{name}/61-80
GET /streams/{name}/81-100
GET /streams/{name}/101-120
```

In this example, the {name} placeholder is replaced with the name of the stream being read, such as underwriting or, even more generally, policy-marketplace. The former would serve only Underwriting-specific events, while the latter would provide a full stream of all events over the various subsystem contexts, including Underwriting, Risk, and Rate.

The disadvantage is that if subscriber polling is not implemented correctly, clients will constantly request the next log, which is not yet available, and those requests could cause a lot of network traffic. Requests must also be limited to reasonably sized logs. This can be enforced by making the resource identities fixed ranges, with the next and previous logs referenced by hypermedia links in response headers. Caching techniques and timed read intervals can be established using response header metadata to smooth out request swamping. Additionally, even a partial log can be served by using a generic minted URI:

```
GET /streams/policy-marketplace/current
```

The current resource is the means to consume the most recent event log resource. If the current log—for example, 101-120—is beyond the previous event logs that have not yet been read by a given client, an HTTP response header will provide the link to navigate to the previous log, which would be read and applied before the current log. This backward navigation would continue until the client's most recently applied event is read. From that point, all events not yet applied are applied, which would include navigating forward until the current log is reached. Once again, caching plays into this approach by preventing pre-read but not yet applied logs from being reread from the server, even when they are explicitly requested by means of a redundant GET operation. This is explained in more detail in *Implementing Domain-Driven Design* [IDDD], and in our own follow-on book, *Implementing Strategic Monoliths and Microservices* (Vernon & Jaskuła, Addison-Wesley, forthcoming).

Server-Sent Events

Although Server-Sent Events (SSE) are well known as support for server-to-browser event feeds, that is not the intended usage here. The problem with browser usage is that not all browsers support the SSE specification. Even so, SSE is a worthy integration option between the events producer and its non-browser, services/applications clients that need to receive the events.

The specification for SSE states that a client should request a long-lived connection to the server for a subscription. Upon subscribing, the client may specify the identifier of the last event that it successfully applied. In such a case, the client would have previously been subscribed but disconnected at some point within the stream:

```
GET /streams/policy-marketplace
. . .
Last-Event-ID: 102470
```

As implied by providing its current starting position, the client is responsible for maintaining its current position in the stream.

As a result of subscribing, the events available will stream from the beginning or from the position of the `Last-Event-ID` and continue until the client unsubscribes or otherwise disconnects. The following is the format that is approved by the SSE specification, though actual applications might contain more or fewer fields. Each event is followed by a blank line:

```
id: 102470
event: RiskAssessed
data: { "name" : "value", ... }


. . .

id: 102480
event: RateCalculated
data: { "name" : "value", ... }


. . .
```

To unsubscribe from the stream, the client sends the following message:

```
DELETE /streams/policy-marketplace
```

When this message is sent, the subscription is terminated, the server sends a 200 OK response, and the server closes its end of the channel. After receiving its 200 OK response, the client should also close the channel.

Event-Driven and Process Management

Earlier sections in this chapter clarified the ideas behind event-driven process management where the focus is on choreographed processes. Choreography requires the Bounded Contexts participating in a process to understand the events from one or more other contexts, and to interpret those events based on their local meaning. Here, the focus shifts to orchestration[2] [Conductor], putting a central component in charge of driving the process from start to finish.[3]

In Figure 9.4, the process manager named *Application Premium Process* is responsible for driving the outcome of a fully constructed quote to an applicant who has submitted an application, the steps for which are described in the list that follows.

1. The event ApplicationSubmitted has occurred as a result of the Aggregate type Application being created from the applicant's submitted application document. For the sake of brevity, the Application instance creation is not shown. The process begins when the process manager sees the ApplicationSubmitted event.

2. The ApplicationSubmitted event is translated to a command named AssessRisk and enqueued on the message bus.

3. The AssessRisk command is delivered to the Risk Context, where it is dispatched to the Domain Service named RiskAssessor. Below the RiskAssessor are processing details (not shown in Figure 9.4).

---

2. Netflix found it was harder to scale choreography-based processes in the face of its growing business needs and complexities. A choreographed pub-sub model worked for the simplest of the flows, but quickly showed its limits. For that reason, Netflix has created its own orchestration framework called Conductor.

3. It is possible that a process might never end because ongoing streams of messages—whether events, commands, queries and their results, or something else—might never end. Here, start-to-finish processes are used for practical purposes, but be aware that there are no limitations imposed by this style.

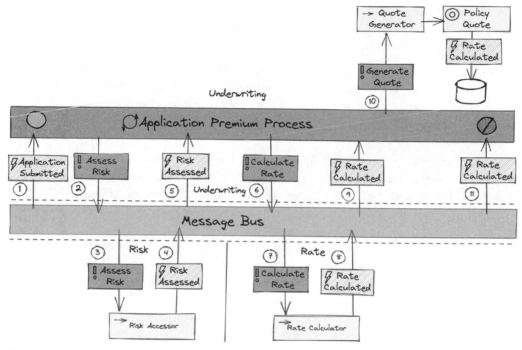

Figure 9.4 *Orchestration: commands are sent on the bus to drive process results.*

4. Once the risk has been assessed, the RiskAssessed event is emitted and enqueued on the message bus.

5. The RiskAssessed event is delivered to the process manager.

6. The RiskAssessed event is translated to the CalculateRate command and enqueued on the message bus.

7. The CalculateRate command is delivered to the Rate Context, where it is dispatched to the Domain Service named RateCalculator. Below the RateCalculator are processing details (not shown in Figure 9.4).

8. Once the rate has been calculated, the RateCalculated event is emitted and enqueued on the message bus.

9. The RateCalculated event is delivered to the process manager.

10. The RateCalculated event is translated to the GenerateQuote command and dispatched locally and directly to the Domain Service named QuoteGenerator. The QuoteGenerator is responsible for interpreting the PremiumRates to QuoteLines and dispatched to the Aggregate named PremiumQuote (see Chapter 7, "Modeling

Domain Concepts," and Chapter 8, "Foundation Architecture," for more details). When the final `QuoteLine` is recorded, the `QuoteGenerated` event is emitted and stored in the database.

11. Once an event is stored in the database, it can be enqueued on the message bus—and this is true for the `QuoteGenerated` event. In the case of the *Application Premium Process*, the receipt of the `QuoteGenerated` event marks the end of the process.

Examining Figure 9.4, it might appear that an attempt to enqueue events and commands on the message bus could fail, causing the overall failure of the process. Consider, however, that all of the events and the commands translated from them are first persisted into a database, and then placed on the message bus, sometimes repeatedly until this effort succeeds. This establishes an at-least-once delivery contract. Steps 10 and 11 highlight the persistence first, enqueuing second sequence. However, going to that level of detail on all steps illustrated in Figure 9.4 would detract from the main flow and obscure the main points that should be gleaned from the example.

With orchestrated processes, the process manager is responsible for driving the process. This generally places the process itself downstream, so that the collaborating contexts do not need to know anything about the process details, only how to perform their core responsibilities.

In the preceding example, the *Application Premium Process* is housed in the Underwriting Context. This need not be the case, however, because the process might be deployed separately. Yet, by default it makes sense for the process to be deployed along with the Bounded Context components that require the process to be accomplished. This design choice has been made for the *Application Premium Process*, which is placed within the Underwriting Context. Such a design tends to reduce the complexity of the overall process.

The question remains: Are the *Application Premium Process* and the contexts involved deployed as a Monolith or as separate Microservices? The use of a message bus, as seen in Figure 9.4, might seem to imply a Microservices architecture. That's possible, but not necessarily so:

- The message bus might be provided inside a Monolith using lightweight messaging, such as with ZeroMQ.

- The teams might have decided that the Monolith should have used more reliable messaging middleware or a cloud-based message bus (or message log) such as RabbitMQ, Kafka, IBM MQ, implementations of JMS, AWS SNS,

AWS Kinesis, Google Cloud Pub/Sub, or Azure Message Bus.[4] Choose whatever works best for your project requirements and SLAs.

- The solution might require using a Microservices architecture, or a blend of Monoliths and Microservices. Reliable messaging mechanisms, whether cloud-based or on premises, are the sound choices for these situations.

As discussed in Chapter 6, the use of a schema registry reduces the complexity of cross-context dependencies and translations into and out of various Published Languages, which is required of the *Application Premium Process*. One such FOSS schema registry is provided with VLINGO XOOM—namely, Schemata [VLINGO-XOOM].

Event Sourcing

It's become customary for software developers to store objects in a relational database. With a domain-driven approach, it's generally a matter of persisting the state of whole Aggregates that way. Tools called *object-relational mappers* are available to help with this task. Of late, several relational databases have innovated around storing objects that are serialized as JSON, which is a good trade-off for addressing the common impedance[5] of the competing forces of the object and relational models. For one thing, a serialized JSON object can be queried in much the same way as relational columns by means of specialized SQL extensions.

Yet, there is an alternative, rather radically different approach to object persistence that emphasizes the opposite: Don't store objects; store records of their changes instead. This practice, known as *Event Sourcing*,[6] requires the records of changes to the Aggregate state to be captured in events.

It's helpful to reference Figure 9.5 for the discussion that follows.

---

4. The number of possible messaging mechanisms is too large to present an exhaustive list here. The options identified here are among some better known by the authors and are generally used extensively.

5. Many architects and developers are familiar with these impedances, so this chapter doesn't offer exhaustive descriptions of them. They generally relate to the desire to structure an object for some modeling advantage, which then runs up against the limits of object-relational mapping tools and/or databases. In such cases, the object-relational mapping tools and databases win, and the object modeler loses.

6. There are more event-driven patterns than the ones described in this book. Extensive descriptions are provided in our follow-on book, *Implementing Strategic Monoliths and Microservices* (Vernon & Jaskuła, Addison-Wesley, forthcoming).

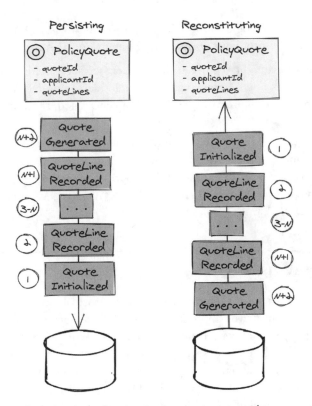

Figure 9.5 *Event Sourcing is used to persist Aggregate state and to reconstitute it.*

The ideas behind Event Sourcing are fairly simple. When a command handled by an Aggregate causes its state to change, the change is represented by at least one event. The one or more events representing the change are fine-grained; that is, they represent the minimal state required to capture the essence of the change. These events are stored in a database that can maintain the order in which the events occurred for a specific Aggregate. The ordered collection of events is known as the Aggregate's *stream*. Every time that a change to the Aggregate occurs and one or more events are emitted, it represents a different version of the stream and the stream length grows.

Assuming the Aggregate instance under discussion goes out of scope and is garbage collected by the runtime, if its subsequent use then becomes necessary, the Aggregate instance must be reconstituted. As expected, its state must once again reflect all changes from its first event to its most recent changes. This is accomplished by reading the Aggregate's stream from the database in the order in which the events originally occurred, and then reapplying them one-by-one to the Aggregate. In this way, the Aggregate state is gradually modified to reflect the change that each event represented.

This approach sounds both powerful and simple, and so far it is. Yet, you must wield this sword carefully, because it can also inflict pain.

Straightforward Except When ...

The challenges arise not with the initial use of Event Sourcing, but primarily for a few other reasons:

- When significant design changes occur in one or more Aggregate types
- When there is an error in an event in an Aggregate stream
- When reconstituting the state of an Aggregate that has a large stream of events
- When complex data views must be assembled from the events

Handling design changes involves producing streams that represent either a dividing of one stream or a merging of two or more streams.

An error in an event in one Aggregate instance stream must be patched. And by "patch," we mean not patching the existing event data in the database, but rather adding a new event, possibly of a different type used only for the patch. This is intended to cause an interpretation that compensates for the error in the reconstituted Aggregate state previously affected, as well as for any downstream consumers of the previous error-containing event. Given an error in one Aggregate instance stream of a given type, there's a good chance that the same error exists in all instances of that Aggregate type, or at least many of them. The issue is with the code that produced the event. Thus, the code must be fixed and the streams must be patched as described.

When an Aggregate's state is constituted by a large event stream, the performance when reconstituting its state can be enhanced by employing state snapshots. Such snapshots are taken of the full Aggregate state at specific version intervals, such as every 100, 200, or any number of versions that achieves acceptable performance. When the stream is read for the purpose of reconstituting the Aggregate state, the snapshot is read first, and then only the events that were emitted following the snapshot version are read and applied to the state in that order.

When using Event Sourcing, you should assume that Command Query Responsibility Segregation (CQRS; described in the next section) will nearly always be needed. CQRS is used to project events emitted by Aggregates into views that are queried and rendered on user interfaces, or that are consumed for other informational needs.

> None of this is easy, but then again, bugs happen in all software, and migrations happen to a persistent state no matter which persistence approach is used or what the chosen database is. There are ways to reduce the pain. It is not within the scope of this book to provide deep guidance on using Event Sourcing, but you can find that information in our follow-on implementation book, *Implementing Strategic Monoliths and Microservices* (Vernon & Jaskuła, Addison-Wesley, forthcoming).

When the potential pain of using Event Sourcing is understood, it tends to cause a bit of wonderment as to why it would be employed in the first place. There's nothing wrong with that—it's generally good to ask why. The worst case arises when Event Sourcing is used without a clear understanding of why and how,[7] as this application is generally followed by regret and a fixing of blame on Event Sourcing. All too often, architects and programmers make technology and design choices based on intrigue rather than business-driven purpose, and then get in way over their heads in accidental complexity. In addition, architects and programmers are often influenced by technology-driven frameworks and tools produced by vendors that try to convince their market that Event Sourcing is the best way to implement Microservices.[8]

Noting the pain ahead of the gain is an important warning sign for the uninitiated, curious, and gullible.

The good news is that there are very definite reasons to use Event Sourcing. Next, we consider the possible gains while understanding that these might require some pain—but that's all part of the software patterns and tools experience. They come with a package deal known as trade-offs and consequences, and there are always positives and negatives with each choice made. The point is, if the positives are necessary, then the negatives are necessary, too. Now, consider what is gained from Event Sourcing:

1. We can maintain an audit trail of every change that has occurred in the instances of every given Aggregate type that uses Event Sourcing. This might be required by or at least smart to use within specific industries.

---

7. Some of the loudest complaints about Event Sourcing that the authors have heard are the outcome of not understanding it, and thus not using it correctly.

8. The assumption that Microservices are good is a weak reason to use them. Microservices are good only when need informs purpose. Vendors who insist that Microservices are always good, and that Event Sourcing is the best way to implement Microservices, are misleading their customers, whether intentionally or not.

2. Event Sourcing can be compared with a general ledger employed in accounting. Changes are never made to existing entries. That is, only new entries are added to the ledger, and no entries are ever changed for correction. Problems caused by one or more previous entries are corrected by adding one or more new entries that compensate. This was described in the sidebar "Straightforward Except When . . . ."

3. Event Sourcing is useful in addressing the complexities of specific business problems. For example, because events represent both what happens in the business domain and when they happen, event streams can be used for special time-based purposes.

4. Besides using the event streams for persistence, we can apply them in many different ways, such as decision analytics, machine learning, "what if" studies, and similar knowledge-based projections.

5. The audit trail as a "general ledger" doubles as a debugging tool. Developers can use the series of factual events as a means to consider every level of change, which can lead to insights into when and how bugs were introduced. This help is unavailable when object states are fully replaced by every new change.

It might be appropriate for some Aggregate types in a Bounded Context to use Event Sourcing, while others do not. Conversely, this mixed approach would not be practical if a totally ordered stream of all changes to all Aggregate types is important to the business.

Although it has motivations in technical solutions, Event Sourcing should be employed only for justifiable business reasons and avoided for others. Considering this, only points 1–3 in the previous list of benefits from Event Sourcing have business motivations. Points 4 and 5 do not, but are advantageous when any of 1–3 are satisfied.

CQRS

Users of systems tend to view data differently than users who create and modify data. The system user must often view a larger, more diverse, coarse-grained dataset to make a decision. Once this decision is made, the operation that the system user carries out is fine-grained and targeted. Consider the following examples:

- Think of all the patient data that a doctor must view before prescribing a medication: the patient's vital signs, past health conditions, treatments, and procedures; current and past mediations; allergies (including those to medications); and even the patient's behavior and sentiments. Following this review, the doctor will record a medication, dosage, administration, duration, and number of refills, probably across a single row on a form.

- An underwriter must view data from a submitted application; all research, such as a property inspection or the applicant's health examination; past claims of losses or health conditions; assessed risks; and the use of all this data to calculate a recommended quotable premium. After considering the entire set of information, the underwriter can click a button to either offer a quote for a policy or deny a policy to the applicant.

This puts the viewable model and the operational model at odds. The available data structures are generally optimized around the operational model rather than the viewable model. Under such circumstances, it can be very complex and computationally expensive to assemble the viewable dataset.

The CQRS pattern can be used to address this challenge. As Figure 9.6 illustrates, this pattern calls for two models: one that is optimized for command operations, and one that is optimized for queries that aggregate the viewable dataset.

The pattern in Figure 9.6 works as follows:

1. The user is presented with a view dataset from the query model as a form.

2. The user makes a decision, fills in some data, and submits the form as a command.

3. The command is carried out on the command model, and the data is persisted.

4. The persisted command model changes are projected into the query model for as many viewable datasets as needed.

5. Go back to step 1.

Figure 9.6 shows storage for the Command model and the Query model as two separate databases. Although such a design makes sense for large-scale and

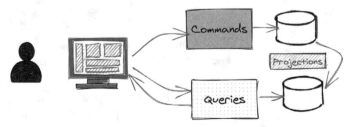

Figure 9.6 *The Command and Query models form two possible pathways.*

high-throughput systems, it is not truly necessary. The model storage might be only a virtual/logical separation, actually using a single database or database schema. Given that the two models are physically one and that a single transaction can manage multiple writes, this design implies that both the Command model and the Query model could be transactionally consistent. Maintaining transactional consistency saves developers the headaches incurred when the two models are physically separated, but eventually consistent.

When using Event Sourcing, it is generally necessary to also use CQRS. Otherwise, there is no way to query the Event Sourced Command model other than by Aggregate unique identity, which makes any sophisticated queries implemented to render broad viewable datasets either impossible or extremely prohibitive. To overcome this limitation, events emitted from the Event Sourced Command model are projected into the Query model.

Serverless and Function as a Service

Cloud-based serverless architectures are increasingly becoming a force in the software industry. This trend reflects the simplicity and savings afforded by serverless designs. The term "serverless" might seem a bit misleading because the solution obviously requires computers.[9] Yes, but the term is actually being applied from the cloud subscriber-developer perspective. Cloud vendors provision the servers, rather than the subscriber taking on this responsibility. To cloud subscribers, then, there are no servers, only available uptime.

To position serverless architectures more explicitly, some have used the term Backend as a Service (BaaS). Yet, thinking only in terms of hosting the application's "backend" does not adequately describe the full benefits. Serverless architecture is also Infrastructure as a Service (IaaS), where infrastructure is not limited to computer and network resources. More specifically, infrastructure from this perspective includes all kinds of software that application developers do not need to create and (sometimes) subscribers do not need to even pay for. This is truly a leap forward in regard to the age-old mantra, "Focus on the business." The following are some key benefits of using a serverless architecture:

- Users pay only for actual compute time, not for the well-known "always up" provisioned servers.

---

9. As software professionals are constantly reminded, naming is hard, and software names are too quickly chiseled in stone. As with HATEOAS, perhaps consider "serverless" to be a glyph that represents a concept.

- The significant cost savings are generally hard to believe, but users can believe them anyway.

- Other than deciding on required cloud software components, planning is easier.

- The solutions use a plethora of hardware and cloud-native software infrastructure and mechanisms that are free or very low cost.

- Development is accelerated due to diminished infrastructure concerns.

- Businesses can deploy cloud-native modular Monoliths.

- Serverless architecture offers strong support for browser clients and mobile clients.

- Because they need to create less software, users can actually focus on the business solutions.

The Ports and Adapters architecture discussed in Chapter 8, "Foundation Architecture," is still useful, and fits quite well with the serverless approach. In fact, if it is carefully architected and designed, there is a good chance that service and application packaging need not change. The greatly reduced overhead in regard to dealing with infrastructure software has great benefits, as previously described. The primary difference relates to how service and application software is architected, designed, and run. The term *cloud-native* refers to utilizing all purpose-built infrastructure, as well as mechanisms such as databases and messaging, that are themselves designed specifically for cloud computing.

Consider the example of a browser-based REST request from a user. The request arrives at an API gateway that is provided by the cloud vendor. The gateway is configured to understand how to dispatch requests onto the service or application. When the dispatch takes place, the cloud platform determines whether the REST request handler (i.e., endpoint or adapter) and its software dependencies are already running and currently available. If so, the request is immediately dispatched to that request handler. If not, the cloud platform spins up a server with the subscriber's software running, and dispatches it to the request handler. In either case, from that point onward the subscriber's software operates normally.

When the request handler provides a response to the client, the subscriber's use of the server ends. The cloud platform then determines whether the server should remain available for future requests, or should be shut down. The subscriber incurs only the cost of handling the request, and any applicable costs for the hardware and software infrastructure required to do so.

If the entire time to actually handle the request is 20, 50, 100, or 1,000 milliseconds, that's what the subscriber pays for to run their software. If no requests arrive for a second or two, the subscriber doesn't pay for that time. Compare that to cloud-provisioned servers, which incur costs just to stay alive and ready, every second of every day, whether or not they are in use.

Function as a Service (FaaS) is a kind of serverless mechanism that supports the software architecture and design for the aforementioned characteristics. Yet, FaaS is typically used to deploy very small components into their operational capacities. The functions are meant to carry out very narrowly focused operations that complete very quickly. Think of creating a single procedure or method within a very large system—that is roughly the scope addressed when implementing and deploying a FaaS.

One difference might be how a request is handled. Thinking in terms of functional programming, a function is implemented with side-effect-free behavior. As was stated in the section, "Functional Core with Imperative Shell" in Chapter 8: "[A] pure function always returns the same result for the same input and never causes observable side effects." Based on this definition, it could be that the entire state on which a given FaaS will operate is provided as input parameters, requiring no database interaction. The result is determined by producing a new value that is then used by the FaaS, just as a function would work. The input might be an event that was caused elsewhere in the system, or it might be an incoming REST request. Whatever the case, it's possible that the FaaS might not itself interact with a database, either reading from it or writing to it. Writing to the database would cause a side effect. That said, there is no restriction to FaaS using a database as a procedure or method could for both reading and writing state.

Applying the Tools

Several examples of applying message- and event-driven architectures have already been given in this and previous chapters. The remaining chapters detail the application of specific architectures and patterns explained in Part III. The companion book, *Implementing Strategic Monoliths and Microservices* (Vernon & Jaskuła, Addison-Wesley, forthcoming), provides exhaustive implementation examples.

Summary

This chapter considered the challenges of using distributed systems and synchronization between subsystems to complete a large use case by completing a number of smaller step-based cases. The message- and event-driven architectures were introduced as a means of carrying out complex, multi-step processes while avoiding cascading failure due to asynchronous messaging and temporal decoupling. Process management using both choreography and orchestration was introduced, along with the differences between these approaches and how each can be used. REST's role in process management was described as well. Event Sourcing and CQRS were introduced, including their use in message- and event-driven systems. Serverless and FaaS architectures show promise in future cloud computing. Here are action items from this chapter:

- Use choreography for decentralized processing of limited multi-step distributed use cases.

- Employ the centralized orchestration pattern when complex processes with numerous steps are needed, driving steps across relevant subsystems.

- Consider the use of REST-based clients and providers of event-driven notifications when familiar technology approaches are desired.

- Use Event Sourcing to persist the stream of event records that represent the state of an entity over time.

- With CQRS, separate the service/application command operations and state from those used by queries to display groupings of state.

This completes Part III. Part IV ties this and the two previous parts together to build business-centric Monoliths and Microservices.

References

[Conductor] https://netflix.github.io/conductor/

[IDDD] Vaughn Vernon. *Implementing Domain-Driven Design*. Boston, MA: Addison-Wesley, 2013.

[Reactive] https://www.reactivemanifesto.org/

[VLINGO-XOOM] https://vlingo.io

Part IV

The Two Paths for Purposeful Architecture

Executive Summary

Here it is, the culmination of a trek to reach the pinnacle of purposeful architecture with well-designed contextual boundaries of expertise. There are two paths, Monoliths and Microservices. Both have purpose, yet the purpose of each does not fit with every system or subsystem situation. The two paths offered between the covers of this book are fitting for a given set of circumstances, and possibly a hybrid of both is appropriate. There is no shame in taking either path as long as the decision to take one over the other is backed by sound reasoning and intellectual honesty.

Chapter 10: Building Monoliths Like You Mean It

Building a Monolithic architecture should not feel like a third-class, cop-out choice—that is, not if you build a respectable, well-modularized Monolith in the way that the authors recommend. Building Monoliths as a first-class choice is the theme of Chapter 10. We'll offer guidance that explains two ways to get there.

- Take a lesson in why Monoliths should be used under specific circumstances, and how to achieve the best results.

- Take a brief history lesson on how the industry reached the mess that it has found itself in. This historical perspective delivers a reliable background on why software went so wrong.

- Every system construction endeavor that does not need to use a Microservices architecture must set out on the path to create a well-modularized Monolith. This is not just an attainable goal, but the only way to avoid the tangled, muddy mess that is the inevitable destination of lesser efforts. The effort includes the proper reference to business capabilities and wise architecture decisions.

- When a Monolith has not been architected, designed, and implemented as a desirable, well-modularized Monolith, a course correction is difficult but not impossible. But how do teams deal with change that's required to maintain the legacy system operational while simultaneously reworking the architecture?

- Either trek can be taken to achieve the best Monolithic architecture result, while keeping the sound software from gradually sliding into a pit of mud. Take advice on how to prevent the slowly creeping doom.

Chapter 11: Monolith to Microservices Like a Boss

Microservices are a suitable architectural decision, especially when certain contextual areas of expertise change more quickly than others. An added advantage of Microservices is that they are delivered as separate deployment units from all other subsystems. When Microservices are appropriately used, they can be a boon to autonomous development and delivery.

- Mental preparation is essential for every software development venture. Even so, we must be especially mentally prepared to take on the challenges of distributed systems architecture. It's not an easy trek to deliver robust distributed systems, but that journey can be made simpler by the use of some techniques and tools that support the techniques.

- The straightforward way to get from a Monolith to Microservices is when the Monolith is well modularized. This might have been because the Monolith was architected properly from the start. Or, instead, it could be that a legacy Big Ball of Mud was heavily refactored to a modularized Monolith using the steps provided in Chapter 10. Either way, starting with a modular Monolith is the best way to get from legacy to Microservices.

- When dealing with a legacy Big Ball of Mud, taking the trek directly to a Microservices architecture will be the most challenging journey. Even so, it is possible to reach that destination by fully comprehending the ruggedness of the terrain. This requires extracting components from the legacy, and implies all of the same challenges as the journey of Big Ball of Mud to modular Monolith that were discussed in Chapter 10. Yet, this is more like attaching new train cars to a train as it is speeding ahead, and then disconnecting those cars one-by-one as self-powered vehicles that arrive at the destination with all others. All the while, the team is working on the top of the train, with individuals simultaneously leaping from car to car as necessary. What could possibly go wrong? The guidance in Chapter 11 offers safety harnesses to the team members and catwalks between cars.

- Decisions, decisions. At what point can the legacy Monolith be decommissioned? There are several different trade-offs involved, not the least of which might be expensive hardware and software support licensing that have locked in businesses for decades. Consider the positive and negative consequences.

Chapter 12: Require Balance, Demand Strategy

After an intense journey to reach solid, high ground with strategy digital transformation and event-first learning and purposeful architecture, making the best choices to use Monoliths and Microservices is possible. This chapter steps through a cooldown with reinforcing reminders to balance choices and remain bent on strategic innovation.

- Because software architecture is a multidimensional discipline, it calls for balance when choosing trade-offs between the competing forces of different quality attributes.

- Outstanding takeaway: Balance is unbiased. Innovation is essential. Demand strategy.

Companies without a software innovation strategy will eventually become obsolete. Don't trade off the opportunity to turn a current core software system into the next generation of SaaS or PaaS in your industry. You now have incentive, inspiration, and tooling to start that journey, or to keep innovating along the path that has already begun.

Chapter 10

Building Monoliths Like You Mean It

Building clean and uncompromised Monoliths is not a pipe dream, and is the best choice for a large number of systems. It's also not as easy to achieve as 1-2-3. It requires thought, skill, discipline, and determination—much the same mindset needed when creating Microservices.

> **Note**
>
> The running case study introduced in Chapter 1, and carried throughout this book, is continued in this chapter. If some context within the examples seems to be missing, please see previous chapters.

To lead off, we'll provide a recap of why Monoliths are a good choice in many cases, at least early on, and how Monolithic architectures can be created effectively by using the previously defined strategic toolset. Organizations should learn to architect, design, and construct Monoliths that meet their business strategic goals and that are maintainable and extensible over a long lifetime.

The Whys and Hows of Monoliths

The following list recaps points made earlier, such as in Chapters 1 and 2, which are helpful in forming new Monoliths and restructuring and refactoring existing ones:

- *Why?* Many software systems don't need to employ Microservices.
- *How?* Experimentation using quick iterations, incremental value creation, and stepwise refinement is the best approach.

- *How?* Being wrong is not lethal, as long as it eventually leads to being right; develop a culture for safe experimentation and quick failures that result in valuable learning.

- *Why?* Monoliths are not bad in themselves; it's the mud that many of them contain that ensures entropy.

- *Why?* Monolith should be an architecture, not the unarchitecture.

- *How?* Build an environment that supports creativity and innovation that is free of technology speedbumps.

- *How?* Effective communication within small teams of virtually flat structures is the only way to reach full success in the face of Conway's Law.

- *How?* Fearlessly champion changes to the *what* or *how* so that your organization can achieve creativity and innovation; conversely, don't be married to anything that stifles creativity and innovation.

- *How?* Reject the *what* and *how* that harms business operations; that is, the next generation of software must be mature enough to support decommissioning the previous generation.

- *Why?* Avoid escalating commitment to systems that have diminished life expectancy, or continuing to invest heavily due to fear of sunk costs from previous efforts.

- *How?* Think and rethink, which requires determination and costs mental and emotional energy.

- *Why?* Beware of overlooking business logic that is missing and compensated for by patching persisted data on a daily or even hourly basis; teams likely lack a full understanding of why expedient data patches were necessary.

- *How?* Fear losing individual changes and the context of changes within the Big Ball of Mud (BBoM) while trying to replace it; carefully track all changes in the subsystems being replaced.

- *How?* Beware of the unknowns associated with refactoring or replacing an existing BBoM; large chunks of time can be lost due to unforeseen complexities perceived as simplicity.

- *How?* Modularize as Bounded Contexts that follow business capabilities, not business lines.

There are three primary concerns and goals with Monoliths:

1. Getting a Monolith right from the start and keeping it that way

2. Getting a Monolith right after it was previously done wrong

3. Getting from Monolith to Microservices

Today, most organizations are pursuing the third concern and goal due to their need to deal with Monoliths done wrong. It's not the authors' place to say that the third concern is the wrong goal, but stakeholders should be willing to consider that it might not be necessary or even the best target to aim for. Assuming that a Monolith-to-Microservices transition is the correct ultimate goal, it's possible that initially focusing on the second concern is the better initial strategy.

Understanding how to succeed when dealing with the second concern is best achieved by observing how to successfully accomplish the first goal. As an analogy, consider people who are trained to recognize counterfeit money. They don't learn about every possible example of counterfeit money, partly because it's impossible to know all of those and the unending attempts at new ways to counterfeit. Instead, they learn everything about the authentic currency by practicing: "touch, tilt, look at, look through." Those trained in these ways are then capable of detecting all sorts of attempts at counterfeiting. They can explain everything that is wrong about the counterfeit and how it would appear if authentic.

Following this reasoning, the first and second listed goals are addressed in that order in this chapter. Chapter 11, "Monolith to Microservices Like a Boss," delves into the third goal, by examining two distinct approaches to this transition. Before jumping in, it's fair to provide a brief historical overview starting at around 20 years before this writing.

Historical Perspective

It's only proper to provide a historical perspective of the industry in the early 21st century, because it's unfair to judge past decisions without understanding the influences of the time the decisions were made. When NuCoverage first started on its journey in 2007, the "software is eating the world" declaration was not yet made. That was still four years in the future. Even before 2001, software had taken on a different role due to the dot-com boom. Although the fledgling global Web had not matured far past brochureware and e-commerce storefronts, it was starting to hit its stride.

By 2001, Software as a Service (SaaS) 1.0 had mostly failed due to overambitious business plans and a lack of experience in developing enterprise-grade systems, the expense of operating on premises (because the cloud was not available), and—most especially—desktop suite lock-in. At that time there was buzz around "intranets," but software was still for the most part an augmentation to human decision making. It was rare to conduct business on the Web, other than to buy from an e-commerce store.

Make no mistake about it: Humans were still carrying a lot of the cognitive load in day-to-day business. Software was responsible for managing the large volume of data that was impervious to human use without augmentation around specific use cases. Business was still being conducted by phone and email. Such business workers had what was sold as software to help deal with their tasks. Commercial enterprise office products, such as SharePoint, were used by low-tech knowledge workers to tuck away a lot of indispensable email. These workers, who possessed business knowledge but far too few technical skills for that sort of responsibility, would hack document management repositories and feed their emails and attachments to these disorganized, quasi–"data warehouses." After only a few months of archiving preexisting emails along with new ones, the warehouses became nearly unusable, and certainly far less organized than many paper filing systems. They were actually glorified network filesystems with no rules or constraints on hierarchies or naming, where finding things was attempted with poor-quality search tools, resulting in many false positives and few true ones. Businesses could forget about attempting to gain business intelligence from that data unless they undertook a major initiative to perform scrubbing, restructuring, and reorganizing, so as to mold the data into useful pools of potential knowledge rather than a usability crapshoot.

Trial-and-error approaches to "office automation" weren't isolated to end-user–designed ticky-tacky document management systems. Still, considering the predominant software development and production platforms is also eye opening. From the late 1990s until perhaps 2004, the Java world was ruled by J2EE. Between 2003 and 2006, the Spring Framework began to disrupt J2EE, even becoming mixed together with the facilities of J2EE application servers by application architects.

On the other side of the divide was the .NET Framework, which arrived in 2002. By 2004, claims of .NET overtaking J2EE in popularity were abounding, yet the reality seemed to be somewhat less than that. One of the better .NET improvements over J2EE was to leave out anything resembling Enterprise JavaBeans (EJB). EJB Entity Beans were an utter disaster, and never truly delivered a convincing solution for database entity objects. Clued-in Java developers quickly realized that TOPLink and the later-arriving Hibernate provided a far superior object-persistence experience. Those who stuck with the Entity Bean bandwagon stumbled many times. On the .NET side, the Entity Framework arrived in 2008 but was met with great disappointment. Odd mapping rules forced impractical object designs, and it was several years before these difficulties were overcome without a lot of help from advanced application developers.

Given the state of the tech world around 2007, NuCoverage did well to bridle its ambitions by initially going no further than building software that assisted underwriters in issuing policies and claims adjusters in determining correct loss coverages. There was no Web-facing application submission or virtual handshake upon issuing a policy or covering a claim. This conservative approach got the company out of the gate, where it could make fast strides toward making a profit while enhancing its system as it learned more through experience.

The problem was that the NuCoverage software teams didn't possess a good understanding of and appreciation for software architecture, or any clue about modularizing their different business capabilities. This gap would have been observable very early on by wiser, more experienced heads. As a result, the team gradually faced the reality of crippling debt and entropy as time advanced. It didn't take long for the initial lumps of mud to take a toll. Unsurprisingly, the unrecognized and unpaid debt, piling up year after year, led to layer of mud upon layer of mud, until the Big Ball of Mud Monolith illustrated in Figure 10.1 had NuCoverage working on a creepingly slow fix and new-functionality conveyor belt.

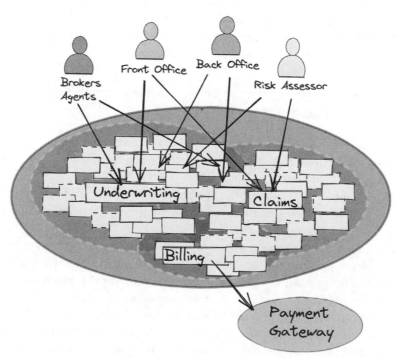

Figure 10.1 *The NuCoverage Big Ball of Mud resulted from years of neglect and expedient changes.*

With an understanding of software architecture that employs modularization of business capabilities, how could the NuCoverage enterprise have been shaped, even as a Monolith, to be welcoming to many years of change?

Look beyond technologies and frameworks. Throwing SharePoint, Enterprise Java, Entity Framework, JPA, database products, and message buses at the problem domain will never spare teams from the need to think. Even while the crazy technology failures were being thrust at every software IT department, CIO, CTO, and developer, there were reasonable approaches and guidelines that could have actually helped.

Domain-Driven Design (DDD) was introduced by 2003 and the Ports and Adapters architecture by 2004. Even earlier, the Layers architecture was available from the first volume of *Patterns of Software Architecture* [POSA1]. Extreme Programming [XP] existed well before DDD, as did the Agile Manifesto [Manifesto]. Several ideas found in DDD bear a striking resemblance to XP and the Agile Manifesto. There was a clear reference to organizational (business) capabilities by 2004 [BC-HBR]. Additionally, the ways of object-oriented design [OOD] and programming [OOP], domain modeling [Domain-Modeling], and class responsibilities and collaborations [CRC] were being used long before NuCoverage entered the fray. Several of the ideas, patterns, and tools in existence by then had the opportunity to influence architecture and development in 2007. Yet, that doesn't mean that they were used, and observing the results of systems developed from the past and in the present, it's clear that to a large degree they still aren't.

Right from the Start

Don't underestimate the importance of hiring top software architects and developers. Do top businesses look for bargains in C-level executives? Then why shop for bottom-shelf software developers when serious practitioners can be recruited? Understand who to recruit—that is, the right people with the right skills. Be aware that expertise in software engineering, although different, is as important as that among executive management.

Even though NuCoverage might have favored the idea that greatly minimizing software development costs would be to its advantage, it definitely wasn't. Taking conservative first steps for an early release of a minimal system doesn't justify poor-quality architecture and design. In fact, quite the opposite is justifiable. Early sound, tested architecture and design would have prepared the system's codebase for continued development of progressively advanced functionality, and actually facilitated much more rapid deliveries over the long haul. First and foremost, attention must be given to commissioning architects and lead engineers to guard architecture and code quality with avid, hawklike awareness and enthusiasm, as their unending priority.

Consider what a 2007 reboot of NuCoverage could have yielded. The context of 2007 must be kept in mind when reading the following descriptions. To be even more explicit, the following discussion does not represent the contemporary context—that is, when WellBank approaches NuCoverage. Instead, these events take place well before then, when NuCoverage is in startup mode.

Business Capabilities

Recall that a business capability defines what a business does. This implies that, while a business might be reorganized into a completely new structure, the new structure doesn't change its business capabilities. The business, for the most part, still does what it did before the new structure came along. Of course, the restructuring might have been undertaken for the purpose of enabling new business capabilities, but no business capabilities that were profitable the day before the restructuring have been jettisoned by the day after. This reinforces the point that it is generally best to define a software model's communication boundaries according to the business capability that it implements.

In Figure 10.1, three business capabilities are apparent: Underwriting, Claims, and Billing. They're obvious choices for an insurance company. Yet, there are other necessary capabilities that must also be discovered and identified by the NuCoverage startup team.

As shown in Table 10.1, the NuCoverage startup team collectively identified their business capabilities. This required walk-throughs of concrete usage scenarios that were understood by unified conversations to develop a shared understanding of the business goals. Each is described in Table 10.1 in terms of its initial purpose and implementation.

Table 10.1 *The NuCoverage Initial Business Capabilities, as Discovered in 2007*

Business Capability	Description	Type
Intake	Receives and validates applications, which can be submitted through the Web, but are often received via fax and email from agents, or as paper forms directly from applicants by way of postal mail. The intake process might require contacting agents and applicants to request missing data or to correct unclear and conflicting information. Approved applications are forwarded to Underwriting by means of an electronic feed.	Supporting

Continues

Table 10.1 *The NuCoverage Initial Business Capabilities, as Discovered in 2007 (Continued)*

Business Capability	Description	Type
Underwriting	Produces a decision on whether a given insurable risk is worth accepting, resulting in either issuing a policy or denying the policy. NuCoverage employs human underwriters to assess insurable risks based on software-based assistance from risk models. Underwriter review of the risk model recommendations, along with any necessary additional research and discussions with other underwriters, lead to a final human decision. The final underwriting decisions are recorded. Any details inside other business capabilities used for the underwriting process are collected in the respective contexts.	Core
Risk	Calculating a risk assessment is central to insurance, as it is a means to determine the degree of loss potential in a given insurable risk. One key to NuCoverage's success is its development of software actuarial risk models that assist human underwriters in decision making by means of automated calculations and recommendations. The initial focus is on auto and driver risks that lead to differentiating rates. This business goal requires careful scrutiny to reduce the risk by accepting the least likely loss potential.	Core
Rate	Calculations of premium rates are based on the risk model recommendations combined with underwriter review and reasoning. The results of combining the data and human effort are recorded here. Over time, the final recorded rate results will be used to gradually improve automated rate calculations, along with providing the reasons applied from past experience.	Core
Policyholder (Accounts)	Keeps the account of every policyholder along with a historical but limited snapshot of all of their policies. When a new policy is issued by Underwriting, a record of that business transaction is entered into the respective policyholder's account. This might require establishing a new policyholder account.	Supporting
Claims	Captures filed losses as claims by policyholders and provides the means to calculate the actual loss and settlement payments. Losses and settlements are available for later renewals and possibly near-term premium adjustments. If the loss is highly likely to be fraudulent but unprovable, it's a classic reason to proactively increase premium rates. If fraud is provable, the policy is certain to be canceled.	Supporting
Renewals	Where the process of renewing a policy begins. The process requires gathering claims against the policy, if any, along with current risk models and possible rate increases due to the increasing cost of covering specific risks. The renewal process includes the claims review, approved risk, and newly calculated rate, which are obtained and sent to Underwriting for renewal approval results. The finalized policy renewal is recorded in Underwriting and the policyholder's account.	Core

Business Capability	Description	Type
Billing	Tracks premium payment schedules and generates invoices based on Underwriting policy issuance. Manages nonpayment and collections, which might lead to recommending policy cancellations. Initially payments are made by check or bank transfer. It's possible that future payments might be made by credit card. Currently card transaction fees might cost as much as or more than NuCoverage's profit margins. This can be overcome in the future when high numbers of payments are built up and new-tech payment gateways become available.	Generic

Figure 10.2 shows the Monolith container with eight Bounded Contexts modules, each representing a business capability. The business capability type, both in Table 10.1 and Figure 10.2, indicates the level of strategic value of each.

At the present time, the Risk business capability is definitely a Core Domain. Because of the urgency to ensure high business value and integrated interactive operations, there are initially four different business capabilities with core value. Underwriters perform their essential workflows and garner valuable decision-making information while utilizing these four core contexts: Underwriting, Risk, Rate, and Renewals. Not surprisingly, underwriters have a lot to say about their workflows and the guiding environment, treating the four core business capabilities as an underwriting product suite.

Over time, the core value will tend to shift. For example, as Underwriting becomes more automated through continuous improvements in the Risk and Rate functions, Underwriting will transition to a supporting role. The same will be true of Renewals. There will be new Core Domains added.

A few years after the successful launch of the minimum platform and subsequent continuous improvements, another business capability arises—namely, Rewards.

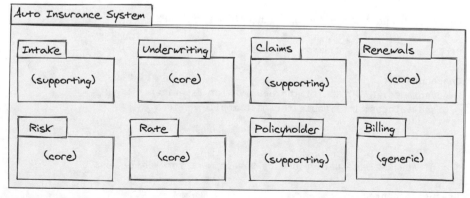

Figure 10.2 *The initial NuCoverage problem space domain was realized as a modular Monolith.*

As explained in Chapter 5, "Contextual Expertise," the Safe Driver Reward was the initial policyholder reward introduced. Initially, it was considered a simple value in the Policyholder Accounts capability. Although this was not a favorable long-term decision, it would suffice until business priorities would drive out the additional Rewards capability.

Architecture Decisions

After identifying business capabilities, NuCoverage now needs to make a few architectural decisions. For example, how will users of various kinds interact with the platform? It might seem obvious that a Web-based user interface will be used. Even so, there is a growing need for devices that support employees' job duties, which require mobility and convenience when those employees are on the go. Is there a sound way to propose, track, and finally determine which architectural decisions are needed and how the user-driven mechanisms and others can be provided by means of eyes-wide-open adoption?

The teams rely on Architecture Decision Records (ADRs) to define, propose, track, and implement prominent architectural choices. Listing 10.1 provides three examples. The ADR approach to decision making was described in Chapter 2, "Essential Strategic Learning Tools." These examples illustrate pertinent decisions made by the Auto Insurance System teams.

Listing 10.1 *ADRs Capture User Interface and Message Exchange Proposals and Decisions*

```
Title: ADR 001: REST Request-Response for Desktop User Interfaces

Status: Accepted

Context: Support Web-based user interfaces with REST

Decision: Use Web standards for desktop clients

Consequences:
    Advantages: HTTP; Scale; Inexpensive for experiments
    Disadvantages: Unsuitable for most mobile devices



Title: ADR 002: Use Native Device Development for mobile apps UI

Status: Accepted
```

```
Context: Support iOS and Android Toolkits for mobile apps

Decision: Use iOS and Android standard toolkits for mobile apps

Consequences:
  Advantages: Native look and feel
  Disadvantages: Multiple device types, form factors, languages,
  toolkits; slow development



Title: ADR 003: Platform Message Exchange

Status: Accepted

Context: Collaborating subsystems exchange commands, events, and queries

Decision: Use RabbitMQ for reliable message exchanges

Consequences:
  Advantages: Throughput; Scale; Polyglot; FOSS; Support available
  Disadvantages: Stability?; latency vs in-memory transport?;
                 support quality?; Operational complexity
```

> **Note**
>
> In the discussions that follow, there are several references to various architectures and related patterns, such as REST, messaging, and event-driven architectures. See Chapters 8 and 9 for discussions of these concepts.

The eight Bounded Contexts in Figure 10.3 correspond one-to-one with those shown in Figure 10.2. Highlighted in Figure 10.3 are the architectures in use—namely, Ports and Adapters; in Figure 10.2, the emphasis is on the modules used to separate each Bounded Context from the others. Actually, in Figure 10.3, it might look as if each Bounded Context has almost exact architectural implementations, but this is drawn only symbolically. In actuality, the various Bounded Contexts could share some resemblance due to the nature of Ports and Adapters. However, the inside application part of the architecture layer, possibly with a domain model, would be implemented differently depending on the need to deal with different levels of complexity. See Part II, "Driving Business Innovation," and Part III, "Events-First Architecture," for more detailed examples.

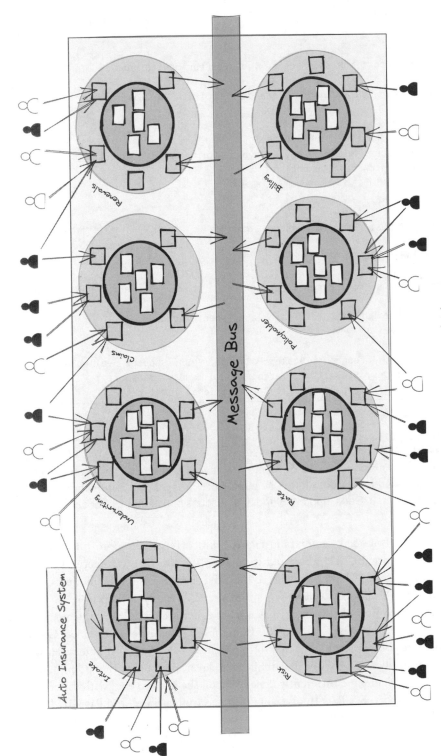

Figure 10.3 *Eight Bounded Contexts inside a Monolith, each employing Ports and Adapters.*

Note that the displays of the user interfaces are not shown in Figure 10.3 for the sake of simplicity, so it appears as if users are interacting directly with adapters. Also, the users would usually be shown strictly on the left of each subsystem. Here the architectures are "rotated" for the convenience of showing users surrounding the system and playing roles in multiple subsystems.

The results of the ADRs can be identified in Figure 10.3. ADR 001 and its REST request–response architecture, as well as ADR 002 for the user interfaces of mobile apps, are recognized in the user interactions with the Monolith. Furthermore, the outcome of ADR 003 is seen in the exchange of messages on the Message Bus (or broker). It is superimposed through the center of the Monolith to represent the means by which all Bounded Contexts collaborate and integrate inside the Monolith. The NuCoverage software development team was impressed by the early releases of RabbitMQ that occurred in the same year as the founding of NuCoverage.

Essential to understanding and properly implementing this Monolithic architecture correctly is a perfectly clean separation between every Bounded Context and the others. In Figure 10.3, this is represented by all contexts using the Message Bus for inter-context communication. Yet, at the boundaries of each context there must be adapters, as explained in Chapter 8, that adapt all input to and output from each Bounded Context in a way that suits the integration situation. As explained in Chapter 6, it's vital to recognize any upstream–downstream relationships. When one Bounded Context is downstream from another, the downstream context must translate its own language to those of the upstream context. This will happen before a message (event, command, query) is placed on the Message Bus. Thus, the coupling between contexts is maintained with the proper directionality, which in most cases should be unidirectional.

Don't conclude that Figure 10.3 insinuates there is only one correct way to communicate between contexts—that is, through reliable (durable messages with at-least-once delivery semantics), asynchronous messaging. The same effect could be accomplished by using inter-context request–response APIs that honor upstream–downstream relationships. Such APIs can even be executed asynchronously, and be fully event-driven.

Even so, if a business chooses to use request–response APIs rather than messaging APIs via a message bus, it must understand that this might impact the smooth transition to future architectural decisions. At such a point, any collaboration and integration between Bounded Contexts will need to deal with failures that are common to distributed systems. As explained in Chapter 11, "Monolith to Microservices Like a Boss," network, server, and additional infrastructure failures will have potentially catastrophic consequences in the face of naive implementations. Be prepared to implement failure recovery schemes.

Generally speaking, by implementing a message bus/broker, some of such problems can be alleviated "out of the box" because of the temporal decoupling. The benefit derives from designing in latency-tolerance rather than relying on Service Level Agreements (SLAs) that are based on time-limited request–response communications. When many messages have queued in a message bus/broker and require delivery, receivers can be overwhelmed by large bursts of messages within a short time frame. Using Reactive Streams can help here because it supports what is known as backpressure, which provides a way for receivers to set limits on deliveries within a processing window. Of course, it's important to select a resilient mechanism in the first place. For both message producers and consumers, temporary loss of live connections to the messaging mechanism can occur, as well as other failures such as broker leadership. Overcoming these challenges by means of retries with persisted data, however, is far simpler than trying to deal with the problems associated with accessing several temporally coupled services REST APIs. Because messaging tends to happen out-of-band, users are usually unaware of temporary failures, whereas using the APIs of temporally coupled services most often puts the problem "in the user's face."

To be clear, each Bounded Context should own its own database(s), and those must not be directly shared or accessed from outside the Bounded Context. No well-designed context with purposeful architecture should directly share its database with any other system-level contexts or any legacy systems outside that context. This is true of any storage at all, as well as any queuing mechanisms meant only for internal use. The only means of integration with such a context is through its public-facing APIs, which may be by means of REST, RPC, and/or messaging. See Parts II and III of this book for more information.

Sometimes it will not be practical to allocate a completely different database instance for each Bounded Context when creating a Monolith. Depending on the database product(s) in use, there might be ways to create a single database with multiple schemas (Postgres and Oracle). With other database products, using a single database instance but with context-specific tables might be a possible solution. In both of these possible database designs, a critical constraint is to provide unique user accounts and credentials to prevent easy access to context-owned database resources that must be protected from direct use by other contexts. The database resources that belong to a Bounded Context must be rendered as virtually invisible to other resources located outside the context. Due to the potential of several or many Bounded Contexts using a single database, all of the scale and performance consequences of many connections and simultaneous operations may occur.

Inside the Bounded Context in the application layer and in the domain model at the center, strictly employing the following tactical patterns will keep both object and temporal coupling to a minimum:

- Modules
- Aggregate-Based Entities
- Domain Events
- Domain Services

The focus of this book is purposely constrained to strategy; it is not meant to discuss the full implementation of such a system. Our follow-up book, *Implementing Strategic Monoliths and Microservices* (Vernon & Jaskuła, Addison-Wesley, forthcoming), describes these and other implementation tools and techniques in full detail.

Right from Wrong

The timeline presented in this section is different from the one just described. This one began in 2007, but the effort resulted in the entire Auto Insurance System becoming a Big Ball of Mud of frightening size. Now, 14 years later, NuCoverage has to turn this enormous wrong into a right. In this case, the task will be accomplished as Monolith-to-Monolith refactoring rather than a Monolith-to-Microservices transition. Chapter 11 describes the leap from Monolith to Microservices in greater detail.

Caution Needed

Transforming a system from a Big Ball of Mud to a modularized Monolith is not easy or even simple. It requires a lot of business-minded strategic discipline, smart tactics, kid-glove care, and even more patience. Note that the skills enumerated here are ones that have *not* been employed from the beginning, or at least not for a long time. Turning the enormous wrong into a right is often imagined as working like this: "Stop everything and give our team three months to make this right." To be frank, although this might be possible, it probably won't meet with success. The dynamics of a live system that is normally run by making continuous expedient fixes will most likely get in the way of a "stop everything" mentality. Software-business as usual will simply get in the team's way (including the kinds of changes required to keep the system running), preventing them from focusing on their short-term goal of "make this right." Thus, this section deliberately avoids selling the fantasy of short-term success. Even if it is believed that a given team can succeed in this way—and it might be possible—the odds certainly don't bode well for them. If success still seems certain, then kudos to that team. For most organizations, since it's taken considerable time to reach this level of entropy, making the necessary adjustments will require a considerable mental shift, along with time and money. (At the risk of making a forward reference, see the section "Deciding What to Strangle" in Chapter 11 for additional cautionary points to apply.)

Chapter 1, "Business Goals and Digital Transformation," and Chapter 2, "Essential Strategic Learning Tools," discussed the reasons why software goes wrong. It's not practical to try to identify every possible reason for poorly implemented software. Most times, the software implementation simply starts out that way. Less often, it starts out well and then drifts into chaos as time changes the team dynamics that instituted sound architecture and effective design. In whatever ways it went wrong, transitioning to right is the new first order of business.

Some of the common ways that component source code exhibits chaos are as follows:

- Technical rather than strategic business focus

- Undisciplined, haphazard structure (the unarchitecture)

- Lack of business-focused modularity; minimal modules that are technically motivated

- No unit tests; some large, slow, inter-layer integration tests

- Anemic model; CRUD-focused application

- Business logic lost in the user interface, and over multiple layers

- Large numbers of program source files within a single, technical module

- Deeply tangled coupling across many component source files (classes)

- Strong, bidirectional coupling across modules

- No separation of concerns; single concerns separated across multiple layers (both can exist together)

No doubt this list could go on, but we note that these are the common "big-ticket" items. In other words, these problems carry a high cost in terms of maintaining the existing code and making any attempts to correct the wrong.

First consider a few of the highest-level problems: technical motivation, poor structure, and lack of meaningful modularization. Listing 10.2 provides a typical modularity failure situation.[1] This module structure and the module names might not be catastrophic if that structure hosted only a single, well-defined business communication context—that is, the realization of a single business capability. But it doesn't, and even if it did, this modular structure is nearly useless.

Listing 10.2 *Modularity Gone Wrong, as Usual*

```
nucoverage.ais.controller
nucoverage.ais.dao
nucoverage.ais.dto
nucoverage.ais.endpoint
nucoverage.ais.entity
nucoverage.ais.helper
nucoverage.ais.repository
nucoverage.ais.service
nucoverage.ais.util
```

This is, in fact, the kind of module structure that would likely be used to "organize" the entire Monolithic Auto Insurance System. Think about that: eight major business functions all tucked away in a set of modules that have zero business meaning. There would be quite literally hundreds of component source files (e.g., classes) in many, if not all, of the individual modules. Only tacit knowledge—employing an elephant-like memory—of the contents of each module could lead to survival of the mayhem within. Those not capable of leaning on their own memory will tax those who do with their constant barrage of questions. But really, mayhem? The inter-module coupling in multiple directions wasn't even mentioned, but it plays a big role in any effort to scoop and reshape meaningful components from a Big Ball of Mud. Yes, mayhem is definitely the right word.

Still, correcting the problems is possible. Where does a team begin to take corrective action, and what steps should be followed throughout the journey?

---

1. Note the meaningless "ais" module nomenclature chosen, which stands for Auto Insurance System. Yet, that's the least of the naming problems for this system's modules. Further, architected and designed properly, a business-centric codebase should never require components known as "helpers" and "utils."

Change within Change

One thing that likely happens on a daily basis is change; that is, change happens daily just to keep the system running by means of expedient bug fixes. That's the norm. Although this seems like a relentless foe, it might actually be a friend when more than one kind of change is needed and the team decides to slow down just a bit. As patch fixes occur, the team can take a bit of extra time to initiate and continue the refactorings leading to cleanup.

One of the first means of corrective action is to add tests to the code that must change due to business drivers, such as for making patches and other bug fixes. Create a corresponding test every time a patch or any other change is made. Consider the following steps to be repeated continuously:

Step 1.   Add tests to verify the ultimate correctness of code that is being changed, and then fix business-driven bugs.

    a. First create tests that fail due to the bug being fixed.

    b. Generally at the beginning of such efforts, the best things to test are not stand-alone units, but rather coarse-grained integrated layers. For example, given a Service Layer backed by an anemic model, creating tests against the Service Layer makes the most sense because testing an anemic model is nearly useless. Tests against an anemic model would test only that attribute/property setters and getters work correctly, which are almost impossible to get wrong, especially when they are generated by an IDE as is typical. Testing that the Service Layer sets the expected attributes/properties is useful at the early stages of this effort.

    c. Correct the code in error so that the test passes. Commit the changes to the primary codebase.

Step 2.   After the tests are in place and the fixes are made, immediately experiment with modularity and attempt to move related business logic from the Service Layer code to the model.

    a. Is it possible to relocate the code with current bug fixes into a new business-centric module structure? If so, take that step. Test that the refactoring doesn't cause regression. It might be necessary to add one or a few more tests to be certain. Create new tests for the relocated code by refactoring relevant code out of the previous tests and into the new tests.

    b. When a Service Layer fronts an anemic model, locate refactoring opportunities in the Service Layer methods. Typically the Service Layer uses a series of Entity attribute/property setters. These setters can be aggregated into a single, behavioral method on the Entity. To do so, migrate the setter invocations to the new method on the model Entity and have the Service Layer now call that new Entity method. The name of the new method should reflect the Ubiquitous Language in context. Test before and after, using tests on both the Service Layer and the model, to ensure that the components are healing from anemia.

c. If other convenient, quick-win opportunities arise to refactor code that is nearby the code being fixed, jump in and make it right. These efforts could focus on additional modularizing of code and/or factoring the Service Layer business logic into the model. Remain somewhat conservative so that this work doesn't result in regression. All such changes should always be tested. These quick-wins must not require hours of labor, only minutes here and there.

d. As each change is made and all tests pass, commit the test and main code changes to the primary codebase.

Step 3. When additional changes are required to fix bugs or add features in code that has already received some care, take the opportunity to discover opportunities for more refactoring.

a. Create preparatory tests for all of the following refactorings.

b. Modularize other source files (e.g., classes) related to the ones that were previously changed but were left in the old modules because they didn't require change at the time.

c. Factor additional business logic from the Service Layer into the model; that is, when the model is anemic, the only chance of finding business logic is in the Service Layer.

d. As each change is made and all tests pass, commit the test and main code changes to the primary codebase.

Step 4. When a Service Layer takes several parameters that will be used for setting data on Entities, refactor all related parameters into their respective Value Object types. Pass the Value Object types into the Entity behavioral methods that were previously introduced upon aggregating Entity setters into a single behavioral method on an Entity.

Step 5. As the codebase becomes more stable and there are fewer bugs to fix expediently on a daily basis, use the time to refactor as defined in the previous steps. At this point, the improvements will tend to accelerate because the team has grown in experience and confidence.

Consider a reasonable module structure for the eight Bounded Contexts of the Auto Insurance System built as a Monolith. As seen in Table 10.2, each of the Bounded Contexts has a corresponding module just under the NuCoverage company identifier. Every submodule under the context-identifying module addresses a specific architectural concern.

In Table 10.2, the submodules of every context module are not shown. Instead, the submodules of the Underwriting context module are shown; they are representative of the common submodules to be found in the other context modules. There are likely to be other submodules, especially within the model of each context. There might be other submodules inside the infrastructure module. For instance, if gRPC is used, there would be an infrastructure.rpc submodule.

Table 10.2 *Business-centric Modules and Structure for the Monolithic Auto Insurance System*

Context Module	Submodule	Description
nucoverage.intake		Primary Intake module
nucoverage.underwriting		Primary Underwriting module
	application	Application Services/Service Layer
	infrastructure	Adapters and data objects home
	infrastructure.data	Data objects used for deserializing from REST requests and serializing to REST responses
	infrastructure.query	Query model interfaces
	infrastructure.messaging	Messaging adapters
	infrastructure.persistence	Persistence adapters
	infrastructure.resource	REST resource adapters
	model	Domain model
nucoverage.claims		Primary Claims module
nucoverage.renewals		Primary Renewals module
nucoverage.risk		Primary Risk module
nucoverage.rate		Primary Rate module
nucoverage.policyholder		Primary Policyholder module
nucoverage.billing		Primary Billing module

Although it might be tempting to immediately break this Monolith into separate executable components, such as Java JAR files or Windows DLL files, it's probably best to leave the entire system in a single source project and single execut-able component for a time. The reasons are explained in the next section, "Break the Coupling."

Working in this way with a gradually but continuously improving codebase for a number of months, and possibly fewer months than anticipated, will take the code from a muddy mess to a much more readable, changeable, and stable version of itself.

A friend of one of the authors, experienced in the construction industry, asserts that it requires one-tenth or less of the amount of time to tear down a building struc-ture in an orderly fashion as was required to build it. The purpose is not merely to destroy the building, but to reuse all of its significant parts. Software construction is not much like the building construction industry, but this assertion might well pro-vide a clue to the orderly refactoring and restructuring of a large system codebase with the intention to significantly reuse its code. Although the codebase has been a liability up to this point, it is possible that existing code is simpler to reshape than it is to newly construct. If it required 10 years to reach a position of deep technical debt, it could require as much as one year for a team to work their way out of that debt by using the stepwise approach to improvement we just described. Assuming a team has the experience to skillfully address this difficult situation, it certainly won't require 10 years to reach a vastly improved state. At a minimum, one-tenth of the original build time frame is a decent goal to set for this refactoring, and the team could potentially even outperform it by a considerable margin.

Break the Coupling

There's still a major challenge to overcome. So far, the team has avoided breaking the strong coupling between most components. That challenge is the most difficult part of successfully chipping away at change to reach a fully refactored system code-base. Breaking the strongly coupled components into loosely coupled or completely decoupled components is hard work. In reality, tight coupling in the Big Ball of Mud is likely one of the biggest reasons for the mysterious bugs that have undermined system quality and plagued the development team. It's been the most difficult kinds of bugs to track down. What is more, some such bugs in the midst of a wildly con-fusing Big Ball of Mud might never be completely understood. The root cause of the relentless system failings must change.

Consider what's happened to this point. All components of a specific type (Enti-ties, for example) that were previously in one very large module are now spread across several contextual modules. Sure, housing components in their contextually correct modules is a desired effect. What isn't desired is the coupling that still exists between the components. This has been purposely left unaddressed because it's the most difficult of refactorings to deal with, and it may be very disruptive to a large team of developers. It's easy to damage the stability of the system and interrupt previously good progress when working through decoupling efforts. That's the bad kind of easy.

Because there is still coupling between contextual modules, it might be best to use a mono-repo for source code revision control for the time being. Some even prefer a mono-repo on a long-term basis. Initially, this might help reduce the complexity of maintaining dependencies across executable components, such as Java JAR files and Windows DLL files.

As Figure 10.4 shows, the legacy `Policy`, `Claim`, and `Policyholder` were previously under a single overly crowded module known as `NuCoverage.ais.entity`, along with all other Entities in the entire system. Now they are all relocated to a specific contextual module and submodule. Good. But examine the lines that indicate coupling between the Entities. Although the coupling was previously the result of major problems, it was nearly invisible to the developers unless they were specifically looking for it. Now it's started to stick out like a sore thumb. Breaking these couplings apart is tedious work, but it can be readily accomplished.

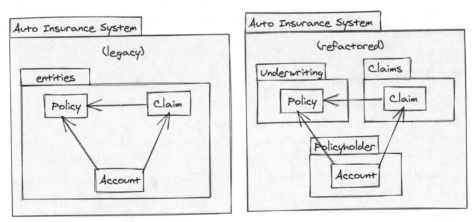

Figure 10.4 *Entities have been relocated to contextual modules, but are still coupled.*

The primary strategy for decoupling can be summed up in two rules:

1. For components that are coupled but have been relocated into separate contextual modules, make it a top priority to break the coupling during this step. Assuming that there are business rules across contextual modules that require consistency between components, employ eventual consistency.

2. For components that have landed in the same contextual module, prioritize these as least important to decouple for the time being. Assuming that there are business rules across contextual modules that require consistency between components, employ immediate, transactional consistency. Address these as potential candidates for eventual consistency after the first priority decouplings are achieved.

Addressing the first priority requires eliminating inter-context component direct coupling. To collaborate and integrate between contexts, there must be *some* coupling. Still, the kinds of coupling can be changed and the firmness of attachment greatly reduced.

As Figure 10.5 demonstrates, coupling is reduced in three ways:

- There is no longer transactional consistency of components in different contextual modules.

- Lack of transactional consistency means that temporal coupling is greatly reduced.

- There are no direct object references from components in one contextual module to those in other contextual modules. References are by identity only.

An example of reference by identity only is seen in `Claim`, which holds the `policyId` of the `Policy` against which the claim was filed. Also, an `Account` holds one or more `policyId` references for each of the policies issued to the policyholder. The same goes for each of the claims filed, with the `Account` holding a `claimId` for each.

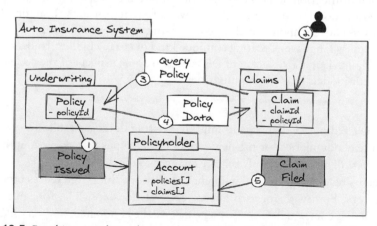

Figure 10.5 *Breaking coupling of inter-context dependencies with event-driven architecture.*

There might be other value data held along with the identity, such as a policy type being held along with its respective `policyId`.

As discussed in Chapter 5, the Renewals Context requires a `Policy` type in its model. The `Policy` in the Underwriting Context is the original record of its issuance. Creating a `Policy` in the Renewals Context is not duplicating code or wrongly disregarding the Don't Repeat Yourself (DRY) principle. The Renewals Context has a different definition for `Policy`, even though it is related to the original record of its issuance. That's part of the purpose of Bounded Contexts. The explicit separation acknowledges and protects the differences from a confusing merger of two distinct languages into one language that is wrong for both uses. The best models reflect a team's ability to sustain elevated communication in a context.

Disregarding DRY (Don't Repeat Yourself)

There is a cost to code unification. It results in coupling and complexity, and leads to increased communication between modules and the teams working on them. Still, code repetition is bad.

The zealous pursuit of DRY is often based on the misunderstanding that DRY is about code. It's not. It's about knowledge. DRY is meant to emphasize that the duplication of knowledge is a poor choice. For example, the Claims Context might have a `Policy` as a Value Object with all the properties needed by Claims. The `Policy` in the Underwriting Context is an Entity, and very different from the `Policy` in Claims. Those holding the wrong view of DRY would insist on unifying both into a single class; however, doing so would result in a complex model, including the creation of a "god class" that is highly coupled to everything else.

Such unification blurs the boundaries between two separate contexts that should purposely model a `Policy` as two different concepts. Bounded Contexts are entirely about dividing concepts into contextually correct models by business language. Creating a unique kind of `Policy` in both Underwriting and Claims is not a violation of DRY, even if some aspects of the code in the different models bear some similarities.

Another tedious challenge is to migrate existing database tables to support the new context boundaries for the new model Entity types. Breaking coupling apart on models will almost certainly require changes to the database.

When using object-relational mapping, usually one Entity references others using foreign keys, both with forward and reverse relationships. The foreign keys constraints across contextual databases/schemas will be eliminated, and very likely present within the same database/schema. Depending on the kind of database in use, one or more columns might be needed to hold identities of associated Entities, or those might be embedded in a fully serialized Entity state. Reference by identity techniques are used both for Entities of the same context and those of inter-context references.

Database migrations are common in enterprise applications, so they should not be viewed as perilous steps. Nevertheless, these migrations must be handled carefully, which further emphasizes the need to be conservative in carrying out these decoupling efforts as gradual, stepwise refinements. As explained in the section "Right from Wrong," the team should create a separate database, database schema, or access-managed database tables for each newly defined context.

Next, the team will take on the second priority refactoring—that is, breaking up as much of the same-context coupling as possible. Using Aggregate (Entity transactional boundary) rules, decouple all Entities from the others unless they require transactional consistency to meet business rules.

Beware of Design for Code Reuse

One of the principles of modularized design is to advocate code duplication over coupling. Clearly, while the ability to reuse code is good, as with many good ideas that are misunderstood and misused, creating more problems by demanding reuse can cause more problems than it solves. Bob Barton[2] said, "Good ideas don't often scale"; in other words, an idea that works for a limited scope will not work when applied to a much broader scope. Think of building a skyscraper with the same principles, tools, and techniques as are used to build a single-family house. It won't work. The same is true for design for code reuse at a larger scale. The developers risk spending far too much time trying to shape the code for future use, and in the end the code will have little or no actual utility. In fact, designing for reuse could render single-use code a failure. Design for use over reuse.

Designing for and implementing reusable code requires foreseeing future needs. Predicting the future is very hard, and few are those who are proved right. That's why this book advocates experimentation with acceptable failure. Thus code duplication, which should actually be viewed as code contextualization, is preferable, and often advisable, to avoid ill-advised coupling.

All "helper" and "util" (or utilities) components can quite possibly be entirely eliminated from the legacy system. There should be no need, or very little need, for extraneous components. That lot is often created to house common code used

---

2. Bob Barton was recognized as the chief architect of the Burroughs B5000 and other computers such as the B1700, and a co-inventor of dataflow.

across business components, such as to enforce rules, to validate and constrain state, and to run simple processes. These components should instead be primarily part of the domain model. If they cannot be placed entirely in Entity and Value Object types, then they would likely be amenable to handling by Domain Services. Otherwise, some "helper" and "util" components may remain or become part of the Service Layer (i.e., Application Services).

Keeping It Right

After all the organization's determination and vigorous effort was focused on the goal of building a strategically significant modular Monolith, whether from the start or by means of laborious correction, it would be most disappointing for the good results to gradually slide into a Big Ball of Mud. This can happen when those who were committed to the original effort leave the project. Although such a migration is likely to happen to some extent, the organization should try to prevent a mass exodus.

On the one hand, system project departures might happen due to normal attrition. Competent and driven engineers want new challenges, and there might be no way to keep some of them on the team. When this occurs, the most experienced hands must be replaced with others who have similar strengths and skills.

On the other hand, oftentimes management will move the more experienced engineers to new projects, and backfill the hole they leave with less experienced engineers. This tends to happen when the well-designed system is considered to be "done" and enters "maintenance mode." The problems with this approach are discussed in Chapter 2 in the section, "Getting Conway's Law Right"—specifically at the bullet point, "Keep the team together." Considering a system that solves complex problems to be "done" when it reaches version 1.0 or even 1.4 is generally the wrong mentality. Some of the most important insights into ways to differentiate value very likely lie ahead.

The very nature of new innovations in an existing large codebase means that significant architectural and model design changes will need to occur. A domain model concept could be split to form multiple new concepts, or two or more could be joined to form a single concept, each with different transactional boundaries, and take on new characteristics—and that means big changes will occur. These kinds of changes must not be left to less experienced developers without any architecture and design supervision. Getting these kinds of changes wrong could easily be followed by a slide down a slippery slope, and end in a new Big Ball of Mud.

Just as with any investment, watchful care is necessary to keep a strategic codebase in good order. A strategic software differentiator is worthy of continued investment and care to keep its dividends flowing for years to come.

Summary

This chapter considered the whys and hows of Monoliths as a choice of architecture. Monoliths should not be mistaken for a Big Ball of Mud. Monoliths are a means to achieve well-architected solutions from the start, or to mold them correctly after they were previously poorly architected. Business capabilities were considered again in this chapter to demonstrate their relationship to software models. Architecture Decision Records (ADRs) can help the team define, propose, track, and implement their major architectural choices. Guidance on how to avoid coupling between components was also presented. Strong coupling generally leads to a tangled Big Ball of Mud—something that should be avoided, and if not, eventually defeated. The chapter finished with advice on how to keep the strategic codebase in good order.

Here are the action items from this chapter:

- Not every system requires a Microservices architecture. Monoliths can be a viable alternative and architecture choice for many teams and enterprise situations.

- Business capabilities define what a business does, and typically do not change even if a business structure is reorganized.

- Understanding the importance of and maintaining a clean separation between every Bounded Context is a key to properly implementing a Monolithic architecture correctly.

- Transforming from a Big Ball of Mud to a Monolith requires a lot of business-minded strategic discipline, intelligent tactics, and patience.

- Event-driven architectures make coupling explicit, highlighting inter-context dependencies.

- Beware of maintenance mode, because it is often a trap that results in overlooking the strategic differentiating value that is still ahead.

Chapter 11 explores a few options for transitioning from Monoliths to Microservices. The first option explores how to get from a well-modularized Monolithic architecture to Microservices. The second option coerces a Big Ball of Mud Monolith to Microservices. The first option is relatively straightforward—but don't plan on the second option being anything other than very difficult.

References

[BC-HBR] https://hbr.org/2004/06/capitalizing-on-capabilities

[CRC] https://en.wikipedia.org/wiki/Class-responsibility-collaboration_card

[Domain-Modeling] https://en.wikipedia.org/wiki/Domain_model

[Evolutionary] Neal Ford, Patrick Kua, and Rebecca Parsons. *Building Evolutionary Architectures*. Sebastopol, CA: O'Reilly Media, 2017.

[Manifesto] https://agilemanifesto.org/

[OOD] https://en.wikipedia.org/wiki/Object-oriented_design

[OOP] https://en.wikipedia.org/wiki/Object-oriented_programming

[POSA1] https://en.wikipedia.org/wiki/Pattern-Oriented_Software_Architecture

[XP] http://www.extremeprogramming.org/rules/customer.html

Chapter 11

Monolith to Microservices Like a Boss

There are circumstances when the use of Microservices is the best choice. These were discussed primarily in Chapters 1, 2, and 8. Despite the advantages of Microservices, making sweeping changes to introduce system-wide use of Microservices might not be necessary. The number of Microservices should be determined by business purpose and technical justification.

> **Note**
>
> The running case study of NuCoverage, which was introduced in Chapter 1 and has been carried throughout this book, is continued in this chapter. If some context within the examples seems to be missing, please see the earlier chapters.

Transitioning from a Monolith-only architecture to some qualified number of Microservices might mean preserving some parts of the Monolith to operate in conjunction with the newly extracted Microservices. There might also be a good reason to entirely replace a Monolith with a full array of Microservices. This chapter addresses both approaches.

Mental Preparation with Resolve

When breaking off Microservices from a Monolith, the freshly introduced distributed system components bring along a significantly higher potential for runtime failure. It's not only the Microservices that introduce failure potential, but also the overall distributed ecosystem required to provide an end-to-end solution. This is largely due to the increased dependency on the network to communicate across different computing nodes, and the fact that both tend to fail: The more nodes, the greater likelihood of failure of both network and nodes. To fathom the new complexities, it's beneficial to consider the effects of falling into the traps of distributed computing. Here is a list of Fallacies of Distributed Computing [Fallacies]:

1. The network is reliable.

2. Latency is zero.

3. Bandwidth is infinite.

4. The network is secure.

5. Topology doesn't change.

6. There is one administrator.

7. Transport cost is zero.

8. The network is homogeneous.

Now, consider the results of believing these and how distributed systems will fail because they are untrue. These are reasons that distributed systems software will fail:

1. The network is unreliable and changes over time without warning, and software lacks resiliency and recovery tactics.

2. Latency is indeterminate and unpredictable, and worsened by the obliviousness common among inexperienced software developers.

3. Bandwidth fluctuates at counterintuitive times, and that inconsistency is exacerbated by naivete.

4. The network is not fully secure due to the Internet's historical openness, as well as the complexity faced by security teams required to balance default openness with corporate security policies, and even complacency and laxness among common users who don't follow mandated security policies.

5. Topology has suboptimal routes and produces unexpected bottlenecks.

6. An unknown number of administrators create conflicting policies that slow or block traffic.

7. Building network transports is nontrivial. and mistakes in their construction can have negative financial and/or functional and quality-associated consequences.

8. Assuming that the network is composed entirely of the same or similar parts leads to the effects of 1–3.

Points 1–3 indicate the primary problems with distributed systems. Most software is unprepared to deal with network failures, or any other failures common to distributed computing. Points 1–8 address network failures alone; they don't account for software failures unrelated to the network. Now add to that list all other kinds of failure: application errors, server and other hardware failures, persistence resources that are slowed or downed, and other general infrastructure failures. All of these problems can lead to catastrophic consequences.

Distributed systems must have non-naive designs. Design with failure prevention and recovery in mind:

- *Failure supervision:* Prevents cascading failures by placing software bulkheads around application components.

- *Circuit breakers:* Prevents cascading failures by blocking access to a failed component until that component is restored to full operation.

- *Retries with capped exponential backoff:* Provides the means for failed requests from a client to a server to retry until the server is restored to full operation, but without overwhelming the network or server by rapidly repeating retries at a constant rate.

- *Idempotent receivers:* When a server receives the same request more than once, it knows how to safely ignore subsequent operations, or otherwise perform the operation again without negative consequences.

- *Out-of-sequence message deliveries:* Generally applicable in the same way as commutative math (2 + 3 = 3 + 2), which works with addition and multiplication, but not with subtraction and division. Additionally, rather than demand a specific sequence, understand what qualifies as the total of all necessary message deliveries and take next step(s) only when the total is reached.

- *Avoid overwhelming requests and/or deliveries using loadshedding, offloading, and backpressure:* To lighten the runtime burdens on subsystems, loadshedding drops/ignores some unnecessarily work. Offloading distributes work to other workers that have capacity. Consumers use backpressure to limit the number of elements that might be received from a producer within a given time frame.

Of course, none of these remedies, by itself, will solve all problems. At a minimum, failure supervision can prevent catastrophic outcomes. Supervision might be difficult to introduce for some architectural designs. The use of the Actor Model will generally provide supervision as a platform requirement, but not always. Still, most software runtime environments are devoid of supervision.

Yet, even employing supervision should not be considered a complete solution on its own. Continual failure with local recovery only, and lack of cooperative stabilizing designs, will not reverse *deteriorating* conditions or prevent compute anomalies. Think of the negative consequences of improperly handled redelivery and wrongly ordered mutating operations. For example, continuously adding to or subtracting from financial accounts because of unrecognized redelivery will inflect monetary damage on multiple parties, and possibly even prove fatal to the party responsible for the error.

Migration to Microservices Should Not Be a (Typical) Project

The characteristics of a project include plans, scheduled workload, allocation of resources and developers, a starting date, various milestones, and probably an end date. For a Monolith-to-Microservices effort, creating a project with the aforementioned constraining characteristics is a mistake. Undue pressure to commit to a date before gaining understanding, confidence, and momentum will lead to problems. Friction will arise between people working on "the new thing" and those tethered to ongoing business pressures and servitude to legacy. There is always underestimation of effort and complexity, and the likelihood that engineers lack skills to drive the needed change.

The transition from Monolith to Microservices should instead be a continuous and uninterrupted effort backed by all stakeholders who are committed to success. It must be a business goal. It's critical for teams to be stacked with the right people—mature developers with advanced skills. Further, the teams should be organized around business capabilities and have cross-functional skills as discussed in the section "Culture and Teams" in Chapter 2, "Essential Strategic Learning Tools."

Teams must prepare mentally and resolve to prevent landslide failures, and anticipate that the small technical failures that arise can become large technical failures. This must be followed up with robust designs and implementations, which are essential for successful distributed systems operations.

Modular Monolith to Microservices

Chapter 10, "Building Monoliths Like You Mean It," outlined two approaches for building modular Monoliths:

- Build a modular Monolith from the start.

- Recover from the negative effects of a Big Ball of Mud by gradually refactoring it into a modular Monolith.

Figures 10.2 and 10.3 in Chapter 10 illustrated the ultimate goal of forming eight contextual modules inside a single deployment container named Auto Insurance System. Using either approach, NuCoverage now has a modular Monolith. Even so, some new dynamics with the system are causing pain.

There are five total teams working on the eight subdomains and contextual modules. Each of the modules changes at a different rate, but two of the eight modules, Risk and Rate, change especially frequently. The business rules change in both, as well as the algorithms that execute the actuarial processing and the pricing calculations, respectively. Additionally, Risk and Rate must scale independently due to their heavy loads and their demand for greater resources. Moreover, the company plans to expand the Rewards offerings, and its addition of new lines of insurance will bring several other impacts. This means that Rewards must be factored out of Policyholder Accounts. The custom-built legacy Billing subsystem is getting long in the tooth and lacks new billing rules and payment options. It will be replaced by a Software as a Service (SaaS)–based billing solution.

All these changes call for extracting some contexts from the Monolith into Microservices:

1. Risk Context

2. Rate Context

3. Policyholder Accounts Context

4. Rewards Context

5. Billing Context

There will be other extractions, but there are enough unfamiliar challenges to be faced with these initial ones. Making stepwise refinements with these five business capabilities will help the teams gain experience with relatively low risk.

The initial tasks extract one contextual module at a time. As Figure 11.1 shows, within a relatively short time, the four existing contexts have been extracted into four autonomous Microservices. Although the Billing Context will eventually be completely replaced, the team takes a conservative step of extracting the existing modular context with a specific purpose in mind. More refactorings follow.

> **Note**
>
> As was the case with Figure 10.3, the user interfaces are not shown in Figure 11.1 for the sake of simplicity, so it appears that users are interacting directly with adapters. Also, the users would usually be shown strictly on the left of each subsystem. Here the architectures are "rotated" for the convenience of showing users surrounding the system and having roles in multiple subsystems. User interfaces are discussed later in the section "User Interactions."

Because the Monolith is already using a Message Bus with reliable delivery, the inter-context communication using commands, events, and queries by means of messaging requires no changes when extracting new contexts. What changes is that any new Microservices must manage security on their own to keep out bad actors and provide authorization to control who can do what. Also, the Rewards model must be extracted from the Policyholder Accounts Context and the Billing Context must be greatly altered, mostly to provide a transport between the existing system and the new SaaS Billing service. And we'll add another item to the technical concerns checklist: Each Bounded Context should own its own database(s).

The SaaS-based Billing service doesn't understand the Auto Insurance System's events or offer a means to stream events to it. As seen in Figure 11.2, to facilitate the integration of the NuCoverage system with the subscription Billing service, we need a small Billing Interchange Context that is responsible for translating the local events into API calls on the SaaS-based Billing service.

There is a feed available from the SaaS-based Billing service that provides a stream of event records that carry information about what has happened there. The NuCoverage Billing Interchange Context translates that stream into events that are published onto the NuCoverage Message Bus and understood where needed. The event types already exist, so the system as a whole does not need to change as a result of using a new Billing subsystem.

The initial extraction of the Billing Context might seem like a wasteful step because much of it will be thrown out. It's true that the legacy business logic in Billing will eventually go away. Even so, taking advice from refactoring guidelines, it would be safer to prove that extracting the current Billing Context doesn't break the system. Once that is done, each of the features provided by the legacy Billing Context can be redirected one-by-one to the new SaaS Billing service.

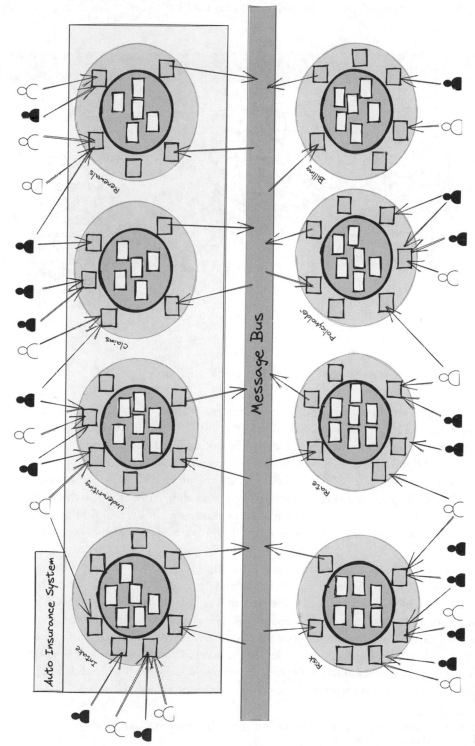

Figure 11.1 *The modular Monolith shrinks in the face of context extractions into Microservices.*

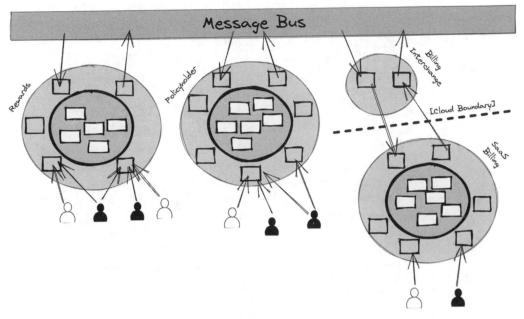

Figure 11.2 *Continued rework and model extractions.*

True, the team could redirect Billing features one-by-one from within the Monolith to the subscription service.[1] Yet, taking the initial step will create the separation that is ultimately desired. Specifically, the Billing capability will no longer be inside the Monolith and there will be one less team to cause a conflicting pace of change for the other teams. This will be especially helpful as the intense refactoring of Billing takes place and several releases begin occurring daily or at least weekly. Consider how much time would be involved in extracting the current Billing Context compared to the value it might or might not provide, and decide how the team should proceed.

Finally, the Rewards model is extracted from the Policyholder Accounts Context into its own Rewards Context and packaged and deployed as a Microservice. This is a fairly simple extraction because the current Rewards support is implemented as just one or a few attributes on the Account type. Nevertheless, migrating these into a new context and ensuring that all Rewards concerns are now addressed in one place will provide at least some opportunities for the team to pause and think. The good news is that the number and types of Rewards can now more readily expand to popularize new lines of insurance as the specific coverage products go live.

---

1. This is a form of the Strangler Fig Application pattern (also known as Strangler), which is discussed in the next section.

Big Ball of Mud Monolith to Microservices

The far more challenging approach to extracting components from a Monolith involves decomposing a Big Ball of Mud directly into Microservices. Considering that this effort requires assuming several complexities at once, it isn't difficult to perceive how challenging it is. All of the steps described in the section "Right from Wrong" in Chapter 10 must be shoved and squeezed through a narrow seam that must be pried open for each rework task. Because this is all done while the existing Big Ball of Mud is still running in production, nothing can be broken or compromised by this decomposition, or at least not for very long. Collectively, the resulting sweeping changes will be comparable to a very big leap forward. Even so, there's a lot of weight to lose and software strengthening required to make that strenuous long jump.

Again, the major change involves transitioning from the troublesome software development behaviors, pivoting on a pebble's radius to become a team operating in a highly optimized iterative process, while employing business-driven strategy with quality assurance. This must happen quickly. A tall order? Absolutely.

Here's a short list of what has to happen:

Step 1.   Identify all business capabilities that exist in the Big Ball of Mud.

Step 2.   Rank business capabilities according to strategic significance: core competitive advantage > supporting functionality > generic operations that could be replaced by third-party solutions.

Step 3.   Gather an inventory of the business rules and functionality that are still relevant and now irrelevant.

Step 4.   Decide which business capabilities will be extracted in priority order.

Step 5.   Plan how the first of the business capabilities will be extracted.

Step 6.   Work iteratively and deliver incrementally on steps 1–5.

Early on, step 4 can bias the teams toward prioritizing its attack to obtain an easy win. An example is replacing the legacy Policyholder Accounts with a new Microservice. This would naturally lead to the Rewards Context being created so that it can be extracted from Policyholder Accounts. These changes are the least complex and can help build the teams' experience and confidence.

Several varied details are inherent within step 5. The sections that follow disclose the details, which are not necessarily given in sequential order. Some steps may be taken at any given time as demand requires. For the most part, this technique is known as "strangling" the Monolith, much in the same way a vine strangles a tree.

User Interactions

The system remains enabled and available for users of the system at all times. Thus, the user interface must remain consistent.

Maintaining the system's contract with users can be facilitated by placing a Facade [GoF] between users and the Monolith. Figure 11.3 shows an API Gateway as the Facade, which works as described next.

1. Initially all user requests are directed from the API Gateway to the legacy Big Ball of Mud.

2. As the features of business capabilities are extracted into Microservices and enabled for the user, the API Gateway is changed to direct some or all respective user requests to the newly enabled Microservice.

3. This scheme can be used for A/B testing to determine if users in groups A and B have good/bad and better/worse experiences.

4. If there are bad or worse experiences with the new Microservice, direct all user requests back to the legacy Big Ball of Mud.

5. If tests determine that the newly enabled Microservice is sound and properly integrated, direct all user requests there.

Repeat these steps for every newly extracted Microservice.

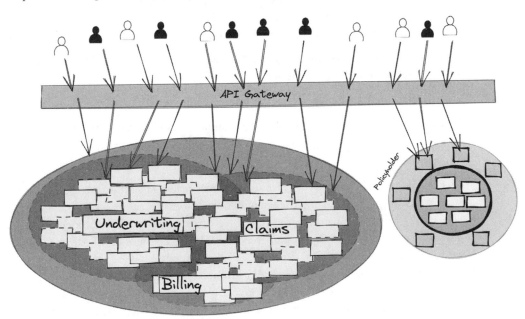

Figure 11.3 *Use an API Gateway to direct user requests to the current live contexts.*

It is possible to succeed in redirecting requests without the use of an API Gateway, but it requires changes to the UI. Although it might be more difficult to perform A/B tests this way, it is still doable. The authors have used this approach with success. Nevertheless, an API Gateway makes it far simpler.

A common complexity here, regardless of the approach used, is the need to deal with single requests that must be split. This occurs when the legacy and one or more new Microservices all provide part of the requested service. Whatever the results they produce, the multiple outcomes must be aggregated. This is much simpler to handle through an API Gateway. A query request and response can often be readily aggregated. By comparison, requests for creates and updates are not so readily aggregated. Some query tools can make this task run more smoothly, but the solution might run the risk of needing full and direct database access rather than using the well-designed application and domain model. A query tool such as GraphQL can also work through REST request–response communications, thus preserving valuable application services and the domain model. The pattern has been referred to as *GraphQL for Server-Side Resource Aggregation* [TW-GraphQL].

The preceding discussion points out a need to rethink how the user interface is designed and built. As data becomes segregated into various modules within the legacy, or as whole business capabilities are reimplemented in autonomous Microservices, the user interface must display the aggregation of the data from multiple sources to provide a meaningful user experience. There is no longer just one place from which to get all the data to render in the user interface.[2] This is yet another reason to use an API Gateway. As illustrated in Figure 11.4, the pattern that changes the way the user interface works is known as Composite UI.

When using this pattern, the UI is aware that different components are assembled within one Web page. This is accomplished by using the relatively simple HTML Web markup language. It provides block-based document segmentation or divisions, which can be used to compose various areas of the Web page to show data from different subsystems. Each segment or division gets its content from a different source. In Figure 11.4, there are three user interface components to be rendered, which are obtained by querying Underwriting in the legacy, and Risk and Rate in the new Microservices. All of this aggregation and composition work can be managed with an API Gateway. The API Gateway can use traditional REST queries or specialized GraphQL queries.

Note that it is possible to accomplish the same goals using other approaches, such as a backend for frontend and micro frontends. These approaches are described in detail in our follow on-book *Implementing Strategic Monoliths and Microservices* (Vernon & Jaskuła, Addison-Wesley, forthcoming).

---

2. Actually, there was never a convenient way to aggregate data into the user interface from the Big Ball of Mud, although there was possibly an illusion that such a way existed from an outside perspective.

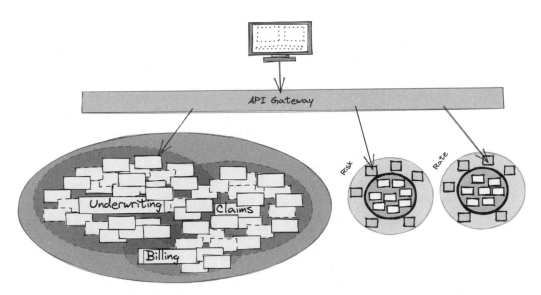

Figure 11.4 *A Composite UI designed by NuCoverage for a rich user experience.*

Harmonizing Data Changes

While strangling the Monolith, the data that is being maintained in a Microservice must be given to the legacy, and the legacy data must be given to the Microservices. Otherwise, users will see inconsistent views of what they perceive as *the same data*. Thus, whenever system state data is mutated in the legacy, or when a Microservice's state is modified, generally the changes must be harmonized on the opposite side. That is, changes to the legacy system state are generally made available to all Microservices that use this data. Likewise, state changes made in a Microservice will likely be needed by the legacy application. Because "generally" and "likely" aren't decisions, each case must be dealt with individually.

> **Note**
> It might seem better to refer to "harmonizing" as " synchronizing," because what is described here is a sort of synchronization. Yet, the data will no doubt take a different shape and possibly change its meaning between the legacy system and the new Microservices. Thus, the authors have chosen the terms "harmonizing" and "harmony." What's happening here is similar to two singers who have different vocal ranges, but can still sing in harmony.

Such cross-process data harmony will be eventually consistent. Thus, if the legacy system state changes, the Microservice that must be harmonized will only be able to merge the changes after some delay. For this reason, the Microservice will have at least a brief discrepancy with the data in the legacy system. The same goes for the legacy system being eventually harmonized with data changes in the Microservices. There isn't much that can be done about this temporary mismatch other than querying the multiple sources of data and merging into the latest snapshot. Even so, changes to the same data may occur before the current use case is completed. In distributed computing, there truly is no "now," and time always wins over consistency.

Harmonizing data modifications on both sides is essential when both remain at least partially dependent on the same data. This might seem odd, but until an entire business capability is replaced by one or more Microservices, all subsystems holding the same data must eventually agree on the system's state. This might be necessary for a while, despite it not being the ultimate goal. The ultimate goal is a single source of truth.

Single Source of Truth

Well-designed systems have single sources of truth, where a given set of data, such as an Entity, is owned by one subsystem of record. During Big Ball of Mud decomposition into Microservices, maintaining a single source of truth as a rule might or might not be possible while complex refactoring and extraction are under way.

Some legacy systems are somewhat simpler to deal with, and maintaining strict single sources of truth throughout decomposition is possible. This could still require that the legacy data be updated from the results of data changes inside Microservices because of the need to easily query the data there. Nevertheless, all changes to the migrated data must be made in the owning Microservices only.

If it is too complex to create strict single sources of truth, the rule might need to be relaxed for a while. Some codebases and database schemas are so convoluted that it is impossible to gradually release multiple Microservices into production while maintaining the strict single source of truth on a given Entity type at all times. To insist on the strict single sources of truth constraint at all times would likely mean that few, if any, Microservices would be gradually rolled out. The result would be more like a waterfall effort with a final big bang release after many months or even years of lift and tuck surgeries. The effort would likely be canceled before any, or at least more than a few, Microservices were deployed.

Eventually, there should be only a single source of truth for each data element, within a system of record. This does not mean that no duplication of data can ever occur. Indeed, we acknowledge that attempting to keep two or more data elements that change often in harmony over the long haul is not only difficult but also quite risky. This series of multiple sources of replicated "truth" must not be maintained for long, and certainly not permanently. At some point, the strangling must prove deadly to the legacy. See the final section in this chapter, "Unplugging the Legacy Monolith."

Of course, having a single source of truth is impossible to achieve at all times because at any given moment the changes in the legacy or a given Microservice will be recorded in only one place. The harmony of system state is achieved only eventually; that is, a true distributed system is always eventually consistent. In reality, in a large and complex system with many constantly changing sources of data, all system states are never fully consistent. Achieving this feat would require defying the laws of physics, so it's best not even to try.

Next, we'll present three primary approaches to achieve eventual data harmony of dependent system states: database triggers, event surfacing, and Change Data Capture (CDC).

Database Triggers

The first approach uses database triggers. When a trigger fires, an event is created to represent what changed, inserted into an events table, and managed by the transaction scope. The event is made available to Microservices through message publishing. A given use case might need triggers to fire on multiple tables in a single transaction. The problem with triggers is that database products other than RDBMS types don't support them. Even when they are supported, triggers can be tedious to work with. Triggers can also be slow when used on a database under heavy load.

The authors have used this technique when no better solution was available. In one case, the legacy Big Ball of Mud was implemented in an arcane language and framework with a sizable amount of reimplementations and new work using a modern programming language. It would have been quite difficult to use anything other than triggers due to the extensive use of the Microsoft SQL Server database in that environment. Fortunately, with SQL Server, all triggers can fire before the transaction commits, enabling the aggregation of multi-table modifications into a single event. At the time, Change Data Capture was not an option. Using database triggers in this situation was challenging, but it worked.

Event Surfacing

The second approach to harmonize data is to create a table in the legacy database that will be used to insert events related to each translation. Call it the events table, and the technique *event surfacing*. We have named this technique *event surfacing* because the original implementation was not designed with events, but now events are being jammed into the legacy system codebase to make strangling it easier. The difference between database triggers and event surfacing is that the first approach creates an event when one or more triggers are fired, while the second approach explicitly creates the event in the application code and persists it into the database along with the entities.

When inserting, updating, or deleting one or more application entities to carry out a use case, a new event is created by the application (perhaps the Service Layer) and inserted into the events table. The Entities and the event are committed in the same transaction. The event will later be queried by a background task and published via messaging.

The complexity here is that it is often difficult to find a good place to create and inject the event. Sometimes multiple Service Layer components will modify the system state independently while being managed within a single transaction scope. Unless some top-level component is orchestrating the subtasks, how and where is a single event created? Perhaps each individual Service Layer component will create a unique event, and the Microservices must deal with multiple events rather than one. If a thread-local or thread-static concept is available, and assuming the legacy code is single-threaded per request, this could be used to advantage in aggregating all in-thread changes into a single event. These technical topics are discussed in detail in our follow-on book, *Implementing Strategic Monoliths and Microservices* (Vernon & Jaskuła, Addison-Wesley, forthcoming).

Change Data Capture

A third approach uses special database tooling that supports Change Data Capture [CDC]. In fact, triggers can be used to implement a form of Change Data Capture, but a class of highly specialized tools for this task are available that work even better. When such tools are applied, the database transaction log holds only changes to be made to the underlying data. An extraction tool runs as a separate process from the database, which eliminates any problematic issues related to coupling and contention. This specific technique is referred to as *database transaction log tailing*.

For example, the tool named Debezium [Debezium] is available as open source. Debezium has had some limitations in regard to the number of database products it supports, but its abilities have been steadily increasing and improving.

Unsurprisingly, Debezium gives priority to supporting open source database products. At the time of writing, there were nine total supported database products—six open source and three fully commercial. Take this product seriously and watch this space.

Using Change Data Capture is very efficient when its proper use is well understood. Such tools can be used for other solutions, and there are patterns to describe those. The additional patterns are described in the follow-on book within this series, *Implementing Strategic Monoliths and Microservices* (Vernon & Jaskuła, Addison-Wesley, forthcoming).

Applying Data-Harmonizing Events

All of the previously discussed approaches to harmonizing data are a means to the same end. They are not intended to make the Big Ball of Mud a better place to work, although that can be a goal (as discussed in Chapter 10). In this case, NuCoverage has decided that its Big Ball of Mud should be decomposed piece by piece, and finally decommissioned.

Likely one of the previously discussed approaches will suit this specific situation, or at least provide some significant clues about what will work in other cases. Once an approach has been chosen, it's time to apply it to harmonizing data. Figure 11.5 and the list that follows explain how this process works from end to end.

1. The user submits a request.

2. The API Gateway directs the request to the legacy system.

3. Data modifications are persisted into the legacy database transaction log.

4. Change Data Capture reads the database transaction log and dispatches to a listener, and the listener creates an event that is placed on the Message Bus.

5. The Message Bus delivers the event to the Microservice, which establishes consistency (database persistence implied).

6. The user submits a request.

7. The API Gateway directs the request to the Microservice.

8. The event emitted by the Microservice (database persistence implied) is placed on the Message Bus.

9. The Message Bus delivers the event to the legacy, which harmonizes the data.

10. The harmonized data modifications are persisted in the legacy database.

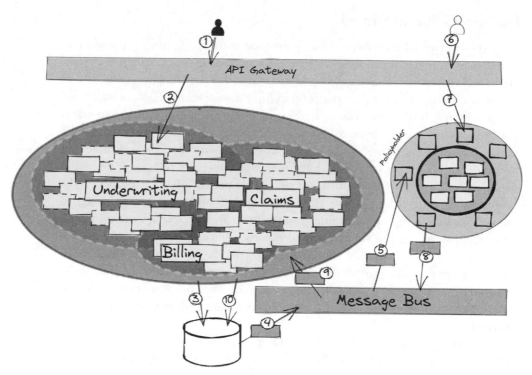

Figure 11.5 *Use change data capture to distribute local data modifications to system peers.*

Note that both sides must understand how to detect and ignore events that are seen during a full round-trip. That is, an event caused by the legacy that harmonizes state in the Microservice will, in turn, emit an event that the legacy system will receive. The legacy system must know to ignore the event that is the result of a full round-trip. The same goes for an event that originates in the Microservice as a result of a direct user action and is used to harmonize state in the legacy, which in turn emits an event from Change Data Capture. The Microservice must know to ignore the event that is the result of a full round-trip. If this consideration is not taken into account, a single database transaction could lead to infinite synchronization. This outcome can be avoided by each event carrying the originator's correlation identity/tag, which must be propagated by all receivers into their emitted events. When the originator's correlation identity/tag is seen back home, the event carrying it can be safely ignored.

Deciding What to Strangle

The previous two subsections describe the procedures for facilitating the use of a pattern named Strangler Fig Application [Strangler-Fig], or simply Strangler [Strangler].[3] Here, we consider how to work within the ecosystem that the Strangler creates.

Interestingly, the physical strangler fig itself, if it were sentient, might be labeled an opportunist. It first gets a ride up a tree from inside an animal, such as a monkey, and is then deposited on the tree in a most unpleasant package. Growth begins by taking in sunlight and nutrients from rain, as well as plant litter from the tree that becomes its host. From its humble beginnings, the strangler fig spouts roots that begin a slow growth following rich and convenient paths. When the roots find the ground, they embed themselves securely into the soil and begin growing aggressively. This opens new opportunities to forcefully overtake the host tree by consuming the nutrients that the tree would otherwise receive. At the point where it covers the whole host tree, the strangler fig tightens its grip by developing thicker roots and squeezes the trunk of the tree. It simultaneously stretches above the host, enveloping the top and blocking the sunlight's reach. Incredibly, it's not only strangulation that kills the tree, but also depletion of sunlight and root monopoly of soil nutrients.

The organic "opportunistic strategy and tactics" provide a framework for succeeding when strangling a legacy Big Ball of Mud. This is a fitting metaphor from which we can learn valuable lessons.

- Things will be ugly and smelly when we first start out, and it might appear to be a long way to fall from our humble beginnings, but starting is a must.

- Begin slowly, and be biased toward prioritizing for an easy win. The example we cited earlier was replacing the legacy Policyholder Accounts with a new Microservice.

- After achieving some early growth and gaining confidence, it's possible to sprout new roots by following a few more opportunities for certain wins.

- Continue in this mode until the team has become grounded in the techniques.

- Start aggressive growth, tightening the grip around the Monolith.

- If the choice is to kill the Monolith, that final squeeze might not be a long way off.

---

3. Interestingly, Martin Fowler later decided that he didn't like the name "Strangler Application," which he originally used, because the word "strangler" has an "unpleasantly violent connotation." Yet, encyclopedias and other sources use "Strangler" as a common name for this plant species. The authors use the name best known in the software industry, which is "Strangler."

One good thing about this approach is that it might not be necessary to carry the baggage of the legacy forward. It's possible that some existing code could be migrated to Microservices, but that should be done with caution. Strangling is not the same as refactoring from a Big Ball of Mud to a modular Monolith, and this is a great opportunity to shed the weight of the legacy and gain strength from a well-designed set of Microservices. This is discussed in more detail later in this chapter in the section "Unplugging the Legacy Monolith."

Consider some cautionary points regarding the decomposition of a Big Ball of Mud Monolith into Microservices:

- *Beware of blurred behavior.* The legacy code has no explicit model of a given business behavior. Other impediments include components that have too many responsibilities, business logic is flung into the user interface and infrastructure, the user interface and service layer yield conflicts, and behavior and business rules have been duplicated. (On a more technical note, these problems may include issues such as low cohesion of related components and high coupling between any two or more components.) This list of impediments is not exhaustive, but the examples chosen are certainly frequently seen in the wild. One of the authors encountered a scenario where the user interface sported business rules that triggered massive technical workflows and processes and integration with business partners.[4] A hierarchical selection list housed business logic, and depending on the list items involved, different categories of data would be updated, triggering the workflows and processes. The codebase provided no practical assistance in understanding the business logic and rules. To change this joyless situation, a deep analysis and extensive archaeological dig, including help from business experts, finally led to knowledge acquisition.

- *Don't carry over the wrong behavior.* Very often some parts of the Big Ball of Mud were wrongly implemented, from both business and technical perspectives. Business people must accomplish their work, even in the face of poorly designed systems. As a result, user-contrived workarounds abound. This tacit knowledge is gained and shared in the user community, and software never answers their needs. Familiarity breeds complacency. Fight it: Don't replicate the same wrong model into the new Microservices. Instead, challenge business experts constantly to help discover breakthrough innovations. Keep checking the pulse of the legacy decomposition, monitoring how results are being received. One heuristic is to observe users accomplishing a

---

4. In case it is not obvious, this is an antipattern that tends to go far beyond wrong.

certain task with the system. Does the user experience appear to be intuitive? Do users require special knowledge to work around problems? Do users need paper instructions, sticky notes on their display, or secret spreadsheets with hacks? The more experienced users might carry most of the knowledge in their head, so user experience issues might be difficult to see in some cases. Observe, yes—but also ask and challenge. Be understanding and empathetic.

- *Don't implement a new feature in the Monolith.* The ongoing decomposition effort might take some time, but the business won't grind to halt while waiting for those tasks to be accomplished. Rather, the business will constantly demand new features. If some business capability currently in the Monolith is supposed to be reimplemented in a Microservice, try to avoid implementing a new feature for that business capability in the Monolith, if at all possible. Doing so would be a waste of time and effort, unless there is a very urgent need to introduce the new feature in one of the remaining vestiges of the Monolith. Besides limiting the growth and size of the Monolith (which should instead be shrinking), building the new feature inside a Microservice will accelerate development and more quickly deliver the business value.

Extracting business capability behavior out of a Big Ball of Mud requires very hard work. There has to be a substantial effort devoted to rediscovering the domain, identifying its rules, and challenging them.

Unplugging the Legacy Monolith

On the one hand, at some point it might be practical or even necessary to put the final squeeze on the legacy and bring about its death. On the other hand, that action might be either impractical or unnecessary. If the decision is to keep some parts of the legacy in operation, it might be possible to rid its codebase of obsolete code. Or it could be that the code was previously so tangled that it's not practical to remove large swaths or even small pieces. The saddest part is knowing that harmonizing data between the legacy and Microservices will very likely be necessary for the foreseeable future and beyond.

If some business capabilities will not be extracted at all, or will remain relevant for a short time, leave the legacy Monolith running. Of course, this is not desirable because the rigging to maintain data harmony will almost certainly be necessary even for the reduced number of business capabilities in the legacy. Naturally, leaving the Monolith running simultaneously with the new Microservices will increase the operational and development complexity, which will certainly lead to greater business risk.

Some situations will not tolerate retaining the legacy system, even when terminating it is associated with great complexity. Consider the cases where companies are themselves in a stranglehold by computing machinery and software that is long obsolete or extremely unpopular, not to mention the grand expense of renewing licenses and support contracts. It can feel like paying the mob for protection from the mob itself. This legacy overhead imposes a huge "tax," and unless the organization takes drastic measures, it never, ever, ends. Even beyond vendor lock-in, in some situations it has become nearly impossible to hire developers to maintain the legacy. The original code might have been implemented by people who now have great-grandchildren, or are no longer with us.

For these reasons and more, a less significant muddy legacy system cannot remain in service beyond a given license and support contract expiration date. A few semi-tractor trailers (e.g., lorries or large hauling trucks) must pull up to a shipping dock, where burly movers push some behemoths into the trailer, and take them to the museum of computing. The team charged with decommissioning the legacy must be the best possible human form of the strangler fig. For some CEOs, CFOs, CIOs, and others who would like to move on from the 1960s and 1970s, unplugging machinery will have never felt so good.

Summary

This chapter considers how to move from a Monolithic architecture to a Microservices architecture. Because it is essential to understanding the challenges of Microservices, an introduction of the issues related to distributed computing was provided first. Next, we considered the simplest step of the transitioning from a well-modularized Monolith to Microservices. With that understanding, we outlined the challenges related to extracting Microservices directly from a Big Ball of Mud, and provided step-by-step guidance for doing so. Lastly, the chapter described the goal of eventually unplugging the legacy Big Ball of Mud in the face of the challenges associated with shedding unhealthy technology lock-in.

The primary takeaways of this chapter are as follows:

- Distributed computing introduces several complex challenges, which are mostly avoidable when employing a Monolithic architecture.

- The simplest and most direct way to realize Microservices architecture from a legacy system is to start with a well-modularized Monolith, like that developed in Chapter 10.

- It is far more challenging to extract components from a legacy Big Ball of Mud system directly into Microservices, because doing so requires assuming several levels of complexities at once.

- Consider an API Gateway as a means to aggregate requests between several Microservices and legacy applications when each implements parts of requested services.

- A composite UI is a great way of aggregating data from multiple services.

- Consider having always a single source of truth for any data when moving features from a Monolith to Microservices.

- Database triggers, event surfacing, and Change Data Capture are patterns to consider when migrating a legacy system to Microservices.

In Chapter 12 (the final chapter in this book), we will look at everything we have seen so far.

References

[CDC] https://en.wikipedia.org/wiki/Change_data_capture

[Debezium] https://debezium.io/

[Fallacies] https://en.wikipedia.org/wiki/Fallacies_of_distributed_computing

[GoF] Erich Gamma, Richard Helm, Ralph Johnson, and John Vlissides. *Design Patterns: Elements of Reusable Object-Oriented Software*. Reading, MA: Addison-Wesley, 1995.

[Strangler] https://docs.microsoft.com/en-us/azure/architecture/patterns/strangler

[Strangler-Fig] https://martinfowler.com/bliki/StranglerFigApplication.html

[TW-GraphQL] https://www.thoughtworks.com/radar/techniques/graphql-for-server-side-resource-aggregation

Chapter 12

Require Balance, Demand Strategy

This book has taken us on an intense journey through many aspects of business strategy, digital transformation, strategic learning tools, event-first modeling, reaching domain-driven results, and purposeful architecture with both Monoliths and Microservices.

In this final chapter, we provide a chapter-by-chapter summary of our journey. First, though, we reinforce a key message: There must be balance between business functional requirements and quality attributes, where the latter must be justified by identifying purpose. This balance is key if the organization is to remain laser-focused on strategic innovation.

Balance and Quality Attributes

Software architecture is multidimensional. The section "Right from the Start" in Chapter 10, "Building Monoliths Like You Mean It," highlights the importance of trade-offs in the face of balancing quality attributes, such as performance, scalability, throughput, security, and others. One such trade-off is to balance between performance and scalability without compromising on either of them. Choosing which one of these requirements is more important is essential, because it's impossible to optimize equally for both. Ultimately, one or the other must have the edge in the realized quality attributes.

Thus, selecting between trade-offs is equally important for modular Monoliths and Microservices. Take another look at the quality attributes in Chapter 8, "Foundation Architecture." Consider how the chosen architecture affects the quality attributes, and how the quality attributes affect the chosen architecture. It's not diffi-cult to understand why finding balance is so important. Here's a summary:

- **Performance:** Network latency affects performance. Microservices require a network, if not multiple networks. There are various options for lowering latency by ensuring there are fewer network requests and by making network requests simultaneously.

- **Scalability:** There is a definite advantage to using Microservices when high scalability is necessary, because they can independently scale the resource-intensive parts of the software. Yet, if a Monolith is designed and imple-mented as a cloud-native system, then it can be deployed as a Function as a Service (FaaS) component, yielding a cloud-scale application.

- **Resilience, reliability, and fault tolerance:** Both Monoliths and Micro-services can be designed and implemented with these important qualities. There is less technical overhead in doing so with Monoliths. Use of the Actor Model and other single-process Reactive architectural approaches can increase these qualities in both Monoliths and Microservices.

- **Complexity:** There are several trade-offs between Monoliths and Micro-services in terms of complexity, which tend to have opposite consequences.

The quality attributes discussed in this section are not exhaustive. For exam-ple, we could include a discussion about usability, and how it is interrelated with the requirements we did discuss. Of course, security and privacy, as discussed in Chapter 8, are not optional. Our focus here is on what are generally the most salient among the quality-related consequences brought from choice.

There is no clear winner between modularized Monoliths and Microservices. As always, it is important to understand the circumstantial trade-offs. Modular-ized Monoliths fit well in the context where performance, reliability, and the least possible complexity are required. Microservices shine when it comes to scalability, availability, reliability, and fault tolerance. Deciding which approach to pursue isn't a binary selection process. Instead, the options can be balanced to ensure the opti-mal application of each.

Finding balance is hard, especially in a large system, but tools are available to help us do so [ATAM]. Sometimes, and possibly even more often than not, a blend of modular Monolith and Microservices will give the greatest payoff. Remember, the ultimate goal is to develop strategically significant software that produces breakthrough innovations.

Strategy and Purpose

The overarching theme of this book has been reaching strategic goals by means of strategic thinking and strategic software development. Recall what has been explored in this journey, chapter by chapter.

Business Goals Inform Digital Transformation

Business goals should be differentiating; otherwise, transformation is just another buzzword that is expensive to chase, but too elusive to catch. Here are the big ideas from Chapter 1, "Business Goals and Digital Transformation."

- If pure invention seems nearly impossible, continuous and tenacious improvement is not. Although you will fail if you attempt to leap from A to Z, moving from A to B, and then from B to C, and then . . . is a feasible way to achieve innovations that outstrip imaginary transformation, such as on-premises to cloud migrations. (For a reminder of why this is "imaginary transformation," see the section "Digital Transformation: What Is the Goal?" in Chapter 1.)

- Software goes wrong when lack of knowledge and necessary shortcuts aren't recognized and then addressed by knowledge acquisition and corrective refactorings. A Big Ball of Mud becomes the destination, where everything becomes slow, and getting out of the hardened mud is difficult after spending a long time encased in it.

- Operating under the effects of Conway's Law is an inescapable fact of life. Communication is the key to knowledge acquisition, and organization structure can either help or hinder this process. Organizing teams around areas of expertise with the right people and clear communication is the best way to innovate with success. Of course, we're not recommending the creation of silos, but rather creating teams within specialized areas of a system that include cross-team communication and overall shared goals.

- Minds can be on autopilot, or they can be engaged in exploratory and deep thought. Rethinking multidimensionally and critically is a good way to challenge the status quo, with the goal of transitioning from a position of ordinary to a fresh strategic vantage point.

- Monoliths are damaging when poorly designed, and Microservices are disastrous when misappropriated. An architecture is good for its intended purpose. Purposeful architecture is the best architecture.

- #Agile is what teams make of it. If it is kept lightweight and focused on satisfying the customer, it will take teams in the direction of success. If it becomes heavyweight and ceremonial, those using it are by definition *doing* #agile rather than *being* #agile. Doing #agile will hinder success.

- A software system that has become deeply mired in debt, and possibly reached maximum entropy, took years or even decades to reach that point. Succeeding under such conditions depends more on attitude than on distributed architectures. Positive attitude is developed through confidence; confidence is achieved by smart choices and continuous improvement.

Use Strategic Learning Tools

A strategy is the *what* aspect of business creation, leading to new initiatives that are intentionally unique and produce a combination of profit sources. Make culture a tool. Learning to learn for strategic advantage is the essence of Chapter 2, "Essential Strategic Learning Tools."

- Decisions are necessary. Deciding when to make decisions is as important as the target decision. Make decisions at the last responsible moment. Being wrong so that you can eventually be right is the purpose of experimentation.

- Failure is not fatal when building an agile, failure-tolerant culture that fosters willingness to experiment. Providing people with the psychological safety needed to experiment and fail will only increase business success and competitive advantage. It makes teams stand up to Conway's Law.

- Design modules first and push long-term deployment decisions as far out as possible.

- Innovating toward strategic, competitive advantage is hard. Achieving this aim requires focusing on software design based on business capabilities and tackling business challenges. Don't allow poor architecture and design to derail business innovation.

Event-Driven Lightweight Modeling

In software development, some fundamental concepts underlie the way that components work well together. Modeling software rapidly while collaboratively applying the fundamental concepts of components is a powerful approach that accelerates knowledge acquisition and success. Put these tools from Chapter 3, "Events-First Experimentation and Discovery," to work.

- Software modeling is a big part of making sense of the complexities of business. The models produced are used to relate everyday business procedures and processes to software components.

- Model with events first, but include commands, policies, entities, and other elements where they benefit learning. This is a low-tech tool for experimentation that leads to understanding innovation within high technology.

- Although intended for in-person collaboration, EventStorming can be simulated online with remote teams using a virtual modeling surface.

- Using EventStorming big-picture modeling is an exercise in discovering the overall flow of the system under exploration. It's an initial step toward dynamic and rapid learning.

Driving Business Innovation

Every business has a specialized sphere of knowledge, which is gained through pre-existing expertise and the activities of collective and shared learning. Once this knowledge is reflected in software products, it has influence on consumers. In actuality, businesses have multiple, if not many, spheres of knowledge, and the chapters in Part II dive into ways to take advantage of the core parts.

- When it comes to business software strategy, understanding where to invest the most and where to invest the least is critical to success.

- Software reaches across the breadth and depth of an entire business. The entire domain or sphere of knowledge of all software in a large enterprise is voluminous. Use the concepts of domains and subdomains to understand the problem space and strategic decision making.

- Separate the context of communication within a specific, focused sphere of knowledge into a Bounded Context. Develop a language around the salient features of the communication, and maintain its consistency of meaning inside the boundary.

- Understand the specific core, supporting, and generic subdomains within a system. Know where to invest in core differentiation, where to provide supporting models, and where commercially available solutions would work best.

- Use Context Maps to recognize and improve inter-team relationships and for selecting the appropriate integrations patterns.

Events-First Architecture

Not every architecture style and pattern will suit any set of arbitrary business, technical, scale, performance, or throughput constraints. The specific set of constraints will drive a purposeful architecture. These are important takeaways from the chapters in Part III.

- Problems are likely to be encountered when there are fundamental differences between the external devices and other mechanisms used to interact with a software service or application. Use the Ports and Adapters architecture to separate the technology from the outside world into consumable stimuli offered to a service or application.

- A message-driven architecture emphasizes sending and receiving messages as playing a prominent role throughout the system. The benefits realized from this architecture include loose coupling of software components and services as well as reduced dependencies on expected outcomes within an arbitrary time dictated by technology. Events are inherently messages, so a message-driven architecture supports an event-driven architecture.

- REST is an architecture style and pattern that supports request–response actions. In consequence, REST can be useful even in an event-driven architecture. The requests are made using verb-based methods. Requests can be used by a consumer to register for events to be published by a system by means of REST-over-HTTP.

- Within the domain model of an event-driven architecture that uses a domain-driven approach, powerful tactical tools can be employed to manage the complexity of the business domain: Entities, Value Objects, Aggregates, Domain Services, and functional behavior.

- Use process choreography and orchestration, where fitting, to manage long-running system-wide workflows. For simpler long-running business software processes that require limited individual steps, choreography is suitable. For more complex processes with a fair number of processing steps, orchestration works best.

- Use Event Sourcing when maintaining an audit log of all past occurrences in a service or application is a business concern. Employ Command Query Responsibility Segregation (CQRS) when queries are complex and the organization can realize advantages from tuning the answers before the queries are executed.

- Managing security and privacy are certainly not the least important among the many architectural decisions. In fact, in recent years these issues have been pushed to the forefront of information technology concerns.

Monoliths as a First-Order Concern

Architecting and designing Monoliths to be both useful and manageable over the long haul is not a pipe dream. For most companies, developing Monoliths for use over the long term makes a lot of sense. Even if the organization decides to use at least some Microservices, starting with a modular Monolith makes it possible to reach decisions at the last responsible moment. Using the following advice compiled from Chapter 10, "Building Monoliths Like You Mean It," can help teams focus on all-important software delivery rather than getting sidetracked by architecture decisions that they might not have ever needed.

- Effectively architecting and designing Monoliths from the start can be accomplished using straightforward steps.

- Seek business capabilities to implement in a Monolith, because the business capabilities of a company are natural places for division between various models. These decisions will be driven by business experts and technical stakeholders who engage in specific capability-centric conversations.

- Even after a Monolith becomes the unfortunate home of a Big Ball of Mud, an organization can use specific measures, as thoroughly explained in Chapter 10, to form a modular Monolith.

- After traveling the bumpy road to form a modular Monolith from a Big Ball of Mud, it might be that remaining with the modular Monolith makes the most sense.

Purposeful Microservices from a Monolith

If there are good reasons to separate some Bounded Contexts from a Monolith into autonomous Microservices, that transition will be most straightforward when the organization starts working from a modular Monolith. If that's not a luxury afforded to you, and the leap from a Big Ball of Mud into Microservices is necessary, you can follow some steps to make this shift happen more easily. When there is a purpose to using Microservices, by following the guidance from Chapter 11, "Monolith to Microservices Like a Boss," you'll be kicking [amorphous] and taking names.

- As with any complex software development undertaking, developing the right mental perspective is quite important before embarking on a journey to develop an architecture. Yet, when pursuing distributed systems with a Microservices architecture, some challenges will stand out quite starkly. Performance, scalability, reliability and fault tolerance, and other complexities must be well understood.

- From team dynamics and technical perspectives, the choice of which Bounded Contexts to extract from a Monolith, even a well-modularized one, is not arbitrary. The best candidates are based on factors such as rate of change; a general need for autonomy, including independent deployments; performance; and scalability.

- Even when working from a modular Monolith, at the early stages the team should extract one coarse-grained contextual module (Bounded Context) at a time into a Microservice. Look for quick wins. After gaining experience and confidence, the team might be able to evolve more than one Bounded Context into a Microservice. If it encounters problems when doing so, the team can fall back to moving one Bounded Context to a Microservice at a time.

- Extracting Microservices from a Big Ball of Mud is very challenging, but the team can use some measures to render this a success. Move with caution and seek opportunities that lead to achievable wins.

Balance Is Unbiased, Innovation Is Essential

Software architecture is multidimensional, and its evolution requires reaching a clear understanding of the current trade-offs. In the face of balancing non-functional requirements, such as performance, scalability, throughput, security, and others, it is essential to understand the trade-offs and make unbiased decisions. If you want uncompromising value delivery, heed these lessons.

- Imagining that Microservices automatically deliver higher performance is wrong. The only way to understand the trade-offs is to measure. In-process method invocations are faster than network operations.

- Performance and scalability can be achieved in different ways, and Microservices aren't always a clear winner in that regard.

- Using "transformation" as an excuse for pursuing Microservices and/or a cloud-native system is not innovative or differentiating. Following this course of action must provide an advantage. Many companies have already adopted Microservices and cloud-native systems when it was not necessary, and have paid a heavy price for those bad decisions, both financially and operationally.

- Business goals must be sought for differentiating value. This does not negate making other strategic or tactical moves, such as moving to the cloud or using Microservices. Ultimately, those decisions should help the business to achieve differentiating value, not hinder it.

- Being wrong so that you can eventually be right is the purpose of experimentation. Knowledge workers must feel safe and be safe while seeking to acquire knowledge.

- Practice deep thinking and critical thinking when asking "Why?" and "Why not?" Experiment toward reaching strategic business goals. Apply strategic thinking and continuous improvement that leads to distinguishing software systems.

Conclusion

In 2011, *Forbes* published an article titled "Now Every Company Is a Software Company" [Forbes-ECSC]. That article asserts:

> The era of separating traditional industries and technology industries is over—and those who fail to adapt right now will soon find themselves obsolete.

Now, at least 10 years after those words were written, many companies have adopted that point of view. Many more companies have not. There are still other companies that are somewhere in between.

Does that mean companies that have not achieved a good amount of progress toward digital transformation are now obsolete? Look for the startup that could well displace that company within a few years. One problem with huge companies is that they can't move quickly. Another problem is that they can't detect their own slow death, because they can't understand that a $20,000,000 loss in a quarter occurred because consumers are moving to the bright, young, agile competition. The company might literally not even be aware of that new startup, or know of only one out of five serious challengers.

The answer to this dilemma is not for large companies to go on a scavenger hunt, looking for all the new startups that could eat their lunch—that is, unless buying their lunch (acquisition) is the only way to prevent this fate. Allowing and actually enabling nimble startups to innovate over your company with the idea of future acquisition is not a great strategy. Those companies could be second in line or off the offering price by a few billion dollars. Unicorns happen.

Don't trade the opportunity to turn a current core software system into the next generation of SaaS or PaaS in your industry. We, the authors, truly hope to have provided both incentive and inspiration to start your journey, or to keep innovating along the path that has already begun.

References

[ATAM] https://resources.sei.cmu.edu/library/asset-view.cfm?assetid=513908

[Forbes-ECSC] https://www.forbes.com/sites/techonomy/2011/11/30/now-every-company-is-a-software-company/?sh=7cfd5ec2f3b1

Index

Register Your Product at informit.com/register

Access additional benefits and **save 35%** on your next purchase

- Automatically receive a coupon for 35% off your next purchase, valid for 30 days. Look for your code in your InformIT cart or the Manage Codes section of your account page.

- Download available product updates.

- Access bonus material if available.*

- Check the box to hear from us and receive exclusive offers on new editions and related products.

Registration benefits vary by product. Benefits will be listed on your account page under Registered Products.

InformIT.com—The Trusted Technology Learning Source

InformIT is the online home of information technology brands at Pearson, the world's foremost education company. At InformIT.com, you can:

- Shop our books, eBooks, software, and video training
- Take advantage of our special offers and promotions (informit.com/promotions)
- Sign up for special offers and content newsletter (informit.com/newsletters)
- Access thousands of free chapters and video lessons

Connect with InformIT—Visit informit.com/community

informIT®
the trusted technology learning source

Addison-Wesley · Adobe Press · Cisco Press · Microsoft Press · Pearson IT Certification · Que · Sams · Peachpit Press

Ⓟ Pearson